SAVE THE CAT!
WRITES A
NOVEL

SAVE THE CAT!
WRITES A
NOVEL

The Last Book on Novel Writing
You'll Ever Need

JESSICA BRODY

Based on the best-selling
Save the Cat! by Blake Snyder

TEN SPEED PRESS
California | New York

CONTENTS

INTRODUCTION

In 2005, a very wise screenwriter named Blake Snyder wrote a very wise book called *Save the Cat! The Last Book on Screenwriting You'll Ever Need*. In this book, Blake set out to teach screenwriters how to structure their screenplays using a template of fifteen "beats" or plot points, claiming that every great movie Hollywood ever made was structured around these same fifteen beats.

The reaction was almost instantaneous. Within a few short years, screenwriters, directors, producers, and studio executives the world over were turning to Blake's fifteen-beat template or "beat sheet" to develop better, tighter, more engaging stories for the screen. "Save the Cat!" quickly became an industry-recognized method.

Meanwhile, in 2006, I was a former-movie-studio-executive-turned-struggling-*novelist*, trying (and failing) to sell my first book. I had a file drawer literally full of rejection letters, which all said the same thing: "Great writing. No story." Essentially, I was clueless about plot structure. Until one day, a screenwriter friend of mine handed me a copy of *Save the Cat!* and told me, "It's a very popular screenwriting book, but I believe it could work for novels too."

He was right.

After reading *Save the Cat!* cover to cover (multiple times), and comparing Blake's fifteen-beat template to popular novels that I'd read and loved, I soon discovered that with some tweaking and adaptation, his methodology could be applied perfectly to novels.

And I set out to prove it.

Now, nearly a decade later, I have sold more than fifteen novels to major publishers like Simon & Schuster, Random House, and Macmillan.

My books have been published and translated in over twenty-three countries, and two are currently in development as films.

Is this a coincidence? Definitely not. Am I just that good of a writer? Debatable. Did Blake Snyder invent something that no one ever had before? Not at all. He simply studied the elements of story and character transformation and noticed an underlying pattern. A secret storytelling code.

And now, after plotting countless novels using the Save the Cat! methodology and teaching thousands of other authors how to do the same, I've come up with an easy-to-follow, step-by-step process for teaching novelists how to harness the power of that storytelling code and turn it into compelling, well-structured, unputdownable novels. And I'm sharing it all with you here in this book.

Because essentially the Save the Cat! Beat Sheet that Blake designed is not about movies. It's about *story*. And regardless of whether you're writing screenplays, novels, short stories, memoirs, or stage plays, whether you're writing comedy, drama, sci-fi, fantasy, or horror, whether you fancy yourself a literary writer or a commercial writer, one thing is nonnegotiable: You *need* a good story.

And I'm going to help you get there.

A Screenwriting Guide for Novelists?

But why should novelists follow in the footsteps of screenwriters? After all, we novelists came first!

The truth is, in today's media-centric, fast-paced, technology-enhanced climate, we novelists are actually *competing* with screenwriters. Like it or not, since the moment that first silent film hit the big screen, novels have had to contend with movies as a source of entertainment. Charles Dickens and the Brontë sisters didn't have to compete with the latest high-octane superhero flick or the newest Melissa McCarthy comedy, but we modern novelists do. (Although, as a side note, I can attest to having found all fifteen of the beats on the Save the Cat! Beat Sheet in *Jane Eyre, Wuthering Heights,* and *Great Expectations,* among many other classics.)

The key is all in the pacing. A well-paced novel with visual elements, compelling character growth, and an airtight structure can step into the ring with any blockbuster film—and win.

But how do we write one?

Enter Save the Cat!

The Method to My Madness

For several years before writing this book, I taught an intensive Save the Cat! workshop for novelists. After years of watching writers struggle to figure out what their novel is about, and how to structure it, I have come up with what I believe is the most logical, intuitive, and effective way to guide you through the Save the Cat! methodology. The beauty of the way I've structured this process is that you can do it alone *or* with a critique group or partner. I've even included exercises and checklists at the end of key chapters to help you hold yourself accountable (either on your own or with your critique group). So whether you prefer to fly solo or flock together, this book will help you develop the best possible story you can.

Even if you bought this book because you're stuck at a very specific part of your plot (like the middle), I still urge you to read the chapters in order. You may *think* you have everything else in the story figured out, but chances are being stuck somewhere (like in the middle) is just the *symptom*, not the real ailment—and your story problem goes much deeper than you realize.

Because despite what you might think, this book is about so much more than just *plot*. The word "plot" on its own is pretty useless. It's just a series of events that happen in a story. But *structure* is the order in which those events happen and, maybe even more importantly, the timing of *when* they happen. Then you add in a character who needs to change and *does* change by the end, and presto! You've got a story worth telling.

Plot, structure, and character transformation.

Or what I like to call the "Holy Trinity of Story."

All together, these three elements are pure storytelling pixie dust. The three essential building blocks of every great story ever told. But the Holy Trinity of plot, structure, and character transformation is a very delicate, intricately connected entity. And that's why years of research, teaching experience, and careful consideration have gone into the organization of this book.

Plotters Versus Pantsers

It is a truth universally acknowledged (in the writing community) that there are two kinds of novelists: plotters and pantsers. Plotters are those who plot out their novels before they begin; pantsers are those who just "write by the seat of their pants" and figure it out as they go. And I realize any pantser who has bought this book is probably freaking out right now and breaking into a cold sweat at the sight of words like "structure" and "checklists." GAH!

But let me be perfectly clear.

This book is *not* an ode to plotters. Nor is it a manifesto to convert all pantsers. Yes, I do consider myself a "plotter," but I didn't write this book to prove that any particular way to write a novel is better than the other. I've learned, through working with thousands of authors over the years, that the creative process is a very mysterious thing and that everyone is different. (Yes, you are all unique, fragile, storytelling snowflakes.) So, no, I'm not here to change your process. I'm here to *enhance* your process.

If you're the kind of person who likes to figure out exactly where you're driving to *before* you turn the key in the ignition, then this book will help you do that faster and more efficiently. On the other hand, if you're the kind of person who likes to get in the car and just drive, confident you'll figure out where you're going along the way, then consider me and this book your personal AAA, ready and eager to give you a jump start whenever you stall out or get stranded in the middle of nowhere with no map, no GPS, and no fuel.

Regardless of which category you fit into, this book will guide you through the inspiring and often daunting process of plotting a novel.

Because whether you've "pantsed" your way through a first draft, and now you have to figure out what to do with it to make it work, or you're just starting out with a shiny new idea and you want to plot it in advance, it's all the same thing in the end. We all have to do the plotting work somewhere, somehow. Honestly, it doesn't really matter if you're a plotter or a pantser; the structure gets added in eventually. Either up front or afterward. It's all the same to me. And it's all the same to this book.

Meaning: Don't worry, I'll help you get there.

The "F" Word

It's around this time in the process of introducing Save the Cat! that people sometimes start throwing around the "F" word.

Formula.

Many novelists worry that following a methodology like Save the Cat! will cause their novel to end up "formulaic" or "predictable." They worry that following a structure guide or template will detract from their art and limit their creative options.

So I want to nip that fear in the bud right here. Right now.

The pattern that Blake Snyder found in almost all movies and the pattern that I've similarly found in almost all novels is not a formula. Like I said before, it's an underlying storytelling *code*.

It's the secret recipe that makes great stories work.

There's something buried deep within our DNA as humans that makes us respond to certain storytelling elements told in a certain order. We've been responding to them since our primitive ancestors drew on walls and tribes told stories around campfires. The Save the Cat! methodology simply identifies that code and turns it into an easy-to-follow blueprint for crafting a successful story, so that we writers don't have to reinvent a wheel that has been used since, well, the time the wheel was invented.

I've studied popular novels throughout time—books published from as recently as today to as far back as the 1700s. And I've found that nearly *all* of them fit the same pattern. All of them can be structurally analyzed using the Save the Cat! methodology.

If you want to call it a formula, go right ahead. But it's a formula that can be found in the works of countless great authors including Charles Dickens, Jane Austen, John Steinbeck, Stephen King, Nora Roberts, Mark Twain, Alice Walker, Michael Crichton, and Agatha Christie.

Regardless of what you call it, it *works*.

The Beginning . . .

So, let's get this party started. We've got a big journey ahead of us, and I, for one, am antsy to get moving.

First things first. What do you need? At the very least, you need an idea for a novel. It doesn't have to be a huge idea. It can be a seed of an idea, it can be a twinkle of an idea. It can even be a character that interests you, or a collection of inspiring thoughts that you hope to somehow string together. Perhaps you've got an idea but you don't know if it's worth writing. You don't know if it "has legs" as they say in the film industry. Can it go the distance? Can it really carry you through three hundred-plus pages of prose?

Or you might already have a novel fully or partially written that's not working, that you know you have to revise. Or maybe you've started a book and don't know where it's going and now you're stuck and in need of some inspiration.

Regardless of your specific situation, I'm excited to have you along for the journey. Here's a quick breakdown of what we'll be covering in the following chapters (the *structure* of this book on structure, if you will):

1. **THE HERO:** First, in chapter 1, we'll talk about the main character or "hero" of your story, who they are, and why they are desperately in need of transformation.

2. **THE BEATS:** In chapter 2, we'll explore the fifteen beats of the Save the Cat! Beat Sheet in great detail so you can begin to map out the compelling, transformative journey of your novel.

3. **THE GENRES:** Then, in chapters 3–13, we'll identify the genre of your story using the ten Save the Cat! story genres. These are not your mother's genres (sci-fi, drama, comedy, and so on). Instead, the Save the Cat! story genres are broken down by type of character transformation and/or central theme. This will help you further develop your novel and make sure your story contains the necessary "genre ingredients" to make it successful. Also in these chapters, I'll give you ten beat sheets for popular blockbuster novels (one for each story genre), so you can see how the fifteen beats apply to some of today's most successful books.

4. **THE PITCH:** By chapter 14, you'll have a pretty good idea of what your novel is about, which will help you distill the story down into a one-page description (the synopsis) and furthermore, into a one-*sentence* description (the logline) that you can use to pitch agents, editors, publishers, readers, and even movie producers.

5. **THE FAQ:** Despite the awesomeness and thoroughness of the previous chapters, I guarantee you'll have problems along the way. Which is why, in chapter 15, I give you practical solutions to the six most common problems novelists face when implementing the Save the Cat! methodology.

What About the Cat?

But wait! We forgot one important thing. The question that I'm sure has been on your mind from the moment you first heard about this book or picked it up in the bookstore.

Why on earth is it called "Save the Cat!"?

The answer dates back to the original *Save the Cat!* book, in which Blake Snyder included several cleverly titled tips on how to avoid common pitfalls of storytelling. "Save the cat!" is one of these tips. If your main character starts off somewhat unlikable, then, in the early pages of your story, they should save a cat (yes, like from a tree or a burning building or a shelter), or do something comparable that immediately makes the reader root for them, regardless of their original likability.

We'll talk more about cats and how to save them in chapter 15, when we break down some of the most common problems writers face when implementing the Save the Cat! methodology. Additionally, throughout this book, I've included several new tips and tricks specifically for novelists to help you improve your story.

So, let's get on with it already. Your main character is waiting, and they have a *huge* problem . . .

Why Do We Care?
Creating the Story-Worthy Hero

The relationship between character and plot is an essential one. It's why we start the Save the Cat! methodology here, with the main character, who from here on out I will be referring to as the **hero** of your story. Because doesn't that just *sound* better? A hero is proactive and important and worthy of having an entire novel revolve around them. In the world of Save the Cat!, we write about memorable characters who do memorable stuff. But most of all, we create heroes (male and female!) who are *destined* to be the center of a plot.

So who is destined to be the center of *your* plot? Let's roll up our sleeves and find out!

Regardless of whether you've already thought up your big story idea, or you're still working on that part, I urge you to put everything else aside for now and just focus on the hero of your story. In this section we're going to talk about how to make your hero *story*-worthy.

How do you create a hero who is interesting, memorable, and relatable, a hero whom readers want to read about? A hero worthy of an entire novel written about *them*?

Easy!

You simply give them:

1. **A PROBLEM** (or flaw that needs fixing)

2. **A WANT** (or goal that the hero is pursuing)

3. **A NEED** (or life lesson to be learned)

If you think about these three things up front, your hero will automatically start to take shape before your very eyes. And they'll be much easier to insert into your plot later on.

So let's take a look at each of these three things in more detail.

Here's a little secret. Readers don't like reading about perfect heroes who have all their sh*t together. Perfect heroes without any flaws or problems whatsoever are *bo-o-oring*. Not to mention, completely unrealistic. (I, for one, have yet to meet a human being whose life is entirely flawless.) So if you want to create a hero for your novel who is believable, relatable, and interesting, they can't be perfect. They must have at least one major problem—or better yet, *lots* of them!

You'll find a **flawed hero**—a hero with problems—in every great novel ever told.

Take Katniss Everdeen of *The Hunger Games* by Suzanne Collins, for example. She's not exactly living in the lap of luxury out in District 12, is she? She's poor, she's hungry, she's fatherless, her mother has completely checked out. And then, boom! Her little sister gets chosen for the reaping. Katniss's circumstances on the outside have also made her hardened, distrustful, and cynical on the inside. This girl's got problems to spare.

Or what about Tom Joad in *The Grapes of Wrath* by John Steinbeck? He's just gotten out of jail (for killing a man!), and he comes home to find his entire family has up and left because of no money, no work, and no food. He's definitely not winning "Farmer of the Year" anytime soon.

And let's not forget about Becky Bloomwood, in *Confessions of a Shopaholic* by Sophie Kinsella, who, as the title implies, *cannot* stop shopping. Which is why she's crippled by secret credit card debt that's starting to wreak havoc on her entire life.

And that brings us to a great tip for writing flawed heroes: Don't let the problem stay contained to just one area of your hero's life. Let the problem(s) manifest and spread and infect! Your hero's problem(s) should be affecting their entire world: their work, their home life, and their relationships.

When someone starts reading your novel, they should be thinking something along the lines of, *Whoa, what a mess this person's life is!*

That's how you know you've done your job.

I realize this seems like a horrible thing to do to your hero—riddle their life with all sorts of difficulties right from the get-go—but it's also an essential thing to do to your hero. Because if your hero's life isn't flawed, what's the point of the novel? Why do we *care*? We turn to story to watch characters *fix* their problems, better their lives, improve upon their flaws. Great novels take deeply imperfect characters and make them a little less imperfect.

So what kind of problem(s) is *your* character facing? That's the first question you must answer as you begin to create your story-worthy hero.

But it's not enough for your hero just to have flaws; your hero also has to *want* something (badly) and be proactively trying to get it. Your hero knows they've got problems. (Or maybe they don't know, and *that's* one of their problems!) Now, the question is: what does your hero *think* will fix those problems, or what does your hero *think* will better their life? (Take note of the emphasis on the word "think"— we'll be coming back to that later.)

Whatever the answer is—a better job, more money, to be more popular in school, gain their father's approval, solve a big murder case, and so on—*that* is your hero's goal. This is what they will be actively striving to achieve throughout the novel (or at least in the beginning).

Giving your hero a goal and having them proactively pursue that goal is the fastest way to get your reader to root for your hero and latch onto your story. *Ooh, this guy wants to find an Easter egg hidden inside a massive online simulation game?* (*Ready Player One* by Ernest Cline). *Let's stick around and see if he can do it!* Or *Ooh, this gal wants to find a suitable husband for her new best friend?* (*Emma* by Jane Austen). *I wonder if she'll succeed!* Readers keep reading because they want to know if your hero is going to get what they want.

So ask yourself, *What does my character want in life?*

And I'm sorry to say, *My hero wants to be happy* is not a good enough answer. I hear this answer a lot in my workshops, and it's just not specific enough. The most effective character *goals* or *wants* are concrete and tangible. The reader should be able to know if and when your hero gets what they want. How can we really know when your hero has achieved this elusive goal of happiness? We can't. That is, unless you give us a concrete thing that the hero *thinks* will make them happy. Like a new house, a new car, a million followers on Twitter, the national championship trophy, passage to a new country, magical powers, to escape from prison. Something tangible that the reader can keep track of and root for.

And speaking of your hero getting what they want: Why haven't they?

Why doesn't Wade from *Ready Player One* just wake up one day and effortlessly collect all three keys to the Easter egg hidden in the Oasis? Why doesn't Emma successfully set up Harriet with Mr. Elton in *Emma*? Because if they did, there would be no story. It would be too easy. There would be nothing left for the reader to root for. That's why it shouldn't be *easy* for your hero to get what they want. It should be hard. They should have to work for it.

Almost every want or goal has an equal and opposite force holding the hero back from achieving it. This force is often presented as a "conflict" or "nemesis." What is standing in the hero's way? Why can't Tom Joad and his family find work in California in *The Grapes of Wrath*? Well, because, the landowners lied about how much work there was, so they could attract more workers and drive down labor prices, and now there's a huge surplus of hungry, angry migrant workers. And why can't Jean Valjean in *Les Misérables* by Victor Hugo just start over and live his life in peace like he wants? Because his nemesis, Inspector Javert, won't let him.

Now, it's important to note two things about wants (or goals).

First, they *can* change as the novel goes on. And they often do. Victor Frankenstein in *Frankenstein* by Mary Shelley goes from wanting to create life to wanting to destroy the very life he created. Alice in *Alice in Wonderland* by Lewis Carroll goes from wanting to find the White Rabbit to just wanting to go home. Louisa in *Me Before You* by Jojo Moyes goes from just wanting a job to help provide for her family to wanting to save Will's life. The *wants*, regardless of whether they change or stay the same, are what drive the story forward. They're what keep the plot moving. Otherwise, you've got a hero who's just putzing around, waiting for something to happen. (Very boring plot.) When a hero wants something, it sets them in motion. It gets them off their butt and into the action, which is *exactly* where we want them to be!

And the second important thing to note is that not all characters actually *get* what they want. Some do. Like Pi Patel in *Life of Pi* by Yann Martel. He *does* eventually achieve his goal of getting off the lifeboat. But others, like Opal in the children's book *Because of Winn-Dixie* by Kate DiCamillo, do *not* get what they want by the end of the story. When the novel begins, Opal just wants to know more about her mother—and maybe even meet her one day. This doesn't end up happening for her. But you know what? That's okay. As we read this novel, we realize that Opal's goal of getting to know her mother is not the true point of the story. It's not where Opal's *real* journey is heading. Because in the end, the want is only half the story. Heroes aren't complete until they also have a *need*.

Heroes are often wrong about what will inevitably lead to their own happiness. Because typically happiness or a better life goes a lot deeper than just a new house, a new car, popularity, or whatever else you've dreamed up for your hero to want.

But it's easier to yearn for a quick fix than to actually do the real life-changing, soul-searching work. C'mon; who among us hasn't thought, for even a moment, that our lives would drastically improve if we only had more money, nicer things, more success at work, the ability to read minds, a date to the dance? When really these wants are just Band-Aids covering a deeper problem. Something that probably relates back to those pesky little flaws and problems we talked about earlier.

True to life, quick fixes in fiction never last long. In the end, your hero must eventually do some hard, soul-searching work. Now I realize I'm coming dangerously close to sounding like a self-help book here, but the truth is, plotting a compelling and engaging novel and crafting a story-worthy hero is a lot like playing psychologist. It's your job to not only diagnose the real problem in your hero's life, but cure it as well.

We call that real problem the **shard of glass**. It's a psychological wound that has been festering beneath the surface of your hero for a long time. The skin has grown over it, leaving behind an unsightly scar that causes your hero to act the way they act and make the mistakes that they do (flaws!). You, as the author and creator of this world, have to decide how that shard of glass got there. *Why* is your hero so flawed? What happened to them to make them the way they are?

And most important, what will *really* fix your hero's life? What does your hero actually *need*? This is the third and biggest question you'll have to ask yourself as you start to develop your novel. This is the crux of your story. This is the real "stuff" that great stories are made of. And *this* is what readers are really looking for when they pick up a book. Sure, they want action, they want mystery, they want body counts, they want kissing (and sometimes *more* than kissing), but in the end, readers want a novel that's *about* something.

What do I mean by that?

I mean, What's the point of the story? What does the hero *really* get out of it? Why *this* hero for this story?

Your hero's want or goal is an integral part of what's called the **A Story**. The A Story is the external story. It's the stuff that happens on the surface. Car chases; wars; fights in the school hallway; new jobs; casting magic spells; taking on an evil, dystopian government; poisoning the king. Essentially, it's the *exciting* stuff. The "cool" stuff. Or what's also referred to as the **premise**.

On the other hand, the **B Story** is the internal story. It's the story that's intricately linked to what your hero needs to learn in order to change their life, complete their transformation, and enter the hall of fame of story-worthiness.

The B Story/internal story/need is what your novel is really *about*.

For example, *Ready Player One* isn't *about* a worldwide Easter egg hunt through a massive online simulation game. That's just the external story (A Story). Underneath, behind the scenes, the internal story (B Story)—the heart of the novel—is about a shy, insecure boy who hides inside a video game and finally has to learn how to make real-life connections.

Misery by Stephen King isn't *about* a guy stuck in a crazy lady's cabin in the mountains. That's just a really creepy premise. It's the A Story. The book is about a writer who discovers how to write the best novel of his career and how that novel (and writing in general) can save a life (B Story).

And *Frankenstein* isn't *about* a scientist who creates a monster (A Story). It's about a man who has to repent for his sins against the natural world (B Story).

What plays out on the surface—what the hero wants—is only half the story. The true soul of a novel lies in the hero's need, which can also be called the internal goal, the life lesson, or the spiritual lesson. And by "spiritual," I'm not necessarily talking about religion. Although your spiritual lesson certainly can relate to religion (as evidenced in countless popular novels like *The Shack* by William P. Young or *The Kite Runner* by Khaled Hosseini), it certainly doesn't have to.

The life lesson is the inner journey that your hero didn't even know they were on, that will eventually lead them to the answer they never expected.

This life lesson should be something universal. Something inherently human. You should be able to walk up to any Joe Schmoe or Jane Schmane on the street, tell them what your hero needs to learn, and they would instantly get it. Or better yet, *relate* to it.

And here's the good news. There are not that many options to choose from. I've found that almost every novel throughout time has an internal goal or need that is in some way a derivative of one of the following ten universal lessons:

- **FORGIVENESS:** of self or of others
- **LOVE:** includes self-love, family love, romantic love
- **ACCEPTANCE:** of self, of circumstances, of reality
- **FAITH:** in oneself, in others, in the world, in God
- **FEAR:** overcoming it, conquering it, finding courage
- **TRUST:** in oneself, in others, in the unknown
- **SURVIVAL:** including the will to live
- **SELFLESSNESS:** including sacrifice, altruism, heroism, and overcoming greed
- **RESPONSIBILITY:** including duty, standing up for a cause, accepting one's destiny
- **REDEMPTION:** including atonement, accepting blame, remorse, and salvation

Now, I know right now some of you might be thinking, *I don't want to write a "lesson" book* or *I don't want my novel to have a deep universal message. I just want to write an action story, or a suspense thriller or a romance novel.*

But here's a tip for you: even the best action stories, thrillers, and romance novels have a spiritual lesson hidden somewhere within. They all feature a hero who learns something and changes in *some* way. Don't believe me? Check out the beat sheet for *Heart-Shaped Box* by Joe Hill (horror/action) on page 251 of this book, or the beat sheet for *The Girl on the Train* by Paula Hawkins (suspense thriller) on page 92, or the beat sheet for *Everything, Everything* by Nicola Yoon (romance) on page 199.

The spiritual lesson or need is what your reader will grab onto. It's what makes your reader feel like they've been somewhere, done something, experienced something—and that their investment in the pages of your novel was worth their time.

Writing about a hero who transforms—who comes out of the story a different person than who they started as—is the secret sauce of best-selling novels. Novels that people talk about. Novels that hit the best-seller list and stay there. Novels that get turned into movies. Novels that *resonate* with readers. And when you can resonate with a reader, that's when you become a true storyteller.

Who Is Your Hero?
(The Answer May Not Be as Simple
as You Think)

Call me an old romantic, but I believe that every hero has one true plot that is meant only for them. And I also believe that every plot has their one true hero. Your job is to play matchmaker and figure out which hero goes with which plot.

Imagine if Harry Potter had started out a confident, powerful wizard. Imagine if the Dursleys had been nice adoptive parents who took Harry under their wing and nourished his magical soul. What a dull first book that would have been! *Harry Potter and the Sorcerer's Stone* by J. K. Rowling works because Harry does *not* start out confident and powerful. He doesn't have cool, supportive guardians who help him find his way in the wizarding world. He starts out timid, isolated, unaware of his true potential. He is the perfect hero for that plot because he has so far to go. He is the character who will get the most out of this particular story line.

Or imagine if Elizabeth Bennet in *Pride and Prejudice* by Jane Austen had *not* been so quick to judge others. Imagine if she were more like her sister Jane. Patient, gentle, always giving people the benefit of the doubt. Well, honestly, there'd be no novel. It's Elizabeth's prejudice—her titular flaw—that marries her so well to Austen's masterpiece. Because it's essentially what keeps her and Mr. Darcy apart for three-hundred-plus pages.

A few years back, I was teaching one of my intensive Save the Cat! for novelists workshops, and a talented writer named Susan walked into my class with her plot and hero all figured out.* Or so she thought. She pitched the class a story about a young woman whose husband was mistakenly killed by a hit man hired to assassinate someone who looked eerily like the young woman's husband. When I asked her who the hero of the story was, she confidently replied, "The young woman. She's the one who has to learn to forgive." I pressed her a little. "Are you sure?" Yes, she was sure. So we moved on. But about halfway through the day, Susan had an epiphany and suddenly shouted, "Wait! The hero *isn't* the young woman who lost her husband. It's the hit man!" I got chills. Because she was right. The hit man *was* the more interesting choice. He had the more interesting journey. Could she have crafted a compelling novel centered around the young woman who had unjustly lost her husband? Sure. But the novel outline she left the class with was ten times more compelling because the hero she chose was better suited for the story. He was more *worthy* of an entire plot because he had more changing to do.

Now that you know what makes a hero story-worthy and what ingredients we use to build all great heroes, are you starting to get an idea of who the hero of *your* novel is? If the answer is no, don't worry; you still have plenty of time to keep thinking. If the answer is yes, then I'm going to ask you the same thing I asked Susan.

Are you sure?

I ask because the answer could easily make or break your novel. The hero is our guide to your fictional world. It's who the reader will use to track the progress of the story. And by story, I don't just mean the various external plot points; I mean the *transformation*. The important stuff. The internal journey. Your hero is who the reader will turn to when trying to figure out, What is this novel really *about*?

The marriage between plot and hero is essential. A bad marriage can equal a bad novel. So how do we ultimately choose the perfect hero?

---

* Names and plot specifics have been changed to protect students' identities and ideas.

Whether you're writing a novel with one, two, three, or more main characters, I still think it's essential to narrow down *one* true hero. Yes, all main characters *should* have compelling and complete character arcs, but whose is the biggest? Who has the furthest to go? Who has the most to gain from being the hero of this novel? And *who* is the most resistant to the change?

When reading other novels with more than one main character, the hero can often be identified as the character who first appears in the story. Or if the story is told from multiple points of view, whose point of view do we read first? This is essentially the author *introducing* you to your guide.

In *The Help* by Kathryn Stockett (whose full beat sheet can be found on page 124), we're introduced to *three* main characters—Aibileen, Minny, and Skeeter—but it's Aibileen we meet first. And although all three characters grow and learn something by the end, I believe it's Aibileen who changes the most. She starts out as a maid in 1960s Mississippi—oppressed as a black woman, alone, broken, and mourning the loss of her son. Unlike Minny, who already speaks her mind enough to often get herself in trouble, Aibileen is aware of the injustices in her world but starts out unwilling to take any risks to change them. By the end of the story, however, she's completely transformed. Which is evident in the memorable and satisfying scene when Aibileen finally stands up to the insufferable Hilly Holbrook.

Likewise, in *The Husband's Secret* by Liane Moriarty, we're also introduced to three main characters—Cecilia, Tess, and Rachel—but it's Cecilia we meet first. It's Cecilia who has to deal most profoundly with the aftermath of the earth-shattering secret her husband has been keeping. Although the secret affects all three women, it's Cecilia's husband who's referred to in the title of the novel, making her the obvious choice for the novel's true hero.

If you're writing a story with multiple main characters and/or multiple points of view and you're still having problems figuring out who the hero is, or whose arc is the biggest, try asking yourself, *Which of my main characters is* most *like my reader?*

Now, that's not to say all heroes have to fit this description. But there's a reason that Harry Potter came from the Muggle world. There's a reason that Winston in *1984* by George Orwell was pretty much an average guy with an average job. Or that Edward, the vampire, isn't the hero of *Twilight* by Stephanie Meyer—it's Bella, the *human*. As readers, we can relate to these people more.

EXERCISE: IS MY HERO STORY-WORTHY?

- Who is the hero of your story?
- What is their *big* problem or flaw (bonus points if they have more than one!). Remember, flaws start internally (from that metaphorical shard of glass) and manifest into external problems in your hero's life.
- How is this problem or flaw affecting your hero's life/world?
- What is causing this problem or flaw? What is the shard of glass? (Time to psychoanalyze, Dr. Author!)
- At the start of the novel, what does your hero want? What is their goal? (What do they *think* will fix their life?)
- How has your hero been actively pursuing this goal?
- Why haven't they achieved this goal yet? (This roadblock can be internal, external, or both!)
- What does your hero actually need? What is their life lesson? (What will *really* fix their life?)

CHECK YOURSELF!

- ❑ Does your chosen hero change more than any other character in the novel?

- ❑ Is your hero's problem or flaw specific?

- ❑ Does the hero's problem or flaw create a desperate need for change?

- ❑ Is your hero's goal tangible and concrete? (Will we, as readers, know when or if they achieve it?)

- ❑ Is there something standing in the way of your hero achieving that goal? (If not, the goal is too easy!)

- ❑ Is your hero's need (or life lesson) universal? Would a random person on the street understand it?

The Save the Cat! Beat Sheet
aka The End of All Your Plotting Problems

So, you've got your hero. You've flawed them up good. You've given them a strong, compelling **want** and an even more compelling **need** that readers will resonate with. Now what?

Well, to put it simply, now we figure out what to do with this beautifully flawed character of yours. Where are they going? What is their big journey? What is their most perfect plot?

In other words: WHAT THE HECK HAPPENS IN THIS NOVEL?

That's right, friends. We've reached the famous Save the Cat! Beat Sheet.

I like to think of writing a novel as a long cross-country road trip. It feels daunting when you're sitting in your car in San Francisco, knowing you have to get all the way to New York. It almost makes you not ever want to leave. Starting a novel is just as daunting.

"I have to write *how* many pages?"

But we can't think of it like that. We can't say we're going to get in our car, turn the key in the ignition, and drive three thousand miles. Otherwise we'll never start. We have to break down the road trip into smaller chunks. We have to set road markers for ourselves—little goals along the way to keep us on the right route, and make us feel like we've accomplished something at the end of the day or week (or month or year).

That's why when I get into my car to start a road trip, I say to myself, "Today, you only have to get from San Francisco to Reno. Tomorrow, you only have to get from Reno to Salt Lake City." And so on and so forth.

Well, that's essentially what the Save the Cat! Beat Sheet is. It's a map. It's a series of road markers we lay out for ourselves so we're not roaming aimlessly around the country (or the book, as it were), not knowing how far we've gone, how close we are to the finish line, or if we're even heading in the right direction! The Save the Cat! Beat Sheet breaks down the daunting task of writing a three-hundred-, four-hundred-, or even five-hundred-page novel into bite-size, achievable goals. These goals help keep us in line and on the right path toward our final destination: a satisfying end to the novel with a satisfying character transformation.

I know you novelists. I *am* one. We like our detours. We love venturing off on our little five-page explorations of poppy fields or the saga-worthy backstory of the hero's ex-girlfriend's grandfather's brother-in-law.

Fortunately, that's why you have me. And this book. To keep you on course.

Regardless of whether you're a pantser or a plotter, whether you're starting something new or revising something old, drafting a beat sheet that lays out a clear transformative journey for your hero will save you, in the long run, weeks or even months of agony and rewrites.

To this day, I have never been asked by an editor to do a from-page-one rewrite. Sure, I have revisions. I have tweaks to make and scenes to cut and characters to flesh out. But I have never had to start from scratch. Why? Because I did my road mapping. Yes, my beat sheet *always* changes along the way as I get into the story and learn more about the world and the characters (see page 296 for an example). But whenever that happens, I pause, pull over to the side of the road, and take a moment to "rebeat" (rewrite my beats to match my new direction) so that I'm never writing without some semblance of a map in front of me.

Your beat sheet (or novel road map) can be as detailed or as sparse as you want. You can use the beat sheet *before* you start writing, somewhere in the middle when you're feeling lost, or not until you've finished your first draft and are going back to revise. Like I said before, I'm not here to change your process; I'm here to enhance it. The structure has to be added in at some point. And *this,* my friends, is your structure cheat sheet.

Read it. Learn it. Love it!

The Save the Cat! Beat Sheet is divided into three acts (or parts), which are further subdivided into fifteen total beats (or plot points). Before we break down each beat in detail and get into the nitty-gritty, here's a quick summary view of all fifteen beats and where they belong in your novel.

ACT 1

1. OPENING IMAGE (0 TO 1%): A "before" snapshot of your hero and their world.

2. THEME STATED (5%): A statement made by a character (typically not the hero) that *hints* at what the hero's arc will be (that is, what the hero must learn/discover before the end of the book). Also referred to as a life lesson.

3. SETUP (1% TO 10%): An exploration of the hero's status quo life and all its flaws, where we learn what the hero's life looks like before its epic transformation. Here we also introduce other supporting characters and the hero's primary goal. But most important, we show the hero's reluctance to change (aka learn the theme) while also hinting at the stakes at risk should the hero *not* change.

4. CATALYST (10%): An inciting incident (or life-changing event) that happens to the hero, which will catapult them into a new world or new way of thinking. An action beat that should be big enough to prevent the hero from being able to return to their status quo Setup world.

5. DEBATE (10% TO 20%): A reaction sequence in which the hero debates what they will do next. It's usually presented in the form of a question (such as "Should I go?"). The purpose of this beat is to show the hero's reluctance to change.

ACT 2

6. BREAK INTO 2 (20%): The moment the hero decides to accept the call to action, leave their comfort zone, try something new, or venture into a new world or new way of thinking. It's a decisive *action* beat that separates the status quo world of Act 1 from the new "upside-down" world of Act 2.

7. B STORY (22%): The introduction of a new character or characters who will ultimately serve to help the hero learn the theme. Also referred to as a helper character, this can be a love interest, a nemesis, a mentor, a family member, or a friend.

8. FUN AND GAMES (20% TO 50%): This is where we see the hero in their new world. They're either loving it or hating it. Succeeding or floundering. Also called the promise of the premise, this section represents the "hook" of the story (why the reader picked up the novel in the first place).

9. MIDPOINT (50%): Literally the middle of the novel, where the Fun and Games culminates in either a false victory (the hero has thus far been succeeding) or a false defeat (the hero has thus far been floundering). Something should happen here to raise the stakes and push the hero toward real change.

10. BAD GUYS CLOSE IN (50% TO 75%): If the Midpoint was a false victory, this section will be a downward path where things get progressively worse for the hero. If the Midpoint was a false defeat, this section will be an upward path where things seem to get progressively better for the hero. But regardless of path, the hero's deep-rooted flaws (or internal bad guys) are closing in.

11. ALL IS LOST (75%): The lowest point of the novel. An action beat where something happens to the hero that, combined with the internal bad guys, pushes the hero to rock bottom.

12. DARK NIGHT OF THE SOUL (75% TO 80%): A reaction beat where the hero takes time to process everything that's happened thus far. The hero should be worse off than at the start of the novel. The darkest hour—just before the dawn—is the moment right before the hero figures out the solution to their big problem and learns the theme or life lesson.

ACT 3

13. BREAK INTO 3 (80%): The "aha!" moment. The hero realizes what they must do to not only fix all of the problems created in Act 2, but more important, fix themselves. The arc is *nearly* complete.

14. FINALE (80% TO 99%): The hero proves they have truly learned the theme and enacts the plan they came up with in the Break Into 3. Bad guys are destroyed, flaws are conquered, lovers are reunited. Not only is the hero's world saved, but it's a *better* place than it was before.

15. FINAL IMAGE (99% TO 100%): A mirror to the Opening Image, this is the "after" snapshot of who the hero is after going through this epic and satisfying transformation.

So there you have it. The Save the Cat! Beat Sheet. This is your blueprint for an engaging, well-structured story with a compelling and complete character arc that will resonate with readers. Don't worry if the beats seem foreign or confusing right now. This is just the overview. We're now going to dive into every single one in such great detail you'll soon be eating, sleeping, and breathing these beats.

And if you're more of a "learn by example" type of person, fear not! I have provided you with ten (count 'em, *ten*) full beat sheets from popular novels in the following chapters.

You're welcome!

What Goes Where

You'll notice that at the start of each beat I've included a handy "beat cheat sheet" (how's that for a rhyme!) that you can reference at any time to quickly remind you of the beat's primary purpose and where it goes in your manuscript. Because novels vary greatly in length, I've chosen to provide these guidelines as *percentages* of the total novel (instead of page numbers or word counts).

Here's a visual representation of how the beat sheet breaks down:

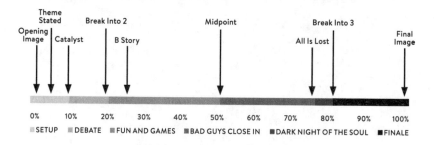

If you need help estimating the total length of your completed novel, these handy tables feature publishing industry standard lengths for middle grade, young adult, and general fiction novels, as well as lengths for a few popular novels.

MIDDLE GRADE NOVELS (READERS 8 TO 12)	WORD COUNT	ESTIMATED MANUSCRIPT PAGE COUNT*
Publishing Industry Standard	40,000 to 60,000	160 to 240
Holes by Louis Sachar	47,079	188
Wonder by R. J. Palacio	73,053	292
Harry Potter and the Sorcerer's Stone	96,000	384

* Page counts calculated from word count using Times New Roman, 12 point font, double spaced, based on an industry standard of 250 words per manuscript page.

YOUNG ADULT NOVELS (READERS 12 TO 17)	WORD COUNT	ESTIMATED MANUSCRIPT PAGE COUNT
Publishing Industry Standard	60,000 to 90,000	240 to 360
The Giver by Lois Lowry	43,617	174
Lord of the Flies by William Golding	59,900	239
The Hunger Games by Suzanne Collins	99,750	399
GENERAL FICTION NOVELS (READERS 18 AND UP)	**WORD COUNT**	**ESTIMATED MANUSCRIPT PAGE COUNT**
Publishing Industry Standard	70,000 to 100,000	280 to 400
Bridget Jones's Diary by Helen Fielding	86,400	346
The Da Vinci Code by Dan Brown	138,952	556
Gone Girl by Gillian Flynn	145,719	582

Remember, however, that novels can vary greatly in length, so it's important that you use these examples only as guidelines. Be flexible. Your novel's length will change as you write and revise, but it's always helpful to have a rough estimated word count or page count in mind when you start so you can calculate where each beat goes.

Okay! Are you ready to dive into the Save the Cat! Beat Sheet? Then, without further ado, let's beat it out!

Act 1

The three-act structure for writing stories is nothing new. It's been around forever. But for the sake of the Save the Cat! Beat Sheet, we're going to look at the three acts not as "acts" but more as "worlds." Three very different worlds or states of being that the hero will traverse on their way to becoming the person they need to become.

But before your hero can go anywhere, or become anyone, they need a place to begin. That is the purpose of the Act 1 world. It is the **thesis** world, or the "status quo" world. It is designed to show the reader of your novel what your hero's life and world look like before everything starts to change. And change it will! But unless the reader understands where your hero has been, they won't fully appreciate who your hero will eventually become.

So let's show 'em!

1. OPENING IMAGE

WHAT DOES IT DO? Provides a quick "before" snapshot of your hero and their world.

WHERE DOES IT GO? 1% (This is the first scene or chapter of your novel.)

In simplest terms, the Opening Image is a "before" snapshot. It's a scene or chapter that depicts your hero's life *before* you've gotten in there as the writer to shake things up. This beat helps the reader of your story understand exactly what kind of journey they're about to go on and *who* they're about to go on it with.

The Opening Image also sets the book's tone, style, and mood. If it's a funny book, this beat should be funny. If it's a suspenseful book, this beat should be—surprise!—suspenseful. This is where your voice (or writing style) as the author shines bright and gives the reader a clear picture of what they're getting into.

But above all else, the Opening Image is an *image*. Yes, that sounds obvious, but you'd be surprised how many writers in my workshops don't really grasp this right away. It should be a *visual* representation of your hero's flawed life.

So what does that mean? It means, open your novel with something active. There's a reason it's not called the Opening Inner Monologue or the Opening Info Dump. We should *see* your flawed hero in action.

Remember all those flaws you jotted down in chapter 1, when we created our story-worthy heroes? Well, here's where you pick one (or two, or three) and *show* us how those flaws are screwing up your hero's life. Is your hero meek and lacking confidence? Well, don't just tell us about it. *Show* your hero being meek and lacking confidence with a specific *visual* scene.

After reading the Opening Image, the reader should be gripping your book, thinking *Aha! So that's how it's going to be, huh? I'm in!*

Think about the first two pages of *The Hunger Games* by Suzanne Collins. Katniss Everdeen wakes up in her house in District 12 on the day of the "reaping" and sneaks out to hunt so her family can eat. In this Opening Image we immediately start to understand her life and the challenges she faces.

Or look at the first chapter of *Pride and Prejudice* by Jane Austen. On page 1, we're immediately thrown into an argument between Mr. and Mrs. Bennet (the parents of the hero, Elizabeth Bennet). The argument is all about whether or not Mr. Bennet will introduce himself to the handsome eligible bachelor who has just moved into the neighborhood. This comical argument gives us a quick taste of the pressures Elizabeth is dealing with as a young woman in nineteenth-century England.

The Opening Image of *Confessions of a Shopaholic* by Sophie Kinsella is just as effective. We *see*, in a very humorous light, Becky Bloomwood opening and reacting to her Visa bill, so we know (1) this character has some serious problems with personal finances and (2) this book is going to be a riot!

The Opening Image has a **mirror beat** (or an opposite beat) called the Final Image, the very last beat of the novel. If the Opening Image shows us where the hero begins, the Final Image shows us where the hero ends. They are bookends of the transformative journey. And you should make them as different as possible. Otherwise, where did the hero go? What was the point of reading this story? The further apart your Opening Image and Final Image are, the more worthwhile the story. It's as simple as that.

It's important to note that the Opening Image is a single scene or chapter. It's *one* piece of information. Katniss's morning routine. The argument at the Bennet house. Which is why I call it a **single-scene beat**. There will be other beats that we'll come across along the way that are **multi-scene beats**, meaning they span across *several* scenes and chapters. As we work our way through the beat sheet, I will always tell you whether or not the beat is a single-scene or a multi-scene beat.

2. THEME STATED

WHAT DOES IT DO? Briefly alludes to the transformative journey that your hero will take and the flaw or flaws they will eventually conquer.

WHERE DOES IT GO? 5% (or somewhere within the first 10% of the novel)

Essentially, the Theme Stated is the hero's need or life lesson, somehow hinted at up front in the story (often by a secondary character).

If that sounds like mumbo jumbo to you, let me put it more simply:

Somewhere in Act 1 (usually within the Setup beat), a character (usually not the hero) will make a statement or pose a question to your hero that somehow relates to what the hero needs to learn by the end of the story. Like this: "Maybe all men got one big soul ever'body's a part of," stated by Preacher Casy to Tom Joad in *The Grapes of Wrath* by John Steinbeck (page 24). Or "Mom is always saying I'm a smart kid but that I just don't 'apply' myself," written in Greg Heffley's journal in *The Diary of a Wimpy Kid* by Jeff Kinney (page 14). Or even something as simple as, "What exactly do you want to do with your life?" stated by Camilla Traynor to Louisa Clark in *Me Before You* by Jojo Moyes (page 22).

And what do you know? By the end of all of these stories, the hero learns these exact themes. Tom Joad learns how to go from independent (someone who looks out mostly for himself) to selfless (someone who looks out for others). Greg learns a valuable lesson in responsibility. And Louisa learns how to take control of her life and live it for *her* (not for anyone else).

Whatever life lesson your hero has to learn, whatever epic transformation your hero has to make, it should be *subtly* mentioned within the first 10 percent of your story. You don't want to shout it from the rooftops or spend five pages delving into it. You just want to delicately plant the seed in the reader's brain. It's writer manipulation at its best. And don't we writers just *love* to manipulate?

Basically, by having a character subtly state the theme of the novel, you are giving the reader a subconscious hint as to what your story is really going to be *about*.

Because although yes, your book can have all sorts of epic space battles or fantasy monsters or swoon-worthy love scenes, if your story is not *about* something, if it doesn't go *deeper* into what it means to be human, it's just not worth reading.

So what *is* your story about?

Well, I've said it before and I'll say it again. It's about *transformation*!

It's about taking an imperfect hero and making them a little less imperfect.

What will it take to make *your* hero a little less imperfect? Well, that's your theme. And now someone's gotta state it.

The Theme Stated is a single-scene beat. It usually comes and goes very quickly. The theme is stated and then the story moves on. But it doesn't necessarily have to be a *person* who states the theme. Although that's more common, I sometimes see themes stated on a billboard the hero passes or in a book or magazine the hero is reading. You can be creative in how you state your theme, just as long as you state it.

Now, don't let the word "theme" confuse you. For the sake of the beat sheet, the theme refers directly to your hero's need or life lesson.

Pride and Prejudice by Jane Austen, for example, has many themes (in the generic sense of the word): love, marriage, wealth, class, and so on. But the Theme Stated, as it pertains to the beat sheet, comes on page 16 when Elizabeth's younger sister Mary says, "Pride is a very common failing, I believe." She then explains why pride is found in all of us and therefore should not be judged too harshly. This is a direct reference to Elizabeth Bennet's life lesson of learning to curb her prejudice. But does Elizabeth listen and take heed? No! Mary is subsequently ignored by everyone in the room.

And *this* is what I love about the Theme Stated.

The hero often *ignores* it!

So, there's your flawed hero. They're traipsing around the Act 1 world, being flawed, making stupid decisions, generally leading an imperfect life, and then someone (usually a secondary character) comes up to them and says, "You know what would really fix your life? *This!*"

Your hero is essentially *presented* with the answer to all of their problems right there at the beginning of the book. But do they listen?

Of course not!

They completely, 100-percent *ignore* this person. Because at the start of the novel, your hero is *resistant* to change. They hear the theme stated and they go, "What the heck does *he* know? He doesn't know *me.*" That's why it's often best to have the theme stated by a *secondary* character—a passerby, a fellow traveler on the bus, a nemesis—as opposed to someone close to your hero. This is by no means a hard-and-fast rule, but it's easier for a reader to *believe* that the hero would ignore the theme if it's stated by a stranger or someone the hero doesn't necessarily know or trust.

But what is your hero going to learn by the end of the book? That very theme that was stated so early in the story. Which means they had the answer to their problems the whole time; they just refused to listen!

Having your hero ignore the theme makes your hero realistic. People rarely change because someone *tells* them to change. People change only when they can see their flaws for themselves. When they've been through some sort of transformative journey and come out on the other side having finally realized the truth. That is the essence of being *human*.

So our job as writers is to create that believable transformative journey that will allow our heroes to see the truth, recognize their flaws, and take action to fix them.

Take a look at the sample beat sheets in chapters 4–13 for some more examples of the Theme Stated beat in action!

Okay, so by now you might be getting a little freaked out, feeling a little overwhelmed at the thought of coming up with an epic life-changing theme to put in your novel. But let me ease your fears a bit.

Remember in the last chapter, when, before anything else, I *forced* you to think about who your hero is, why they're flawed, and what they need to learn by the end of the story?

Well, that need you came up with? That life lesson I made you brainstorm? That *is* your theme. You already have it.

Huzzah! Now you just need to figure out *how* the theme is stated and *who* states it.

3. SETUP

WHAT DOES IT DO? Sets up your hero's life and their status quo world *before* everything changes.

WHERE DOES IT GO? 1% to 10% (This beat usually takes up the first tenth of the novel.)

In the Opening Image, you gave the reader a glimpse of what to expect in this story. A small *sliver* of the hero's life. Now it's time to show us the *rest* of the hero's world.

The Setup is a multi-scene beat. Meaning you get several scenes or chapters to accomplish all that you need to accomplish in the Setup. And get ready, because it's a *lot*.

First and foremost, you need to set up your hero. What kind of person are they? What kind of character tics do they have? What do they want? It's very important that your hero have a *goal*. We talked about wants and goals in chapter 1. Your hero has to be actively pursuing something when the book begins. Even if it's not something they'll pursue throughout the entire story, something has to be there from the start. This is the thing your hero *thinks* will fix their life. Will it actually fix their life? Of course not! Because it's their want, not their need. And, as I explained in the Theme Stated beat, the need (or life lesson) is what will *really* fix the hero's life in the end. They just don't know it . . . yet.

In the Setup is where you'll introduce everyone who exists within your hero's Act 1, status quo world. These can be friends, family, bosses, coworkers, teachers, enemies, fellow students, peers, and so on. Basically anyone who is important when the story begins, before your hero's life changes. These are also called the **A Story characters**, because they represent the A Story (or external story) of the novel. (As opposed to the B Story character[s]—we'll meet them later.)

Finally, the Setup is where you show your hero's flaws in all of their glory. How do these flaws affect all aspects of the hero's life? A hero who is greedy and selfish isn't *only* greedy and selfish at work. They're greedy and selfish at home too. And with their friends. And with their family. The best way to show this is to include scenes or chapters that take place at home, work, and play. This means you may want to take time in your Setup to show your hero at home (with family, with spouse, with kids, or maybe alone in their apartment), at work (in the workplace, at their job, or at school), and at play (how your hero unwinds with friends or by themselves). Think about when we first meet Becky Bloomwood in *Confessions of a Shopaholic* by Sophie Kinsella. Not only are her finances a mess because of her shopping addiction, but she hates her job (work), she's just broken up with her boyfriend (play), *and* she lies to her roommate and her parents about her money situation (home). The more we see your hero in different aspects of their life, the better we will understand them as people.

Remember, your hero's life can't be perfect. Otherwise, where do we go from here? What's the point of reading this novel? Your hero's world needs to be riddled with problems. In the world of Save the Cat!, these problems are referred to as the **things that need fixing**. Basically, it's a laundry list (however long you want) of things that are wrong with the hero's life. She's lonely, doesn't communicate with her father, and has no friends (Opal in *Because of Winn-Dixie* by Kate

DiCamillo). She's an orphan with an evil guardian, gets locked in a scary room with scary things, and has a foster brother who bullies her (*Jane Eyre* by Charlotte Brontë). His whole family was murdered and the killer got away, he's lost his job and his health is failing, and he has a rare brain condition that never allows him to forget anything (Amos Decker in *Memory Man* by David Baldacci). She's lost her job and has no real skills to get another one, her family relies heavily on her income, and she has a boyfriend who bores her (*Me Before You* by Jojo Moyes).

The possibilities are endless, but the objective is the same: to make the reader understand why this person needs to go on a journey of transformation. Because clearly things aren't working out in this status quo world of Act 1.

The things that need fixing all will reappear throughout the rest of the story. They will serve as checkpoints along the journey to demarcate change. As we move through the story, we check in on these things and ask, *What about now? Does he still hate his job? Is she still being bullied? Is his family still hungry?* If some of these things don't start changing along the way, then we know we're not doing enough to transform our hero and their world.

Wow. That's a lot of work to do in the Setup! But it's important, ground-laying work that I guarantee will make for a better and more satisfying read in the long run.

But we can't stay in the Setup forever, any more than your hero can stay in their status quo world forever. If you've done your job well, you've already been hinting at the need for change. And your reader is already getting the sense that if something doesn't happen soon to bring about that change, this hero is pretty much doomed.

Think about the moment in *Me Before You* right after Louisa loses her job. Her father says to her mother, "There are no bloody jobs, Josie . . . We're in the middle of a bloody recession" (page 9). Or the scene in *Jane Eyre* when she gets locked in the seemingly haunted red room by Mrs. Reed, freaks out, and then faints from her fright. Or the moment in *The Outsiders* by S. E. Hinton when Ponyboy and his friends are walking with Cherry and Marcia and a fight almost breaks out with the Socs. Ponyboy says, "I felt the tension growing inside of me and I knew something had to happen, or I would explode" (page 43).

This is called the **stasis = death** moment. It's the moment that comes somewhere in the Setup beat that shows the reader that change is *imperative*; otherwise, things are going south. Fast.

Whether you employ a specific stasis = death moment or you just impart a general sense of urgency, without the obvious need for change in the hero's life, it's difficult to get your reader to continue on the rest of the journey with you. So it's your job, in the Setup, to plant the seed in the reader's mind that change is crucial. That staying in this status quo world for much longer just isn't an option.

Something needs to happen.

Enter . . . the Catalyst.

4. CATALYST

WHAT DOES IT DO? Disrupts the status quo world with a life-changing event.
WHERE DOES IT GO? 10% (or earlier)

Congratulations. You've done a fantastic job constructing your hero's life and world. Giving them flaws and character tics and friends and family and a tangible goal. Bringing to life a realistic world that your reader can really sink their teeth into.

Now it's time to knock it all down.

A dead body is found at the museum (*The Da Vinci Code* by Dan Brown), the king proposes (*The White Queen* by Philippa Gregory), a professional football team is bequeathed to an unsuspecting daughter (*It Had to Be You* by Susan Elizabeth Phillips), a dying girl meets a quirky boy at a cancer support group (*The Fault in Our Stars* by John Green), an arrest is made on an eighteen-month-old cold case (*Memory Man* by David Baldacci), a woman gets a job as caretaker for a quadriplegic man (*Me Before You* by Jojo Moyes), a young girl meets a stray dog (*Because of Winn-Dixie*), an innocent boy is shot by the police (*The Hate U Give* by Angie Thomas).

These are all harbingers of change. The Catalyst will crash land in your hero's life and create so much destruction, your hero will have no choice but to do something different. Try something new. Go somewhere else.

Catalysts often come in the form of bad news (a letter in the mail, a phone call, a death, getting fired, being diagnosed with a deadly disease). Not always, but often. Why? Because most people won't change their ways until something bad happens. Bad news often paves the way to good things. Without any bad news, your hero would be perfectly content just going about their flawed little life, being their flawed little self. Maybe even forever! But would your reader be just as content? No. Your reader wants to see something *happen*. They want action. They want a twist. They want drama.

Whether they realize it or not, they want a *Catalyst*.

The Catalyst is a single-scene beat in which something happens *to* the hero to send their life in an entirely new direction. Notice that I emphasize the word "to." The Catalyst always happens *to* your hero. It's something *active* that will bust through the status quo and send them on the road toward change.

Essentially, it's a wake-up call. Or a call to action. Time to open your eyes and start looking at the world in a new way. The Catalyst should be BIG. Don't wimp out on me with a weak little Catalyst. I see this happen all the time in my workshops. Students will pitch a Catalyst for their story and the rest of us will go, "Yeah? So?"

Conflict is what makes for good fiction. It's what makes for good *story*. Without it, you run the risk of your readers saying, *Yeah? So?* And that's the last thing you want your reader to say. Your reader's response to your Catalyst should be *Whoa! I didn't see that coming! How are they ever going to recover from* that?

Now that sounds like an effective Catalyst.

So how do you know if your Catalyst is big enough? Ask yourself the following question: *Can my hero easily return to their normal life and continue doing what they were doing after this happens?*

If your answer is yes, your Catalyst isn't big enough.

If your answer is *Heck no!* then you're on the right track.

5. DEBATE

WHAT DOES IT DO? Shows how resistant your hero is to change and/or prepares your hero for the break into Act 2.

WHERE DOES IT GO? 10% to 20% (This beat takes us from Catalyst to the end of Act 1.)

For every action, there is a reaction. And for every Catalyst, there is a Debate. For every breakup, firing, disease diagnosis, arrest, dead body, and phone call with bad news, there is a period in which the hero of the story sits down with a huge sigh and goes, *What now?*

It is a reaction beat, and it usually comes in the form of a question. Like *What do I do? Should I go? Should I stay? How will I survive? What happens next?*

And along with the hero, readers will be asking the same Debate questions: "Will Robert Langdon help solve the murder of the museum curator?" (*The Da Vinci Code*). "Was the marriage to the king real or just a ploy to sleep with Elizabeth?" (*The White Queen*). "How will Phoebe handle the football team's head coach?" (*It Had to Be You*). "Will Hazel and Augustus get together?" (*The Fault in Our Stars*). "What will Decker do now that someone has confessed to the murder of his family?" (*Memory Man*). "Can Louisa *do* this job?" (*Me Before You*). "Will Opal *keep* the dog?" (*Because of Winn-Dixie*). "Will Starr speak up about what she saw on the night Khalil was shot?" (*The Hate U Give*).

The Debate is the time in your story for your hero to take a step back and decide how they're going to proceed after this life-altering Catalyst has knocked them down.

But why do heroes debate? Why can't they just get their life-changing news and move on? Because it's not realistic. Pondering and weighing options and gathering more information is what we do as humans *and* heroes. Remember, no one accepts change right away. No one goes, *Oh well, I guess my status quo life didn't work out after all; time to change my ways!*

Nope. Heroes drag their feet. They hem and haw.

They *debate*.

It's a multi-scene beat in which you visibly show us how resistant your hero is to accept the change that's been thrown at them. An effective way to do this is to take your hero back to home, work, and play. Show them struggling to decide what to do next in *all* aspects of their life. Because if they decide too quickly, you risk losing credibility with your reader.

Now, I should note, the Debate doesn't *always* have to be a decision. Sometimes it's not a matter of whether or not your hero will go or stay, act or not act. Sometimes that part is obvious. Like in *The Hunger Games* by Suzanne Collins. Katniss is clearly not going to change her mind after volunteering to take her sister's place in the reaping. Or in *Harry Potter and the Sorcerer's Stone*. After learning he's a wizard and has been accepted to Hogwarts, Harry doesn't have to think that hard about whether to go.

So, what does your hero do in these situations? They *prepare* for the big journey. They gather supplies. They train. They prep mentally, physically, and emotionally. The question in this type of Debate is usually something like, *I know I'm going, but am I ready?*

Whether your Debate is a decision or a preparation, all Debates are designed to do one thing: get your hero and your reader ready for what they're about to encounter in Act 2.

Because trust me, it's going to be unlike anything they've ever seen before.

Act 2

You need to know one very important thing about Act 2, arguably the most important thing to know about the entire beat sheet:

Act 2 is the *opposite* of Act 1.

If Act 1 is the thesis—the status quo world—then Act 2 is the upside-down version of that. The polar opposite. The inverse. The **antithesis**.

I can't overstress this. I see so many fantastic, beautifully written, *promising* novels fall apart in Act 2 because the author forgot to build this simple, yet crucial element into the blueprint of their story. Act 2 needs to be as different as possible from Act 1. So, let's see what we're dealing with in this upside-down world.

6. BREAK INTO 2

WHAT DOES IT DO? Brings the hero into the upside-down world of Act 2, where they will fix things the *wrong* way.

WHERE DOES IT GO? 20% (Before you get one-quarter of the way through your novel, there should be a clear Act break.)

The game is afoot! The challenge is accepted! The adventure is upon us! The new way of life has begun! The Debate is over, our hero knows what they have to do, and now it's time to do it.

This is our clear and defined break into the upside-down world of Act 2. Ta-da!

If you've designed your Act 2 world well (that is, different from Act 1!), then the transition should seem *very* obvious to the reader. There's no doubt about it. We are *not* in Kansas anymore.

Katniss Everdeen enters the Capitol (*The Hunger Games*), Auggie Pullman starts middle school (*Wonder* by R. J. Palacio), Robert Langdon is now on the run from the French police (*The Da Vinci Code*), Jack escapes Room (*Room* by Emma Donoghue), Elizabeth moves into the castle in London (*The White Queen*), Jane sets out for Thornfield to be the new governess (*Jane Eyre*), Hazel and Augustus start a relationship (*The Fault in Our Stars*).

It's important to note that heroes don't have to physically *go* anywhere in order to Break Into 2. But they *do* have to try something new. A new relationship, a new way of approaching life, a new job, a new persona at school. Regardless of whether your hero goes on a literal journey or a metaphorical one, the Break Into 2 is the moment when we leave the old world and old way of thinking behind and step into a new world and new way of thinking. It's a single-scene beat. You get one scene or chapter to break your hero into Act 2. That's it. So make it a good, effective break.

How do you do that?

You make sure the choice to Break Into 2 belongs *to* your hero.

They must be proactive about it. The decision can be put before them by someone else, but the actual choice to act must be theirs and theirs alone.

Regardless of the flaws you've set up in Act 1—regardless if your hero is meek or indecisive, or foolish, or selfish, or cowardly—this is where all heroes prove they have something in them worth rooting for. Something worth *reading* about. This is where all heroes show they're at least somewhat willing to try something new.

No one wants to read about a lazy hero who sits around all day doing nothing about their imperfect life (well, at least not beyond Act 1). If, in the Debate, the hero asks, "What should I do?" then the Break Into 2 is the hero saying, "I should do this! And I will!"

Does this mean that your hero has learned the theme and has finally figured out how to fix their life? Not quite.

Let's briefly return to the wants and needs. Remember those external and internal goals we set up in the last chapter? If you asked your hero, "What do *you* think will fix your life?" they would probably answer with something *external*, like "A better job!" "A new girlfriend!" "To win the world championship!" "To kill the evil queen who murdered my whole family!"

If you've set up your wants and needs correctly, your hero's external goal (want) is *not* what will inevitably fix their life. They think it is. They'd bet their life on it! But in the end, it's their internal or spiritual goal (need) that will make them a better person.

At this point in the story, as our hero is making their proactive decision to Break Into 2, they are still being motivated by what they *want*. They're still chasing after that external goal. Maybe they'll get it, maybe they won't. But by the end of the novel, it won't matter, because they'll have gotten what they *need*. They'll have learned their life lesson. They'll have learned the theme.

That's why I like to call Act 2 **fixing things the wrong way**.

Louisa Clark starts working for the Traynors in *Me Before You* only because she *wants* a job so she can help provide for her working-class family. Eventually, yes, that job will help her learn her life lesson of independence (needs), but that's not why she's doing it now.

Opal Buloni adopts Winn-Dixie in *Because of Winn-Dixie* because she *wants* a friend. And eventually, yes, that dog will bring her and her father together (needs), but again, that's not her reason for adopting the dog.

And Tom Joad is setting off for California with his family because he *wants* work, not because he knows he's destined to become an advocate for the migrant working community (needs). That comes later.

At this point in the story, your hero is making an effort. They're getting off their butt. They're rallying. They're doing what they think has to be done to solve whatever problems you've set up in Act 1, and we have to give them credit for that. They're *trying*.

But they're making uninformed decisions. They're still motivated by those wants. They're fueled by the A Story (the external story). So yeah, in Act 2 they might be slaying dragons and solving clues and kissing boys and flying spaceships in intergalactic wars, but these things, while übercool, are not the answer. They won't fix what needs to be fixed in the long run.

Don't get me wrong. We want to see this stuff. This is what great books are made of. You can't write a story that's *all* theme and life lessons. (Yawn!) You need the fun stuff too. You need the A Story.

But whatever decision your hero makes when they Break Into 2 is a temporary solution. It's the Band-Aid they're slapping on to hide the wound underneath. It's not true healing. Because those flaws are still in there, wreaking havoc. That shard of glass, which has made them who they are, is still buried. And so, at the Break Into 2, your hero is not yet solving anything on a deeper, spiritual level. Ergo, they're fixing things the wrong way.

That's not an insult to your hero. It's just part of the master plot manipulation. Because you can't figure out the right way until you've first tried the wrong way.

And trust me, the wrong way can be a *lot* of fun, as you'll soon see in the Fun and Games beat.

But first, it's time to meet some new people.

7. B STORY

WHAT DOES IT DO? Introduces the character who will somehow represent the B Story/spiritual story/theme and help your hero learn it.

WHERE DOES IT GO? 22% (Usually happens right after the Break Into 2, but can come earlier. Just make sure it happens in the first 25% of the novel.)

Remember when I said Act 2 is the upside-down version of Act 1? That means everything in Act 2 should be upside-down versions of everything in Act 1. Even the people.

In the Setup, we introduced the A Story characters. These are people who come from the hero's status quo world. They represent the external story. They don't necessarily have to go away after the hero enters Act 2, but they will inevitably take a backseat to the person or people we're going to meet in this new world.

Enter the **B Story character!**

The B Story character is a helper character—the person who's ultimately going to somehow *help* your hero learn the theme. They usually come in the form of a love interest, a new friend, a mentor, or a nemesis. Yes, B Story characters can be enemies! I've seen it done well many times.

There are only two criteria for being a successful B Story character (others need not apply):

1. They must in some way represent the upside-down Act 2 world.

2. They must in some way help guide the hero toward their life lesson or theme.

The first criterion means that the hero could never have met or noticed this character in Act 1. It was only because of the Catalyst and subsequent Break Into 2 that this B Story character fully came into the hero's life.

Think about Peeta Mellark in *The Hunger Games*. Yes, he's lived in District 12 with Katniss his whole life. And yes, they did have a few brief encounters in the past. But it isn't until Katniss volunteers as a tribute and gets shipped off to the Capitol that Peeta becomes a major player in her life.

In *Jane Eyre*, the mysterious and ill-tempered Mr. Rochester very much embodies the equally mysterious residence of Thornfield Hall where Jane kicks off her Act 2 adventure.

And what about Peter Van Houten, the reclusive author that Hazel and Augustus meet in Amsterdam in *The Fault in Our Stars*? Sure, Hazel was obsessed with him before, but it's not until after she meets Augustus that Peter enters Hazel's world in a real way.

All of these B Story characters are, in some way, *products* of the Act 2 world.

But why should the B Story character be a product of the new world? Because—remember?—the hero can't learn the theme and complete their transformation in their Act 1, status quo life. That's why we gave them their Catalyst to kick them *into* Act 2. Therefore, the person who's helping them learn that theme should exist in this *new* world. Otherwise, they could have learned that same theme by staying exactly where they were. And where's the fun in that?

The B Story character can help guide your hero toward their life lesson in a variety of different ways. For example: Your B Story character can be the embodiment of the theme. Like Peeta Mellark in *The Hunger Games*. Right before the Games officially begin, Peeta says to Katniss, "I keep wishing I could think of a way to . . . to show the Capitol they don't own me. That I'm more than just a piece in their Games" (page 142). This is the ultimate lesson (theme) that Katniss will learn: how to defy the Capitol, instead of just playing by their rules to survive. And it's Peeta, the B Story character, who helps her get there.

Or your B Story character can be someone who, by their very nature, brings out the theme in the hero. Like Mr. Rochester in *Jane Eyre*, whose bossy, cantankerous nature actually inspires meek Jane to be bolder and assert herself and her independence more.

Or your B Story character could be someone who suffers from the same flaws as your hero, but in an even more exaggerated way, thus holding up a mirror to your hero's flaws and allowing them to see the truth for themselves. Think about how sad, bitter, and lonely author Peter Van Houten has become in *The Fault in Our Stars*. Witnessing this only pushes Hazel to love Augustus more fully, regardless of how badly she might get hurt.

However you choose to do it, helping the hero learn the theme is the ultimate role of the B Story character. And they're introduced here, in this single-scene beat, somewhere in the first half of Act 2 (usually during the Fun and Games beat). The B Story character will appear all throughout the second and even third act of the novel, but here's where they *first* come into the story. Either in the form of a new love interest, new friend, new mentor, or new enemy. It can really be anyone. Just as long as they can effectively bring out your hero's flaws, and make them *want* to change.

So, right now you might be thinking, *Wait, I only get to introduce one new character in the second act?*

No, you can introduce as many characters as you want in Act 2. But the B Story character will be that *special* character that fulfills that very special role as the ambassador of the life lesson.

And if you're having trouble figuring out *who* that special person will be, good news! You can have more than one B Story character! That's right. Many great novels have what are called **twin B stories**. This can happen in the form of a love interest *and* a mentor. Or a love interest *and* a new friend. Or even *two* new friends, as is the case with *Because of Winn-Dixie*, in which Opal meets her two thematic guides—Gloria Dump and Miss Frannie Block—both *because* of Winn-Dixie, the dog. And both teach her a valuable lesson about her theme of loneliness.

But if you're going to have more than one B Story character, make sure both characters are fulfilling their duties in this role. And make sure they're fulfilling it in different ways. Otherwise, why do we need both?

8. FUN AND GAMES

WHAT DOES IT DO? Delivers on the promise of the premise of the novel and shows us how your hero is faring in the new Act 2 world (either having fun or floundering).

WHERE DOES IT GO? 20% to 50% (This beat spans the entire first half of Act 2.)

The Fun and Games beat is probably the reason your reader picked up this book in the first place.

It's also called the **promise of the premise**. Because when a reader starts reading a book, they were most likely told something about this particular beat—either from the summary on the back of the book, a book review, or a fellow reader.

They were promised an astronaut figuring out how to survive on a lifeless planet (*The Martian* by Andy Weir), a school for witches and wizards (*Harry Potter and the Sorcerer's Stone*), a boy stuck on a lifeboat with a tiger (*Life of Pi*), a tattooed punk girl working to solve a forty-year-old mystery of a girl's disappearance (*The Girl with the Dragon Tattoo* by Stieg Larsson), a man with a perfect memory solving the murder of his family (*Memory Man*), or a directionless girl acting as caretaker to an acerbic quadriplegic man in a wheelchair (*Me Before You*).

So now you, the author, must deliver on that promise. Right here. Right now.

I see a lot of writers get confused by the *name* of this beat. They look at the Fun and Games beat of novels like *The Hunger Games* and think, *Twenty-four teens killing each other in an arena? That doesn't sound like a lot of fun for Katniss!*

The key to figuring out the Fun and Games beat is realizing that this part of the story might be fun only for the *reader*. Not necessarily for the *hero*.

Yes, Harry Potter has a blast when he first gets to Hogwarts. He is having *fun* in his upside-down magic world. Katniss Everdeen in *The Hunger Games*? Not so much.

Readers, though, are loving it. Not because they're sadistic and evil and wish they *too* were in that arena killing people. But because reading about Katniss's struggle is interesting and engaging. It's an Act 1 hero living in an Act 2 world. And if you've built your Act 1 and Act 2 worlds to be as different as possible (like I told you to do!), this is automatically fun.

Plus, Katniss fighting in the arena delivers on the premise of the book. Heck, it even delivers on the *title* of the book!

So to avoid confusion, let's define the Fun and Games beat like this: a multi-scene beat in which your hero either shines in their new upside-down world or flounders in it.

Because those are your only two options. They're either loving it or hating it. They're either grateful they made this leap of faith and went on this adventure, or they're severely missing their old way of life.

Think about who your hero is. Think about how they're feeling as they step into their Act 2 world. Are they happy to be there? Or are they miserable? Are they excelling in their new way of life? Or are they struggling?

Now, that doesn't mean your entire Fun and Games beat has to be all struggle or all success. In fact, I recommend it not be. The Fun and Games is nearly 30 percent of your novel. You have to vary the action.

I call this the **bouncing ball** narrative. Your hero is up, your hero is down. Things are going swimmingly, things are going horribly. The hero succeeds at something, then fails at something. The girl gets the boy, the girl loses the boy. The detective makes a breakthrough on the case, only to discover it's a false lead. The king wins a battle, then loses a battle. Up, down, up, down, and so on and so forth. This unpredictable dynamic is how you make your Fun and Games rich, engaging, and most of all, *fun!*

But despite how many times your ball bounces, in the end there should be a general direction in which the beat is heading: success or failure. This is something you must decide. Is this beat an **upward path** (the general direction heading toward success) or a **downward path** (the general direction heading toward failure)?

Once Louisa in *Me Before You* accepts the job as Will's companion and decides to convince him not to take his own life, it's a generally upward path toward the Midpoint. Louisa is making a good wage (wants), and is having a *positive* effect on Will, which is evident from his improved mood and appearance. The two even share an (ambiguously) romantic night at the symphony together.

Same goes for Mark Watney in *The Martian*. Despite the Catalyst being catastrophic (Mark Watney is stuck on Mars with no crew and no way home), Mark's Fun and Games beat is a decidedly upward path as he successfully figures out how to communicate with NASA and grow potatoes in the Hab. So far, it *seems* as though he'll actually survive until the next Mars mission arrives.

On the other hand, the Fun and Games beat in *The Hunger Games* is a decidedly downward path. As the Hunger Games kick off, Katniss is hit from all sides by challenges including dehydration, fire, and tracker jackers (genetically engineered wasps), not to mention twenty-three other teenagers trying to kill her.

Similarly in *The Grapes of Wrath,* Tom Joad and his family are faced with nothing but failures as they set off for California in search of work in the Fun and Games beat. The family unit even starts to unravel when Grandpa dies and Noah, Tom's older brother, abandons the group. It's a clear downward path to the Midpoint.

The general direction of your Fun and Games is a critical decision to be made as you structure your novel. Because as you'll soon see, whichever path you choose for this beat—upward or downward—will ultimately define not only the next beat (the Midpoint) but the rest of the second act.

9. MIDPOINT

WHAT DOES IT DO? Marks the middle of the novel with either a false defeat or a false victory while at the same time raising the stakes of the story.

WHERE DOES IT GO? 50%

Huzzah! We've reached the Midpoint! The very aptly named *middle* of the book.

The Midpoint is a crossroads of things. *Many* things.

It's the middle of the book, yes, but it's also the middle of the second act, which is a crucial middle of the hero's transformation.

Wow! That's a lot of middles!

I've heard many authors refer to the middle of a novel as the *muddle*. Meaning, it's a messy thing to write. It's hard to slog through. It feels cumbersome and sloppy. It lacks focus.

When I read a manuscript (or even a published novel), I can tell *instantly* whether the author understands the function and purpose of the Midpoint. If it feels unfocused and clunky, then they've missed a golden opportunity.

The Midpoint is *magic*. It's the pivot point in the story. The nail in the wall on which all other beats hang. It is precisely the center of the hero's transformative arc, and we must use that to our advantage and make the middle as dynamic and exciting as possible.

So what exactly *is* the Midpoint?

Basically it's a single-scene beat in which three very essential things happen:

1. The hero experiences either a **false victory** or a **false defeat**.

2. The stakes of the story are raised.

3. The A and B stories intersect in some way.

First things first: false victories and false defeats.

Remember when we were in the Fun and Games, and I asked you if your hero was on an upward path or a downward path? Well, if you've answered that question, then the good news is, you're already well on your way to figuring out your Midpoint. See how sneaky I was about that?

The Midpoint is the culmination of whatever path you chose for your Fun and Games. Because essentially, the whole goal of the Fun and Games is to *drive* the story toward the Midpoint, and to give the Midpoint definition.

If your hero is shining in their upside-down world, if things are generally working out well for them (aside from a few bouncing balls), and Act 2 is proving to be a pretty decent place, then you ultimately have a false victory in your Midpoint. Your upward path has reached a peak. Your hero has *seemingly* won. Yay for them!

Why is it called a *false* victory? Because the novel is only halfway finished. If your hero were to really win here, the book would be over at the Midpoint.

Why else is it a *false* victory? Why haven't they really, truly *won*? Because your hero still hasn't learned the theme.

In false victory Midpoints, heroes are usually feeling fairly good about themselves. Maybe they've gotten what they want (that external goal you set up in Act 1), or maybe they're getting close. But unbeknownst to them, their victory is incomplete. Because they have not yet changed the *right* way. They still have those pesky flaws that have been dragging them down their whole life. They still haven't dealt with the *big* issues. And by giving the hero exactly what they want at the Midpoint, you, the author, are essentially shining a spotlight on those bigger issues. You're showing the reader that the victory was false and that the hero's wants were superficial because (1) the book isn't over yet and (2) your hero is still the same flawed person they were in Act 1.

In *Me Before You*, Louisa's Midpoint is a false victory. She has a job (her initial goal) *and* she seems to be making great strides in helping Will live his life to the fullest (her new goal). But has she done anything to live her *own* life to the fullest (theme)? Not really. Which is evident at the Midpoint (a birthday party at Louisa's house, which Will attends) when her long-term boyfriend (whom she's clearly not meant to be with) gives her a gift that proves that, after years of dating, he still doesn't understand her. Whereas Will, whom she's known for only a few months, clearly does.

By the Midpoint in *The Martian*, Mark's harvesting his potato crops, it looks like he will have enough food to last until he can be rescued, and he's able to communicate with NASA and even receive emails from his family. All things considered, Mark's outlook is pretty good. He's achieved all of his smaller goals from the first half of the book (grow food, communicate with Earth). But his larger external goal of getting off the planet is still yet to be realized, as is his internal goal (theme) of conquering his fears.

On the other hand, if your hero has been floundering like a fish out of water in the Fun and Games beat, then your Midpoint will inversely be a false defeat. The downward path has reached a low point. Your hero has seemingly lost. Maybe they haven't gotten what they want, or maybe they have and quickly realize it's not all it's cracked up to be. They might even feel like giving up at this point.

Why is it a *false* defeat? For the exact same reasons it was a false victory. The book isn't over! And your hero still hasn't learned what you put them into this story to learn.

By creating a Midpoint in which your hero fails to get what they want (fails to achieve their external goal), you are also shining a giant spotlight on the bigger issues. You're saying to the reader, "Hey! Look! My hero thinks their life is over because they didn't get this thing that they thought would fix everything." But obviously that thing wasn't that important if there's still half a novel to go. *Obviously*, there's a bigger story here.

By the Midpoint in *The Hunger Games*, Katniss is dealing with dehydration and painful flesh burns. And she's recently discovered that Peeta (her B Story character) has teamed up with the Career tributes (the teenagers who train all their lives to compete in the Games). After she drops a tracker jacker nest on the Careers, they come after her, ready for revenge. Things are looking pretty grim for Katniss at this point. Her external goal of surviving the Games seems further away than ever, as does her internal goal or theme (of defying the Capitol).

The Grapes of Wrath also features a false defeat Midpoint when the Joad family reaches their destination of California (external goal) only to find that they've been deceived. California does *not* offer the prosperity and jobs they expected. And Tom Joad hasn't yet fulfilled his thematic destiny to help organize workers and fight for equality (internal goal).

We writers set up these false victories and false defeats so we can do one very crucial thing (the second essential Midpoint element): to raise the stakes of the story.

Up until this point, your flawed hero has been given an *opportunity* to change their ways and fix those flaws (via the upside-down world of Act 2), but they really haven't taken advantage of that opportunity yet. As we said, they're still being piloted by what they want, not by what they need. By raising the stakes of the story at the Midpoint, we're essentially saying, "Time's almost up, buddy! No more messing around." We're forcing the hero into a new course of action that will inevitably lead to the change they so desperately require.

For this reason, I like to call the Midpoint the "sh*t just got real" beat. In other words, it's no longer Fun and Games (literally). It's time to get serious.

So, how do we raise the stakes? Well, that's up to you. But here are some common stakes-raising methods that you'll often find in popular novels:

- **LOVE STORIES RAMP UP:** This usually happens in the form of a kiss (or more!), a declaration of love, a marriage, a proposal, anything that ups the ante of a relationship and makes it even more difficult for the hero to go back to their old way of life. Once you're in love, you're in love. And even though your hero can still screw it up (and they probably will!), they can't simply walk away and pretend it never happened. At the Midpoint of *The Hate U Give* by Angie Thomas, Starr and her boyfriend, Chris, exchange "I love yous" for the very first time. Up until this moment, Starr has been hiding her true self from Chris (by not telling him that she was the key witness in the police shooting of Khalil), effectively still keeping her home world and her school world separate (just as she was doing at the beginning). By upping the stakes of their relationship, author Thomas is essentially saying, "You can't stay hidden forever, Starr. Things are getting very real, very fast."

- **TIME CLOCKS APPEAR:** Nothing raises stakes and refocuses your story faster than a ticking clock. A bomb is discovered. A kidnapper sends a ransom note with a deadline. A doctor gives someone two weeks to live. A wedding invitation arrives in the mail with a date three months from now. A terrorist threatens to assassinate a politician at an upcoming rally. These are all great ways to give your story a thrilling boost into the second half of the book. Ticking clocks grab the hero's (and the reader's) attention and force them to really think about what's important and what needs to be done. In *The Martian*, just as things seem to be going well for Mark Watney, BOOM! The airlock on the Hab breaks, and all of his potato crops are destroyed. His ticking clock (to get off Mars before his food runs out) was just put on fast forward. This will eventually force Mark to put his courage to the ultimate test (theme) if he wants to survive.

- **A MAJOR GAME-CHANGING PLOT TWIST:** This is one of my favorite ways to raise the stakes in a novel, because I *love* writing plot twists. Essentially, a plot twist is you saying to the hero (and the reader), "You don't even know the half of it yet. Here's what you're *really* dealing with!" I call this the **Midpoint twist**, and writers of thrillers and mysteries employ it quite often. In *Memory Man*, just when Decker and his partner Lancaster start to make some headway on the case involving the school shooting and the death of Decker's family (false victory), suddenly one of the FBI agents on the case turns up dead at Decker's front door, and the evidence reveals that the cops are dealing with not *one* suspect, like they originally thought, but *two*. This is a double whammy stake raiser. First, someone close to the investigation is dead; *then* Decker discovers a twist that no one saw coming and that completely changes the case: the killer is working with someone else! Both of these events put extra pressure on Decker to solve the case, not only for the families of the school shooting victims (A Story) but for his own personal closure regarding the murder of his family (B Story).

- **BIG PARTY, CELEBRATION, OR PUBLIC "OUTING":** If you look at some of your favorite novels, you'll often find that some kind of big party or celebration with lots of people happens right around the middle of the book. I realize a party or celebration may not *seem* like something that would naturally raise the stakes, but it is. Up until this point, your hero might have been *existing* in Act 2, but were they really shouting from the rooftops that this is who they are now? Probably not. Because they probably still had a piece of their heart left in Act 1. But having them attend what I call a **Midpoint party** (a social gathering or large celebration with tons of people) essentially gives your hero a chance to step out into their Act 2 world and declare themselves a part of it. In front of everyone. It's a public "outing" of sorts, which is difficult to back away from. The Midpoint of *Me Before You* (Louisa's birthday dinner party) is the first time in the book when Louisa's parents and boyfriend meet Will, the quadriplegic man she's been hired to take care of (and is slowly falling in love with). This is essentially a collision of her two worlds and a public outing of this new Act 2 version of Louisa. And by putting these two worlds in the same room together, author Moyes shines a spotlight on how different Louisa has become in the few months she's been spending with Will.

In all of these Midpoint examples, you might have noticed a subtle **shift from wants to needs.** This is no coincidence. The third essential Midpoint element is the intersection of the A and B stories, when your hero *starts* to let go of what they want in lieu of figuring out what they need. Now, granted that's not all going to happen on the very next page or even in the very next chapter. Your hero still has quite a ways to get there. A whole three more beats, to be exact. But it's at this moment, when the stakes are raised, that your hero begins to realize they can't keep going the way they've been going. Because either it hasn't worked (false defeat!) or it *has* worked (false victory!), but they still feel like they're missing something.

So this subtle shift from the wants to the needs is often illustrated by a crossing (yes, another Midpoint crossroads!) of the A Story and the B Story. Remember, your A Story is the external story—the whole flashy premise of your novel that you've been setting up and paying off since Act 1. And the B Story is the internal story, the spiritual journey that's represented by the B Story character. Often at the Midpoint the **A and B stories cross**, meaning A Story characters and B Story character(s) intertwine or cross paths in some way. This is done to *visually* cue the reader that we are shifting from the wants (the external A Story) to the needs (the internal B Story), even if the reader isn't quite aware that you're doing it (more writer manipulation).

In the Midpoint of *The Hunger Games*, Peeta Mellark (B Story character) saves Katniss's life just as the other tributes in the Games are about to kill her (A Story characters). This crossroads not only ups the stakes of Katniss's journey (because she now knows that Peeta really does care about her and it wasn't just an act for the cameras) but also demarcates a pivotal moment in her transformation. From here on out, it becomes more and more difficult for Katniss to *only* think about surviving (A Story); she is now forced to also think about how she will stand up against the Capitol (B Story).

To sum it up, the Midpoint changes the direction of your story, making it (yet again!) harder for the hero to go back to who they were before. Does this sound familiar? It should. Because it's exactly what you did with the Catalyst. You raised the stakes so it was more difficult for your hero to turn around and run back to the safety of their status quo Act 1 world.

This, too, is no coincidence. A great story is a continual raising of the stakes. It's one plot device after another that keeps your hero moving *forward*. Because each time you raise the stakes, you make it that much harder for them to move backward.

10. BAD GUYS CLOSE IN

WHAT DOES IT DO? Provides a place for your hero to rebound after a false defeat Midpoint or fall down after a false victory Midpoint, all while the internal bad guys (flaws) are closing in.

WHERE DOES IT GO? 50% to 75%

The good news is, you've already gotten the longest beat of the novel out of the way (the Fun and Games). The bad news is, this is the *second* longest beat of the novel.

I'm not gonna sugarcoat it. Act 2 is a *beast*. It's more than 50 percent of the story! By the time you finish the Midpoint and reach the Bad Guys Close In, you think you're nearly to the end of Act 2. But then you look at how much ground you have to cover before the All Is Lost beat, and you may really feel like All Is Lost.

But fear not! We're going to get through it together.

Like the Fun and Games, the Bad Guys Close In is a multi-scene beat, and it spans a fairly large chunk of pages (approximately 25 percent of your novel). But if done right, these can be some of the most exciting pages of the story.

The beat itself is named after the sequence in an action movie where the bad guys regroup (after having failed to enact their evil plan at the Midpoint) and come back stronger, more organized, and with bigger, badder weapons.

Well, that's all fine and dandy if you're writing a thriller. But what about the rest of us? What if we don't even have traditional "bad guys" in our story? What then?

First of all, don't panic. And secondly, don't be fooled by the *title* of the beat. Just because it's called Bad Guys Close In doesn't mean that you need to have *literal* bad guys (or what I call **external bad guys**) in your story. It doesn't even mean that *only* bad things can happen in this beat. The direction of the beat is actually highly dependent on what you did with your Midpoint.

If your Midpoint was a false victory (your hero seemingly "won"), then yes, your Bad Guys Close In is going to be a steady downward path to the All Is Lost, meaning things are getting progressively *worse* for your hero, and more and more *bad* things are happening (with a few bouncing balls thrown in there to keep things interesting and unpredictable!). Because remember, the victory at the Midpoint was *false*. The hero didn't actually win. They only *thought* they won. So now it's time to show them (and the reader) just how wrong they were. This can be done with *literal* bad guys, like the perpetrators in *Memory Man* who start killing more and more people after the Midpoint. Or it can be done by simply inflicting more "bad" things on your hero, like in *The Martian*. After the airlock on the Hab breaks, raising the stakes for Mark, things go from bad to worse. Mark suffers from injuries; the supply probe NASA tried to send to him explodes; and then Mark loses all communication with Earth. It's a fairly steady downward path for Mark.

On the other hand, if your Midpoint was a false defeat (your hero seemingly "lost"), your Bad Guys Close In beat is actually going to have a steady, upward path. Life is getting progressively *better*. Things are looking up! Your hero is making great strides. Improving their situation. Conquering obstacles. Maybe this upside-down world is not such a bad place after all!

In *The Grapes of Wrath*, after a difficult Midpoint, the Joad family's predicament starts to improve. They find a nice government camp (a vast improvement over the Hoovervilles they've been staying in), and they even find work picking peaches.

Similarly, in *The Hunger Games,* even though Katniss is still dealing with the bad guys of the Capitol and the other tributes, things start to look better for her in the second half of Act 2. She's earning some wins in the arena. She forms an alliance with Rue, and together the two blow up the supplies of the Career tributes. When the Bad Guys Close In is an upward path, false victories like this are often found right before the All Is Lost. Your hero has a small win right before everything falls apart.

But regardless of whether your Bad Guys Close In beat is a downward path or an upward path, whether there are literal bad guys or just bad things are happening to the hero, there is one kind of bad guy that does exist in *all* stories.

And that's **internal bad guys.**

By this, I mean your hero's flaws. Those pesky things you set up all the way back in Act 1 that you promised (via your Theme Stated) that your hero would eventually deal with.

Despite everything that Louisa Clark has been through in *Me Before You,* despite trying to convince Will to enjoy his life, she *still* hasn't done the same for herself. She still hasn't answered the thematic question: "What exactly do you want to do with your life?" (page 22). She's still living the same unfulfilling existence that she was at the beginning. She hasn't even broken up with her incompatible boyfriend. In fact, just the opposite. She moves in with him! This is a prime example of Louisa's internal bad guys—those flaws from Act 1—closing in and stopping her from making any real change.

And that's what the Bad Guys Close In beat is all about. No matter what strides your hero has been making in Act 2, those internal bad guys are still hard at work inside your hero's psyche. Messing up relationships, sabotaging successes, destroying happiness. Because until your hero learns the theme and fixes their life the *right* way, those internal bad guys are going to keep wreaking havoc, pushing your hero toward that lowest-of-the-low point.

Welcome, my friends, to the All Is Lost.

11. ALL IS LOST

WHAT DOES IT DO? Illustrates your hero's rock bottom (lowest moment) of the story.

WHERE DOES IT GO? 75%

Rock bottom. Your hero has finally hit it. It's a truism that no one really changes until they've hit rock bottom. Because until they've tried *everything* else, until they've lost everything that's important to them, they can't see the true path. It's a human condition. And therefore it's a *hero* condition. Because our heroes are, if nothing else, human. That's why they resonate with us.

So before our heroes can find that *true* path to real transformation, we have to bring them so low, so far into despair, that they have no other choice but to change.

Change the *right* way.

No matter which direction your hero was headed in the Bad Guys Close In beat (upward or downward), all heroes must eventually fall.

And fall they will!

That's the function of the All Is Lost. It's a single-scene beat (one scene or one chapter), approximately 75 percent of the way through the novel, in which something happens *to* your hero that tosses them deep, deep down into defeat.

The totalitarian government arrests the hero (*1984*). The king dies, leaving the hero and her family in crisis (*The White Queen*). The two lovers break up (*It Had to Be You*). Justice is *not* served (*The Hate U Give*). The killers strike someone close to the hero (*Memory Man*). The hero discovers that the love of her life is already married (*Jane Eyre*). The hero is betrayed by someone they trust (*The Da Vinci Code*).

Whatever it is, it's BIG. Even bigger than the Catalyst! It seems insurmountable. Your hero must be worse off than they were at the start of the book.

All really does *seem* lost.

I see too many writers in my workshops try to tiptoe around the All Is Lost. They're afraid to do something really awful to their hero. Don't be afraid. Kill people! Fire people! Break people up! If your All Is Lost isn't big, and I mean *big*, your final transformation will feel contrived. It won't be believable. Rock bottom means *rock bottom*.

ALL. IS. LOST.

So how do we make sure this beat is as epic and moving and transformative as it needs to be?

We insert something called the **whiff of death**. Nothing spells despair more than death itself. So this is the point in stories where a lot of characters die or almost die. I'm not trying to sound callous here; it's just the way it is. In *The Fault in Our Stars,* Augustus dies at the All

Is Lost. In *Me Before You,* Will tells Louisa that, despite her efforts, he has not changed his mind about ending his own life. In *Room* by Emma Donoghue, Ma tries to commit suicide. In *Memory Man,* Amos Decker contemplates suicide. In *The Hunger Games,* Rue is killed.

Just look at some of your favorite books, find the All Is Lost, and see for yourself. So many characters die in this beat. Particularly mentors. Killing of a mentor character at the All Is Lost is especially effective because it forces the hero to do the rest on their own. It forces them to look deep inside and realize that they had the answers—the power, the ability, the "force"—in them all along. It's not until Preacher Casy is killed in *The Grapes of Wrath* that Tom Joad finally realizes his true purpose is to continue Casy's teachings and help mankind.

And even if there's not an *actual* death in this beat, there's a hint at death. There's a *whiff* of it. Like a dead plant in the corner, a dead fish in the fish bowl, maybe even the death of an idea or project or relationship or business. In *Something Borrowed* by Emily Giffin, there's a death of a lifelong friendship. Even in the comedy *Confessions of a Shopaholic* by Sophie Kinsella, there's a whiff of death in the All Is Lost when Becky tries to buy something only to find that all her accounts have been frozen and the cashier confiscates her card. It's the death of her credit!

Basically, something must end here. Because the All Is Lost is where the old world/character/way of thinking finally dies so a new world/character/way of thinking can be born.

I like to think of the All Is Lost as yet *another* Catalyst. It's an action beat that serves a very similar function to the Catalyst beat in Act 1. If the first Catalyst pushed your hero into the Debate and then into the Break Into 2, then the All Is Lost will push your hero into the Dark Night of the Soul and finally into the Break Into 3.

And even though whatever happens in the All Is Lost is happening *to* your hero, it should be, at least somewhat, your hero's fault. Why? Because that stubborn fool still hasn't learned the theme! Your hero's internal bad guys have been working behind the scenes, tripping them up, causing them to make mistakes. And now it's led to disaster. Even if the action itself isn't their fault, their dismal predicament is.

In *The Diary of a Wimpy Kid,* Greg is completely to blame for the end of his friendship with Rowley. He's been a *bad* friend. He hadn't yet learned the theme of taking responsibility. In *Pride and Prejudice*, although Lydia makes her own decision to run away with Mr. Wickham, if Elizabeth hadn't been so prejudiced against Mr. Darcy, she would have realized Mr. Wickham's true character earlier and possibly prevented the whole thing.

The hero must be in *some* way responsible. Otherwise, there's no lesson to be learned. And that is the whole point of the All Is Lost. Now your hero has nothing else to do but wallow in their defeat and reflect upon their choices and their life. Little do they know that it'll be the most powerful, life-changing reflection they've ever done.

12. DARK NIGHT OF THE SOUL

WHAT DOES IT DO? Shows how your hero reacts to the All Is Lost and how they eventually break through to a resolution.

WHERE DOES IT GO? 75% to 80% (This beat takes us to the end of Act 2.)

If the All Is Lost is another Catalyst, then naturally, the Dark Night of the Soul beat is another Debate. After hitting rock bottom, what does your hero do? What does anyone do? They *react*.

They think about everything that's happened. They ponder. They contemplate.

They wallow.

I like to call the Dark Night of the Soul "the wallowing beat." Because that's pretty much what heroes do here. They sit around or walk around, feeling hopeless and sorry for themselves. And there's often rain involved.

Jane runs away from Thornfield Hall and nearly starves to death (*Jane Eyre*). Katniss mourns Rue's death by burying her in flowers (*The Hunger Games*). Winston wallows in his jail cell, uncertain of his future (*1984*). Louisa sits in her room for days, refusing to come out (*Me Before You*).

Not all heroes wallow, however. Some get angry, like Starr in *The Hate U Give*, who, after finding out justice won't be served for Khalil, just wants to riot and destroy. Some slip into denial, like Greg in *The Diary of a Wimpy Kid*, who tries to convince himself he's better off without his best friend, Rowley, by hanging out with someone else.

Your hero's specific reaction depends solely on who your hero is as a person. How do *they* react to this low point in their lives?

The All Is Lost was a single-scene beat. It happened fast. It was one scene or one chapter and then it was over. Now your hero needs time to process it all. That's why the Dark Night of the Soul is a multi-scene beat. You get several scenes or chapters to show how your hero is dealing with this defeat.

But it's not *just* wallowing (or brooding) in the rain. The Dark Night of the Soul has a very important and useful function. It's the darkness before the dawn. It's the moment before the big breakthrough realization.

It's the last moment before the *real* change occurs.

That's why most revelations in stories happen in this beat, during what I call the **Dark Night epiphany**. The final clue falls into place, the hero sees something in a new light, the truth they've failed to see all this time suddenly becomes clear. Lots of mysteries (in both mysteries and other types of novels) get solved right here in the Dark Night of the Soul. In David Baldacci's *Memory Man*, at the end of the Dark Night of the Soul is when Amos Decker *finally* realizes why he has been targeted by the killers (the last piece of the puzzle). In *Confessions of a Shopaholic*, the end of the Dark Night of the Soul is when Becky Bloomwood discovers that Flagstaff Life (a major financial institution) has been scamming its investors.

So even though your hero is pretty down and depressed about their life right now, something deep inside of them is working. Analyzing. Processing. They're breaking down their life and looking at their choices; they're thinking about everything they've tried thus far and failed to achieve. They're slowly coming to an ultimate conclusion.

Which is why, similar to the Debate, the Dark Night of the Soul will often revolve around a question. What will the hero do now? How will they cope with this despair? How will they Break Into 3? After Tom Joad kills Preacher Casy's killer in *The Grapes of Wrath*, the Dark Night of the Soul question becomes "What will the Joads do now?" After Mark loses contact with NASA, the Dark Night of the Soul question becomes "How will he get himself to the Ares 4 site to rendezvous with his crew?"

This is also the one beat in the novel where your hero is allowed to move *backward,* instead of forward. I call it the **return to the familiar.** After Becky Bloomwood has reached her financial and emotional rock bottom in *Confesions of a Shopaholic,* she goes to her parents' house, where she feels safe. After Louisa Clark storms off, leaving Will at the airport in *Me Before You,* she moves back in with her family.

If possible, take your hero back to where they started. Reunite them with an old friend. Get them back together with an ex. Give them their old job back. Somehow return them to their original status quo Act 1 life. Because when you're wallowing and feeling lost, it's only natural that you'd start searching for something familiar and safe. But here's the clincher: it doesn't *feel* familiar and safe anymore. And it certainly doesn't feel the *same.*

A return to the familiar essentially shines a giant spotlight on how much your hero has already changed. They're no longer that Act 1 thesis person anymore. They've gone through the upside-down antithesis world, and it's altered them. Therefore, inserting them back into that Act 1 world only exaggerates how *much* it's altered them. They feel like a complete stranger in a place that once felt familiar. This points out to the hero (and the reader) that they don't belong there anymore. That they can't go back to the way things were.

That it's time to make the tough choices.

It's time to rip off that Act 2 Band-Aid, face the deep wound underneath, and *finally* start to heal it.

It's time to make the real change.

Act 3

We're nearly there! We've reached the third and final act, also called the **synthesis**.

Remember, Act 1 was the thesis (or the status quo world), Act 2 was the antithesis (or the upside-down world), and Act 3 is the synthesis (the fusion of those two worlds).

Here's another way I like to look at it:

Who the hero was in Act 1 + What they've learned in Act 2 = Who they will become in Act 3

If the Midpoint was the *crossroads* of all things, then this final act is the *blending* of all things. The hero will combine their Act 1 self with their Act 2 self, to create a brand-new and improved Act 3 self. Friendships are repaired. Relationships are mended. Jilted lovers are reunited. The A and B stories will meet again, but this time they will intertwine and become one. It's the ultimate combination: the fun and excitement of the external story, combined with the knowledge and wisdom of the internal story to create a dynamic, engaging, and powerful third act that will resonate and leave your readers breathless!

13. BREAK INTO 3

WHAT DOES IT DO? Brings the hero into the synthesis world of Act 3, where they will finally fix things the *right* way.

WHERE DOES IT GO? 80%

Voilà! The answer! The solution! The fix!

The Break Into 3 beat is literally a *breakthrough*. At this very moment, thanks to all their struggles in the upside-down world, thanks to all the lessons they've learned from their thematic B Story character(s), thanks to this emotional roller coaster you've put them on, your hero finally realizes what they must do to not only fix all of the problems they've caused in Act 2 (and there are plenty!) but also, more important, how to fix *themselves*.

If the Break Into 2 was the hero figuring out how to fix things the wrong way, then the Break Into 3 is when the hero finally figures out how to **fix things the right way**. No more shortcuts. No more cheats. No more avoiding the bigger issues. They've lost everything, they've hit rock bottom and gone through a Dark Night of the Soul, and now they know what they have to do.

Louisa Clark has to get on that flight to Switzerland to be present at Will's death (*Me Before You*). Becky Bloomwood has to write the article of her life and expose the wrongdoings of the financial institution (*Confessions of a Shopaholic*). Mark Watney has to figure out how to get to the Ares 4 site without NASA's help (*The Martian*). Amos Decker has to confront his family's murderers alone (*Memory Man*). Starr Carter has to use her *real* weapon—her voice (*The Hate U Give*). And Tom Joad can't run away from his problems anymore; he has to help organize the workers and put an end to injustices (*The Grapes of Wrath*).

The Break Into 3 almost always includes the following realization for the hero: *It was never* them *who had to change; it was always* me.

Up until this point your hero has tried everything they can to avoid the real issues in their life. They've ignored the Theme Stated, they've chased after what they want instead of what they need, they've tried to fix their life the wrong way and failed, they've blamed everyone else but themselves. It's time to wise up and face the cold, hard truth:

I am flawed. But now that I know that, I can fix it.

This is a single-scene beat. You get one scene or chapter to show this realization and the decision that comes out of it. (Although I've seen it done successfully in as little as one page or one paragraph.) This is the beat you will use to guide your hero (and your reader!) swiftly and surely into the third and final act.

14. FINALE

WHAT DOES IT DO? Resolves all the problems created in Act 2 and proves that your hero has learned the theme and has been transformed.

WHERE DOES IT GO? 80% to 99%

Your hero has finally wised up and figured out what they have to do. What comes next? Well, now they have to, you know, actually *do* it. It's one thing to sit around and talk about change; it's quite another to enact it. It's time for your hero to put their money where their mouth is and put their brilliant new Break Into 3 plan into action! This is the final test. Can they pull it off? We'll soon see.

You might have noticed that the third act has only three beats, compared to the first act, which has five, and the second act, which has a whopping seven beats. Which means that the Finale beat is often a very *long* beat. It's a multi-scene beat that spans pretty much the entire third act (nearly 20 percent of the novel!).

So what is happening over all of those pages and chapters?

The hero is enacting their new plan, yes. But how do we stretch that out over the *entire* third act so it feels compelling and exciting and not too rushed?

The answer is a dazzling and genius thing called the **Five-Point Finale**, and I guarantee it will change your life!

The Five-Point Finale breaks down the Finale into five sub-beats, giving us even more road markers to break up the last section of our trip. And thank goodness, because we're nearing the finish line of this very long journey. We've been driving forever. We're tired. We're weary. We need smaller goals and shorter driving distances to get us to the end.

The Five-Point Finale is a blueprint for what every third act is essentially all about: storming the Castle! The castle is a metaphor. It can be anything. Getting to Switzerland before Will's death (*Me Before You*), winning the Games (*The Hunger Games*), reaching the Ares 4 landing site (*The Martian*). And of course, it can be a *literal* castle like the royal ball that Cinder must get to in order to warn Prince Kai of Queen Levana's evil scheme (*Cinder* by Marissa Meyer).

Basically, the castle is the *plan*. And the Five-Point Finale helps you masterfully execute that plan to give you the most compelling third act possible. So let's take a look at it, point by point.

Point 1: Gathering the Team

Before the hero can "storm the castle," they need some help. They need allies. They need to assemble troops! These troops can be literal troops or just some good friends to help out. However, keep in mind your hero might not be on speaking terms with some of their friends after the All Is Lost. They might have to mend a few fences in order to solicit help. That's also a big part of the Gathering the Team sub-beat (and the third act in general). Your hero has to make amends and admit that they were wrong and stupid and blind. It's just another step in the completion of their transformative arc. In *The Hunger Games*, after the Gamemakers announce the rule change that allows for *two* victors, Katniss knows she needs to team up with Peeta. But first she has to find him.

Your hero doesn't necessarily need a team to storm the castle, however. Plenty of memorable heroes have stormed a castle on their own. This sub-beat can also be a Gathering of the Tools (strapping on weapons, making plans, collecting supplies, laying out the route, and so on). Before Mark Watney can set out for the Ares 4 site in *The Martian*, he has to prep the rover and plot his course. This is essentially a preparation section before the hero executes the big, exciting plan they came up with in the Break Into 3 beat.

Point 2: Executing the Plan

In this sub-beat, we storm the castle (either literally or figuratively.) The team is assembled, the weapons are strapped on, the supplies are collected, and the route is all mapped out. It's *go* time! Mark Watney sets out for the Ares 4 site (*The Martian*), Louisa boards the flight for Switzerland (*Me Before You*), Katniss and Peeta defeat the rest of the tributes until they are the only two left in the arena (*The Hunger Games*).

As your hero and their team (if they have one) execute the plan, there should be a sense of impossibility in their endeavor. A *Can this really work?* moment. The plan should at first seem *crazy*. But then, as the team works together and makes progress, there's a growing sense of accomplishment. Maybe some quirky secondary characters will "have their moment" here. Maybe some strange skill or device or idiosyncrasy you've set up earlier in the book will pay off. But little by little, the plan *seems* to be working. The team *seems* to be making progress. Maybe this plan wasn't as crazy as they thought! Maybe this is going to be—dare they say it?—*easy!*

This sub-beat is also where a lot of secondary characters or team members make a **B Story Sacrifice**, sacrificing themselves for the cause. They start dropping off. Maybe they die, maybe they take a bullet for the hero, or maybe they simply move aside to allow the hero a chance to shine. In *Harry Potter and the Sorcerer's Stone* by J. K. Rowling, after the three kids go down through the trap door looking for the Sorcerer's Stone, both Ron *and* Hermione sacrifice themselves so that Harry can reach the final room. This is purposeful. Because with every team member who falls away, the hero is forced to do it on their own—showing us that they really do have what it takes.

Point 3: The High Tower Surprise

The hero and their team have executed the plan; they've stormed the castle, and all *seems* to be going well. But you should know by now that in the world of Save the Cat! nothing is ever what it *seems*. Enter the High Tower Surprise. This sub-beat is named after that moment in a classic fairy tale adventure when the hero storms the castle to save the princess only to find . . . surprise! The princess isn't there! And worse yet, the bad guys have led the hero right into a trap!

Sure, you may not have literal bad guys or a literal high tower or even a literal princess, but the purpose of this beat is the same, regardless: to show just how overconfident and naïve the hero and their team have become. This plan was never going to work! It was never going to be that easy. After Katniss and Peeta survive the Hunger Games, the Gamemakers announce another rule change: Only one person can win. After Louisa arrives in Switzerland, she still has one last hope that Will will change his mind. He doesn't. Once Mark Watney reaches the Ares 4 site, NASA tells him about the "invasive procedures" he'll have to do to the MAV in order to get it off Mars. His reaction: "Are you f*cking kidding me?" (page 330).

The High Tower Surprise is simply another twist, another challenge to force the hero to really prove their worth. In a way, it's yet *another* Catalyst. A curve ball thrown at your hero that they now must figure out how to deal with. And this time, pure effort, brawns, weapons, even smarts won't get your hero through. Your hero must dig *deeper* than that.

Point 4: Dig Deep Down

If the High Tower Surprise was yet another Catalyst, then the Dig Deep Down is—you guessed it—another Debate! Are you starting to sense a pattern here? Cause and effect. Action and reaction. That's the underlying pattern of the storytelling code. It's why the beat sheet works, and it's what makes stories work.

This sub-beat is the moment we've been waiting for throughout the entire Finale, or—dare I say it?—the entire *novel*. It's when the hero has once again seemingly failed (in the High Tower Surprise) and has nothing left. No plan. No backup. No hope. And yet, they still have *something*. They may not realize it just yet, but there's something deep down inside of them that will turn out to be the most important weapon of all.

It's the theme of the story.

It's the flaw they've overcome.

It's the proof that they've changed.

And above all else, it's something your hero would never have done at the start of the book. They've come a long way since their days as that flawed little caterpillar. It's time to show us what a beautiful, powerful butterfly they've turned into.

Remember all of those flaws we set up in chapter 1? Remember when I forced you to look at your hero as an imperfect soul in need of transformation, and to think of a small shard of glass that has been buried inside your hero for years?

Well, now it's time for your hero to dig deep down and pull out that shard of glass. Remove their flaws at the source and become victorious. This is the memorable moment in *The Hunger Games* when Katniss prepares to eat the poisonous berries, defying the Capitol and proving once and for all that she's *not* a pawn in their games. This is the moment when Louisa finally accepts Will's choice, realizing that she can't live anyone else's life but her own (*Me Before You*). This is the moment when Mark Watney faces "the real possibility that [he] will die today" (*The Martian*, page 340).

This sub-beat is also called a **touched-by-the-divine** moment. No, your story doesn't have to be spiritual or religious to have a touched-by-the-divine moment. But your story does have to have a soul. It has to speak to us on some deeper level. And here's where the hero takes a final leap of *faith*.

Point 5: The Execution of the New Plan

Only now, when your hero has dug deep down to find the truth, removed that shard of glass, and leaped off the bridge with no net to catch them, can we really see them triumph.

Katniss and Peeta start to eat the berries, but the Gamemakers stop them and announce that they've both won (*The Hunger Games*). Mark Watney blasts off into space in his stripped-down "convertible" MAV (*The Martian*). Louisa Clark says goodbye to Will (*Me Before You*).

In this final sub-beat, your hero puts their bold, innovative, *new* plan into action—and of course, it works! Because after all that soul-searching and all that transformative effort, we need to know that the human spirit and perseverance do prevail. That's how we resonate with readers. We take our heroes to hell and back, we make them work for every last victory, we force them to search deep within themselves to find the answers, and only *then* do we give them the ending they now rightly deserve.

Or if your hero ultimately fails in the end, then there's a *point* to the failure. There's a human lesson to be learned from that too. It's better to try and fail than to never try at all.

So that is the Five-Point Finale. It's the flashy end to your brilliant, transformative tale. It's the climactic finish to your stunning fireworks display. It pulls the entire "message" of your story into focus and leaves the reader with something to remember. Something to ponder. Something that resonates deep in their soul.

Is the Five-Point Finale absolutely necessary? No. I've read plenty of novels that are still captivating and engaging with shorter finales that don't include all five points. Do I recommend at least giving the Five-Point Finale a try? Absolutely! Just like the fifteen beats as a whole, these five sub-beats will help you focus your story and bring it to an exciting and rewarding conclusion.

Regardless of how you approach it, your Finale should be engaging. It shouldn't be an automatic win for your hero. Your hero shouldn't figure out what to do in the Break Into 3 and then just do it—with no obstacles, conflicts, or struggles. Make them *work* for their transformation. Finales that happen too quickly and with no heroic effort run the risk of getting a review that reads, "Great story, but was tied up too easily in the end."

If you put in the extra work to make your third act just as dynamic and turbulent and wrought with action and emotion as the rest of your story, your novel as a whole is going to be elevated to another level. And your very last, final beat is going to feel all the more earned for your hero, your reader . . . and you.

15. FINAL IMAGE

WHAT DOES IT DO? Provides an "after" snapshot of your hero and your hero's life to show how much they've changed.

WHERE DOES IT GO? 99% to 100% (This is the final scene or chapter of your novel.)

Well, you've done it. You've reached the final beat.

If the Opening Image was the "before" snapshot, then the Final Image is the "after" snapshot. It's a single-scene beat in which you *show* us what your hero looks like after this epic transformative journey is complete.

How far have they come? What have they learned? How much have they grown as a human being? What does their life look like now that they've journeyed through the Dark Night of the Soul, faced their demons, ripped out their shard of glass, and come out the other side better and stronger than ever before?

In *Me Before You*, we see Louisa sipping coffee in a café in Paris, finally living her life. It's a far cry from the Opening Image in which she's trapped in her quiet little English town. In *The Martian*, we see Mark Watney boarding the *Hermes* and reuniting with his crew, an exact opposite beat to the Opening Image in which he had just been abandoned by that same crew on Mars. In *The Hunger Games*, we see Katniss boarding the train back to District 12 with Peeta. She's no longer the poor girl we met in the first chapter, just trying to get by. Now she's a victor. And a rebel.

In this one scene or chapter, the reader should be able to very clearly identify how this story has changed your hero for the better. If the Opening Image and the Final Image aren't starkly and obviously different, then it's time to rethink your beats. The farther apart these two versions of your hero are, the more you've proved that there was a point to this journey.

We didn't just travel in circles. We *went* somewhere.

So make it count. Set up a flawed hero in Act 1, take 'em on a wild ride through Act 2, make 'em prove their worth in Act 3, and pay off all your hard work with a Final Image that leaves the reader with only one word floating through their mind:

Wow.

The Transformation Machine

So there you have it. The fifteen beats. The Save the Cat! Beat Sheet. The *magic*.

The beat sheet is often also called a **transformation machine**, and you can probably see why. A flawed hero enters on one side and comes out the other side magically *transformed*! Essentially, the transformation machine is designed to reprogram heroes. To change the way they think, act, and operate. Think of heroes in novels as little robots bebopping around, operating by a strict (and highly *flawed*) set of programming that causes them to make mistakes. The transformation machine is the process that will crack open those robots and fiddle around with the wiring and programming inside until they can operate properly and can make better choices.

In the end, that is what all great stories do. They reprogram heroes. They *transform* human beings. And the beat sheet is essentially your reprogramming manual. It shows you which wires to cut, which code to alter, and in what order.

Pretty cool, huh?

But wait! Do the beats have to come in the *exact* same order that I outlined in this chapter?

Not necessarily. As you'll see in following chapters, where I break down ten popular novels into the fifteen beats, every once in a while *some* of the beats get a little jumbled up. Sometimes the Theme Stated comes after the Catalyst. Sometimes the Catalyst comes so early that the Setup and Debate get mushed together. Sometimes the false victory or false defeat of the Midpoint comes slightly *after* or *before* the literal middle of the story. Sometimes the B Story character is introduced in Act 1 but doesn't actually become important until Act 2.

The point is, the beats are all there. In almost every great story ever told. Because, again, these beats do not create a formula. These beats are what make stories work, because they're what makes *humans* work. Without a Catalyst, your hero would be stuck in their ho-hum Act 1 world forever. Without a Midpoint that raises the stakes, your hero would continue to meander around in the Fun and Games, never knowing that there's more important stuff to be dealt with out there. Without an All Is Lost rock bottom moment, your hero would never really change the right way.

This is story, folks.

Because this is *life*.

If you're having trouble visualizing how the beats fit together, or if you're just more of a visual learner, check out "Help! I Need More Structure!" in chapter 15 (page 277) for another look at the beat sheet in action.

EXERCISE: THE TRANSFORMATION TEST

Is your hero's transformation as big as it can be? Have you hit all the beats hard enough?

Use this handy Self-Workshop Checklist to make sure your beats pass the transformation test!

Opening Image

❏ Is your Opening Image *one* scene or one group of interconnected scenes?

❏ Is your Opening Image *visual*? (Are you showing, not telling?)

❏ Is one or more of your hero's flaws evident in this scene?

Theme Stated

❏ Does your theme directly relate to your hero's need or spiritual lesson?

❏ Is your theme stated by someone (or something!) *other* than the hero?

❏ Can your hero easily and believably dismiss this theme?

Setup

❏ Have you shown at least one thing that needs fixing in your hero's life?

❏ Have you introduced at least one A Story character?

❏ Did you clearly establish your hero's want or external goal somewhere in this beat?

❏ Have you shown your hero in more than one area of their life (such as home, work, and/or play)?

❏ Are your hero's flaws evident in this beat?

❏ Have you created a sense of urgency that imminent change is vital (stasis = death)?

Catalyst

❑ Does the Catalyst happen *to* the hero?

❑ Is it an *action* beat? (No revelations allowed here!)

❑ Is it impossible for the hero to go back to their normal life after this?

❑ Is the Catalyst big enough to break the status quo?

Debate

❑ Can you sum up your Debate with a question? Or if it's a preparation Debate, have you clearly defined what your hero is preparing for and why?

❑ Have you created a sense of hesitation in your hero?

❑ Have you shown your hero debating in more than one area of their life (such as home, work, and/or play)?

Break Into 2

❑ Is your hero *leaving* an old world behind and entering a new one?

❑ If your hero isn't physically going somewhere, are they trying something new?

❑ Is your Act 2 world the *opposite* of your Act 1 world?

❑ Is the break between Act 1 and Act 2 clear and distinct?

❑ Does your hero make a *proactive* move or decision to enter Act 2?

❑ Is your hero making a decision based on what they *want*?

❑ Can you identify why this is the wrong way to change?

B Story

❑ Have you introduced a new love interest, mentor, friend, or nemesis character?

❑ Can you identify how your B Story character (or characters!) represents the theme?

❏ Is your new character in some way a product of the upside-down Act 2 world? (Would they stick out like a sore thumb in the Act 1 world?)

Fun and Games

❏ Do you clearly show your hero either floundering or succeeding in the new world?

❏ Does your Fun and Games deliver on the promise of your premise?

❏ Does your Fun and Games visibly illustrate how your Act 2 world is the upside-down version of your Act 1 world?

Midpoint

❏ Can you clearly identify either a false victory or a false defeat?

❏ Have you raised the stakes of the story?

❏ Do your A (external) and B (internal) stories cross in some way?

❏ Can you identify a shift from the wants to the needs (even if it's subtle)?

Bad Guys Close In

❏ Is the path of this beat a direct opposite of your Fun and Games? (That is, if your hero was succeeding in your Fun and Games, are they floundering here? And vice versa?)

❏ Have you shown or identified how the internal bad guys (flaws) are working against your hero?

All Is Lost

❏ Does something happen *to* the hero in this beat?

❏ Is your All Is Lost *big* enough to push your hero into Act 3? (That is, have they really hit rock bottom?)

❏ Have you inserted a whiff of death?

❏ Does this beat feel like another Catalyst for change?

Dark Night of the Soul

❏ Is your hero reflecting on something in this beat?

❏ Is this beat leading your hero toward an epiphany?

❏ Does your hero's life seem worse off than it did at the beginning of the book?

Break Into 3

❏ Does your hero learn a valuable *universal* lesson (theme) here?

❏ Does your hero make a proactive decision to fix something?

❏ Is the decision based on what your hero needs?

❏ Can you identify why this is the *right* way to change?

❏ Is your Act 3 world a synthesis of Act 1 and Act 2?

Finale

❏ Does your hero struggle to enact their plan? (That is, does your Finale have conflict?)

❏ Is there a Dig Deep Down moment when your hero proves they've really learned their theme?

❏ Do the A Story and B Story somehow intertwine in this beat?

Final Image

❏ Is your Final Image *one* scene or collection of interconnected scenes?

❏ Is your Final Image *visual*? (Are you showing, not telling?)

❏ Is it evident how your hero has *transformed*?

❏ Does your "after" snapshot somehow mirror your "before" snapshot (Opening Image)?

Not Your Mother's Genres
Ten Genres to Fit Any Story
(Yes, Even Yours)

This should come as no surprise: if you want to write a good story, you have to know what good stories are made of. Along the same lines, if you want to *write* a successful novel, you have to *read* successful novels. You have to study how they work, what makes them successful, why they resonate with so many people. You have to break them open, peek inside, and study their inner mechanics, the way a medical student would study the inner workings of the human body.

How do the pieces fit together?

Why does this part go there?

How are certain stories similar and how are they different?

In short, the first step to being a successful writer is being a reader.

There's just one *teeensy* problem.

There are quite a few novels out there. Like, tens of millions of them. There's no possible way to read them all. But here's the good news: you don't have to!

What if we could sort every great novel ever written into one of ten categories and study the categories instead? What if we could group similar stories together into story types, figure out what elements each type has in common, and then design a template to follow when writing our own novel within that same category?

You've probably guessed what I'm going to say next.

We *can*.

Actually, we already have.

They're called the Save the Cat! story genres.

In the last chapter about the Save the Cat! Beat Sheet, we studied the mechanics of story in general. Now it's time to dig deeper and study the mechanics of different *types* of stories, so that when you sit down to write your own novel, you have solid blueprints to help you craft a successful, compelling story.

As the chapter title suggests, don't be fooled by the word "genre." I'm not talking about comedies, dramas, horrors, mysteries, or thrillers. Those are categories of *tone*. I'm talking about categories of *story*.

What *kind* of story are you setting out to tell?

What *type* of transformation does your hero undergo?

What central theme or question does your novel set out to tackle?

These questions are much more useful to us as we develop our novels. And they are exactly the kinds of questions that the Save the Cat! story genres were designed to answer.

And here's the *best* news about the Save the Cat! story genres: there are only ten of them. If you look back to the dawn of storytelling, from epics like *The Odyssey* by Homer to classics like *Pride and Prejudice* by Jane Austen to modern-day blockbusters like *The Girl on the Train* by Paula Hawkins, all can be sorted into one of ten story genres.

And as you study the genres, you'll start to see that, in almost all of the novels included in that genre, certain elements or conventions appear over and over again.

Now before you go throwing the "F" word around (formula), I'll tell you exactly why: for the same reason the fifteen beats appear in almost all great novels.

It's what makes these types of stories *work*.

As human beings, we are hardwired to respond to certain types of storytelling elements. And when they are strung together in the right order, these stories make our hearts sing, our souls cry out, our inner humanity vibrate like a tuning fork. If we study the elements of each story genre, and the patterns that make those elements successful, we can easily see why the novels in each genre are successful. And why these elements and patterns appear over and over again, in novels as old as *The Canterbury Tales* by Geoffrey Chaucer and as new as *Ready Player One* by Ernest Cline (which, by the way, are in the same story genre).

Just like the fifteen beats, the Save the Cat! story genres are a *codification* of the ten story types. These genres distill thousands of years' worth of literature into ten easy-to-follow templates.

No more tearing your hair out, wondering *Why is my story not working?* Figure out what genre your novel belongs in, make sure your novel has all the required elements, and your story *will* work.

Don't believe me? Just look at the centuries' worth of novel titles I've included as examples of each genre. All of those famous authors have made it work using the same templates I'm giving you in this book. Whether they actually *knew* they were doing it is another story. But they did it.

And so can you.

In the next ten chapters, we'll be diving into each genre in great detail. But first, here is a quick overview of the ten Save the Cat! story genres.

1. **WHYDUNIT:** A mystery must be solved by a hero (who may or may not be a detective) during which something shocking is revealed about the dark side of human nature. (See chapter 4.)

2. **RITES OF PASSAGE:** A hero must endure the pain and torment brought about by life's common challenges (death, separation, loss, divorce, addiction, coming of age, and so on). (See chapter 5.)

3. **INSTITUTIONALIZED:** A hero enters or is already entrenched inside a certain group, institution, establishment, or family and must make a choice to join, escape, or destroy it. (See chapter 6.)

4. **SUPERHERO:** An extraordinary hero finds themselves in an ordinary world and must come to terms with being special or destined for greatness. (See chapter 7.)

5. **DUDE WITH A PROBLEM:** An innocent, ordinary hero suddenly finds themselves in the midst of extraordinary circumstances and must rise to the challenge. (See chapter 8.)

6. **FOOL TRIUMPHANT:** An underestimated, underdog hero is pitted against some kind of "establishment" and proves a hidden worth to society. (See chapter 9.)

7. **BUDDY LOVE:** A hero is transformed by meeting someone else, including (but not limited to) love stories, friendship stories, and pet stories. (See chapter 10.)

8. **OUT OF THE BOTTLE:** An ordinary hero is temporarily "touched by magic," usually involving a wish fulfilled or a curse bestowed, and the hero learns an important lesson about appreciating and making the most of "reality." (See chapter 11.)

9. **GOLDEN FLEECE:** A hero (or group) goes on a "road trip" of some type (even if there's no actual road), in search of one thing and winds up discovering something else—themselves. (See chapter 12.)

10. **MONSTER IN THE HOUSE:** A hero (or group of heroes) must overcome some kind of monster (supernatural or not), in some kind of enclosed setting (or limited circumstances), and someone is usually responsible for bringing the monster into being. (See chapter 13.)

Give Me the Same Thing . . . Only Different

Have you ever heard someone say there's no such thing as an original story? Well, as you'll see throughout the next ten chapters, it's true. Original is not an achievable goal in novel-writing. So just throw that word out the window right now.

What *is* achievable is *fresh*.

A fresh "take" on an ancient story type is what readers and publishers are looking for. What's your personal spin on a story that's been told over and over again? How will *you* make this story archetype different? Our job, as writers, is to tell a new *version* of a familiar story that we already know readers are hardwired to respond to.

Basically, readers want the same thing . . . only different. Readers want to read something they *know* they will like, told in a way they've never heard before.

For instance, did you know that *The Help* by Kathryn Stockett and *1984* by George Orwell are actually the *same* Institutionalized story? Or that *The Martian* by Andy Weir and *Misery* by Stephen King share the same Dude with a Problem genre elements?

Writing a novel is a lot like baking. Whatever you make, you know there are certain ingredients you must include to get the outcome you want. If you're baking a cake, for example, you know you're going to need butter, eggs, flour, and sugar. Otherwise, you won't end up with a cake, you'll end up with a salty cracker. But once we have our basic cake formula—once we learn how a cake is properly made—we can start adding our own flavors and embellishments to the recipe, like chocolate and sprinkles and blueberries and orange glaze.

Is anyone else suddenly getting hungry?

Think of the following chapters as your cookbook, the ten story genres as your recipes, and the elements of each genre as your ingredients. Learn the recipes, study the genres, choose the right basic dish, and then give us your own twist on it. After all, you can't bend the rules until you know what the rules are. You need to learn how story *works* before you can start getting all fancy with it.

Why We Need the Genres

Studying your story genre can help you not only structure your own story but also break free from writing and plotting blockages. Whenever I get stuck on a certain part of my story, I always bust out the old Save the Cat! genre breakdowns, find novels and movies that are in my chosen genre, and get studying. Seeing how my predecessors tackled the same genre elements inspires me with new ideas and almost always busts me out of my blockage.

And at some point you're going to have to pitch your book to someone else. Whether it be to an agent, editor, or movie producer, or directly to the reader, you're going to have to quickly sum up what your book is about and why this person simply *has* to read it. And nothing gets this job done faster and more effectively than telling them what your book is similar to.

When someone asks you what your book is about, what they're really asking is this:

What is it most like? And how is it different from that?

They're asking about the story genre—without even knowing it!

Now, of course, you're probably not going to start off saying, "Well, it's a Dude with a Problem story . . ." because unless the other person has read this book, they're going to give you a very funny look. But you *are* going to use what the publishing industry calls "comparable titles," or "comps" for short.

And where will you *find* those comparable titles? You got it. You'll go straight to your story genre.

So the Save the Cat! story genres will not only help you *write* your novel, they might eventually help you *sell* your novel, too.

Final Note: Bleeding Genres

But let's face it. Novels are complex. They don't always fit neatly into just one category. Take *Les Misérables* by Victor Hugo; as you'll soon see, I placed it in the Institutionalized genre because it focuses on the lives of many as they pertain to the "institution" of post-revolutionary France. However, there's an equally compelling argument for *Les Misérables* being a Superhero story, given that Jean Valjean, the hero, is imbued with a power (a mission to be good); is challenged by a self-made nemesis, Javert; and has to overcome the "curse" of being a convict in nineteenth-century French society. But in the end, the true genre of this epic doesn't *really* matter. Victor Hugo is not going to haunt us from beyond the grave until we get it right. (Although what a cool Monster in the House novel that would be!)

We can debate the genres until we're blue in the face, but ultimately, the genres are here to help us focus our own stories and make sure we are including all the right elements.

So as you set out to plot and write your own novel, try not to stress *too* much about finding the exact perfect genre match for your story. You might find that your story exemplifies several genres. Your job is to pick the genre that your book is *most* like. Nothing is black or white. Many things in life are fifty shades of gray (which, by the way, in case you're wondering, is a Buddy Love).

Find the genre that feels *most* right to you and keep in mind that it *can* (and very well might) change as you write and revise.

My novel, *Unremembered*, changed genres about three times while I was writing it. It started out as a Dude with a Problem (girl survives a plane crash with no memories—huge problem!) Until I decided not to reveal *how* she survived the plane crash until the very end. That's when it became a Whydunit (what really happened to this girl and why?). Finally, I realized that she's wasn't an "ordinary" hero. She had *extra*ordinary abilities. She was special. That's when I discovered that the point of the novel was her coming to terms with who she is and how she differs from the rest of humanity. And so it remains to this day a Superhero story.

It's also important to note that individual books within a series *can* have different genres.

For instance, *The Hunger Games* by Suzanne Collins solidly fits into the Dude with a Problem camp. Innocent hero thrust into the action without asking for it, life-or-death battle. But the second book in the series, *Catching Fire,* is clearly an Institutionalized story. As a victor, Katniss is now a "naif" (aka a newcomer) in the system. The big question of the novel is: What will she do about it? And the answer to that question is that she "burns it down" (or at least sets it on fire). And book three, *Mockingjay*, is a Superhero story. It's about Katniss coming to terms with her special status as the "Mockingjay," the leader of the rebellion, and going up against her self-made nemesis, President Snow.

So if after reading the following chapters you feel the burning urge to argue one genre over another, here's my advice: Take a deep breath, relax, and channel that energy into a more worthwhile endeavor—namely, figuring out what's going to make *your* story work.

Because isn't that, after all, why you bought this book?

Whydunit

Detectives, Deception, and the Dark Side

Agatha Christie once wrote, "Very few of us are what we seem."

Appearances can be deceiving. Truth can be slippery. Secrets are inevitable. This is why in almost any bookstore you'll find an entire *section* dedicated to a type of book we call the *mystery*.

We turn to stories to find out more about ourselves. And we turn to mysteries to find out more about the *dark* side of ourselves. What evils lurk inside human hearts? What sins are we, as a species, capable of committing? And most important, *Why?*

If we look closely at what makes good mysteries so compulsively readable, it's not the *who*, but the *why*. It's the reason behind the crime, more than the criminal, that captures our interest and keeps us turning pages. In Agatha Christie's classic *And Then There Were None*, although we're dying to find out *which* of the ten guests on Soldier Island is killing people, it's the *motive* behind these deaths—the theme of judgment—that really fuels the story and resonates with us.

In *The Da Vinci Code* by Dan Brown, the organization responsible for Jacques Saunière's death is not as interesting as the *reason* he was killed and the secret he was killed for. It's the *why*, not the *who*.

Why would someone commit such atrocities?

And what does that say about who we are as humans?

Those are the two questions at the heart of the Save the Cat! story genre called the Whydunit.

Whether you're writing a classic murder mystery (like an Agatha Christie), a detective mystery (like the Harry Bosch series by Michael Connelly or the Dublin Murder Squad series by Tana French), a political mystery (like the Camel Club series by David Baldacci or the Jack Ryan series by Tom Clancy), or an amateur sleuth mystery (like *The Da Vinci Code* by Dan Brown or *In a Dark, Dark Wood* by Ruth Ware), all Whydunits share a common core. They all center around a crime that has been committed and a dark secret that lies at the heart of it. And it's your job as the writer to keep the reader guessing at every turn. Because regardless of whether your Whydunit detective is an amateur who's never solved a mystery or a private eye who's "seen it all," in the end the reader is your true gumshoe. It's the *reader* you have to wow with each shocking **turn of the cards**—clues and reveals set to detonate like bombs at just the right moment, stopping the story in its tracks and sending the mystery in a new direction. And it's the *reader* who must be forever changed by what you ultimately reveal about human nature.

Every Whydunit is like a series of increasingly dark rooms that we readers must walk through. We're not sure what we'll find at the end—or who. But we're along for the ride because we know it's going to answer the fundamental question behind every good mystery: *Why?*

If you think your novel fits into the Whydunit category, you'll need three key ingredients to ensure its success: (1) a **detective**, (2) a **secret**, and (3) a **dark turn**.

Let's take a look at each of these ingredients in more detail.

The *detective* of your story can truly be anyone. It can be someone who's seen a thousand dead bodies or someone who's never seen a single one. But two things must be true of this person: They must be wholly unprepared for what they're getting into (regardless of their job and/or experience), and they must have a *reason* for being dragged into this mess. Again, why *this* hero for *this* plot? The connection can *seem* random at first, but if you don't marry your hero to your plot—or your detective to your mystery, in this case—your reader will leave the novel saying those dreaded words: "Yeah, so?"

Think about Amos Decker, the detective hero of the Whydunit novel *Memory Man* by David Baldacci. At first, the murder of his entire family (which starts off the story) seems completely unrelated to the school shooting that happens over a year later. But ballistic evidence soon reveals that it's the same perpetrator behind both crimes, making Amos much more important in the investigation.

Or think of how shocked *The Da Vinci Code*'s Robert Langdon is when he's brought into the Louvre in the middle of the night and finds a dead man lying naked on the floor, next to a cryptic message written with the man's own blood. It's not your everyday occurrence for a symbologist. But, as Langdon soon learns, the part of the message that was erased by police included *his* name. He's definitely involved. But *why*?

Agatha Christie's *And Then There Were None* has an interesting twist on the detective ingredient. Although all the guests on Soldier Island are desperately trying to figure out who the murderer is before they become the next victim, the true detective in the story is—the reader! True, we are *always* the ultimate detective of every Whydunit, but in this case, we are the only one!

What all detectives have in common, however, is that they are *not* prepared for this case, regardless of how many cases they've solved before. Because if *this* case in *this* novel doesn't show them something they've never seen before, then what's the point? If the secret that is ultimately unveiled is something your hero or detective has dealt with before, then what's the mystery?

Which brings us to our second ingredient. As the detective unravels the clues, and you, the author, continue to turn over the cards, the *secret* is finally revealed. This secret is why we search for the truth to begin with. It's the heart of the Whydunit. It's what we find in the last dark room. It's not just the who and the why. It's the what, where, and when, too! It's what keeps the reader guessing until the very end. The bait that pulls us through the entire story. Because we (and the detective) *need* to know. We need to find out what really happened to

Harriet Vanger in *The Girl with the Dragon Tattoo* by Stieg Larsson. We need to discover what the Priory of Sion is hiding in *The Da Vinci Code*. We need to find out what happened to Jessica in that wood in *In the Woods* by Tana French.

And you, the author, need to make sure the secret is a good one.

The secret often starts out small but grows as the detective digs deeper into the case and uncovers more clues. In *Memory Man*, we first learn that the same gun was fired at both the murder of Decker's family *and* the recent school shooting. But as author Baldacci continues his skillful turning of the cards, the secret grows, and we soon discover that the murderer is actually targeting Decker specifically and trying to send him a message through both homicides.

In *And Then There Were None*, one death turns to three deaths turns to seven deaths! The plot (and the secret!) thickens with each dead body that turns up.

But as the secret grows deeper, so does the detective's desire to solve the case, which leads to their *dark turn*, the third ingredient of a Whydunit. The dark turn is the moment when the hero breaks or abandons the rules (either their own or society's) in pursuit of the secret or the truth.

Like when Amos Decker in *Memory Man* heads off on his own to confront the killer by himself in the third act, without backup and without sharing his latest breakthrough with the other agents working the case, a huge violation of police investigation rules.

The rules broken can be moral, societal, or personal. The point is to show how *this* case has affected your detective. They're now doing things they've never done before—going to places they've never gone before—all in pursuit of this secret. But ultimately it's almost always that dark turn that leads the hero to the theme that will transform them.

And it's what makes the novel worth reading.

Another popular (although not required) element found in many a Whydunit is the **case within a case**. The detective will sometimes start out investigating one mystery, only to find it intricately linked to another (often a case that was just ending at the start of the novel). We see this prominently in *In the Woods* by Tana French. The novel starts out in 1984 in a small Dublin town. Three kids go out to play in the woods. Only one comes back: Rob Ryan, who later becomes a detective sent to investigate the disappearance of a young girl in the same town. It's no surprise that as author French turns over the cards, the cases start to blend together, and our detective's involvement in the old case starts to blur his view of the new case. Even if the old case is never solved (as in *In the Woods*), it's usually this case within the case that reveals the story's theme and teaches the detective some type of lesson about themselves.

In the end, the detective, the secret, and the dark turn all serve one inherent purpose: to show us something about the dark side of human nature. We leave novels like *Memory Man, In the Woods, And Then There Were None,* and *The Girl with the Dragon Tattoo* feeling satisfied that we've solved the mystery and that the hero has been transformed by it, but also feeling just the slightest bit uneasy. Yet, it's this very unease, this little nugget of truth about ourselves, that keeps us reading and that has made the Whydunit one of the most classic and widely read story genres.

To recap: If you're thinking of writing a Whydunit novel, make sure your story includes these three essential ingredients:

- **A DETECTIVE**: whether that's a professional, an amateur, or even the reader! It just needs to be someone with a case on their hands. A case that they are not fully prepared for (whether they realize it or not!).

- **A SECRET**: the key to unraveling the whole thing. What is inside the last, darkest room of our hunt for the truth? It should illuminate something about the dark side of humanity. Something we didn't think was possible before the case began.

- **A DARK TURN**: the moment when the hero or detective finds themselves so deep into the mystery that their own rules, morals, and/or ethics are compromised. The hero must do something (usually in the second half of the novel) that somehow breaks the rules or threatens their integrity or even their innocence. These are the harrowing stakes of a good mystery. And the dark turn is why readers care about this particular case. Because the pull of *this* secret has become so strong, even the straightest arrows are helpless against it.

POPULAR WHYDUNIT NOVELS THROUGH TIME:

The Adventures of Sherlock Holmes by Arthur Conan Doyle
The Secret of the Old Clock (Nancy Drew series) by Carolyn Keene
Rebecca by Daphne Du Maurier
And Then There Were None by Agatha Christie
The Westing Game by Ellen Raskin
A Is for Alibi (Kinsey Millhone series) by Sue Grafton
The Black Echo (Harry Bosch series) by Michael Connelly
Along Came a Spider (Alex Cross series) by James Patterson
One for the Money (Stephanie Plum series) by Janet Evanovich
The Da Vinci Code by Dan Brown
The Girl with the Dragon Tattoo by Stieg Larsson
In the Woods (Dublin Murder Squad series) by Tana French
Gone Girl by Gillian Flynn
Ten by Gretchen McNeil
The Cuckoo's Calling (Comoran Strike series) by Robert Galbraith
The Girl on the Train by Paula Hawkins (*beat sheet included on the following page*)
Memory Man (Amos Decker series) by David Baldacci
In a Dark, Dark Wood by Ruth Ware
All the Missing Girls by Megan Miranda
Watch the Girls by Jennifer Wolfe

THE GIRL ON THE TRAIN

BY: Paula Hawkins
STC GENRE: Whydunit
BOOK GENRE: Mystery/Thriller
TOTAL PAGES: 323 (Riverhead Books Paperback Edition, 2016)

This instant blockbuster by Paula Hawkins debuted at number one on the *New York Times* best-seller list and went on to become a hit movie starring Emily Blunt. *The Girl on the Train* successfully uses a popular mystery-novel device, "the unreliable narrator," to pull you into the story and leave you guessing until the very end. But like so many great mystery novels, the most compelling question of the story is not *who* killed Megan Hipwell, but *why*. And that's what makes this page-turner such a fantastic example of a successful Whydunit novel.

1. Opening Image (pages 1–2)

This book opens up, not surprisingly, on a train. It's a fitting Opening Image, as so much of this book will take place on a train. We meet Rachel, aka "the girl on the train," one of three female protagonists and our primary **hero** of the book.

We soon learn that Rachel is obsessed with other people's lives—a flaw, introduced on the second page, that will drive the entire story.

2. Theme Stated (page 1)

On page 1, Rachel says, "My mother used to tell me that I had an overactive imagination; Tom said that, too." The book's theme is reality, how easily it can be manipulated, and how the three protagonists—Rachel, Megan, and Anna—refuse to accept it. It's not until Rachel learns the theme of accepting reality and comes face-to-face with the biggest truth of them all, that she finally solves the A Story mystery as well as the B Story (internal) mystery of her own life.

3. Setup (pages 2–38)

Rachel's status quo world is bleak. In the first 12 percent of the novel, Paula Hawkins effectively introduces Rachel's **things that need fixing**:

- Rachel is an alcoholic who drinks (and blacks out) way too much.

- Rachel lives in a fantasy world, making up stories about the wonderful life of a couple she's named "Jess" and "Jason" who live at 15 Blenheim Road in Witney.

- Rachel can't get over her ex-husband, Tom, who happens to live three doors down from "Jess" and "Jason" with his new wife, Anna (whom he had an affair with while still married to Rachel).

- Rachel has frequent blackouts in which she calls Tom (sometimes even stopping by his house), and he and his new wife are getting sick of it.

- Rachel's roommate is losing patience with her and her drinking.

- Rachel has already lost her job because of her drinking and rides the train every day only to avoid telling her roommate.

Also in the Setup is where we first meet our second protagonist, Megan (eventually revealed to be "Jess"). Megan's chapters are all told in flashback, starting a year earlier and steadily leading up to the present. Here, in only a few short pages, we learn that Megan's life is nothing like the fantasy Rachel has conjured up for her. She's restless and deeply troubled (we will soon learn by what), she's seeing a therapist, and her marriage is not perfect. In the first Megan chapter, we're introduced to the mysterious "him," a character who will continue to play a role in the story and whose identity will keep us guessing. Here is where Paula Hawkins first starts to use her great powers of misdirection to keep us in suspense and show us that, in this world, nothing is what it seems.

4. Catalyst (pages 38–41)

Although there's a smaller inciting incident on page 29, when Rachel sees "Jess" (Megan) kissing another man (effectively shattering her idealized view of her favorite couple), the real Catalyst of this story comes when Rachel wakes up on a Sunday morning—after blacking out from drinking—to find a lump on her head, blood in her hair, bruises on her legs, and vague memories of going to Blenheim Road the night before.

Now the real fun of *The Girl on the Train* begins. Did she go there to pay her ex-husband and his new wife another drunken visit? Or did she go there because earlier, when she saw "Jess" kissing another man, she swore, "If I saw that woman now, if I saw Jess, I would spit in her face. I would scratch her eyes out"? (page 31).

Rachel also vaguely remembers a red-haired man with her on the train. He will prove important, but for now, he's just another detail lost in the black void of her memory, along with—well, everything else that will make up the pages of this masterfully plotted thriller.

5. Debate (pages 41–62)

The big Debate question of this novel is: What happened on Saturday night, and what will Rachel ultimately do about it? Rachel can't shake the feeling that something bad happened that night and that she's somehow responsible. Meanwhile, in a **stasis = death** moment on page 41, Rachel's roommate, fed up with her drinking, threatens to kick her out of the apartment.

Rachel continues to try to piece together what happened, but it isn't until Rachel learns that Megan went missing on Saturday night that she finally gets her act together and decides to *do* something about it. This second Catalyst (called a **double bump** in Save the Cat! terms) is what will push Rachel into Act 2.

Meanwhile, in more flashbacks, we learn that Megan was having an affair with the mysterious "him," which Hawkins's clever sentence structuring leads us to believe is Megan's therapist, Kamal Abdic. We also start to suspect that Megan's husband, Scott ("Jason") might be responsible for her disappearance, thanks to subtle little hints like,

"We got into a fight. One of the bruising ones." Is Scott capable of hurting his wife?

6. Break Into 2 (pages 62–64)

Rachel leaves her status quo Act 1 world behind when she decides to take action and try to solve the mystery of Megan's disappearance (or more important, the mystery of her possible *involvement* in Megan's disappearance).

7. B Story (page 89)

Rachel's B Story (internal story) relates to her past. She must face up to it before she can truly break through these mysteries of the present. And that internal story is represented by **twin B Story** characters in this book: Scott Hipwell, Megan's husband, whom Rachel befriends and bonds with after Megan's disappearance, and Anna Watson, Tom's new wife, the source of Rachel's painful past. On page 89 Rachel visits Scott Hipwell to tell him about the man she saw kissing Megan before she disappeared. Scott will eventually help Rachel learn the theme by turning out *not* to be the man she thought he was (fantasy versus reality). Then, on page 108, we read our first chapter from Anna's perspective and get a glimpse of the other side of the story. This novel is all about that other side of the story. What aren't we seeing? What don't we know? What is our unreliable narrator unwilling or *unable* to tell us?

8. Fun and Games (pages 64–136)

The upside-down version of Rachel's life is illustrated through her involvement in investigating Megan's disappearance. She researches at the library, comes up with theories, visits Witney (where her hazy memories of Saturday night take place), meets with Scott (B Story), and tells the police about seeing Megan kissing another man (who turns out to be Megan's therapist, Kamal Abdic). Meanwhile, she stops drinking! She's feeling (and looking) better than she's ever felt before. "I am interested, for the first time in ages, in something other than my own misery. I have purpose. Or at least, I have a distraction" (page 85).

Rachel is clearly on an **upward path**. But as she points out in her own narrative, it's just a distraction. Has she successfully dealt with the *source* of her drinking (her painful past)? No. She's just found a replacement for it. A new way to numb the pain. She's **fixing things the wrong way**, as so many heroes do in Act 2. And it's working! The case seems to be making progress, thanks to her tip about Kamal Abdic.

But until she actually faces her reality (theme!), she won't be able to truly solve the mystery (both Megan's and her own).

Paula Hawkins does an excellent job of putting readers in the same boat as Rachel, believing what we see, and trusting our own minds. By the time we reach the Midpoint, we've come to the same conclusion as Rachel: Kamal Abdic is behind Megan's disappearance. He was (almost) definitely the one she was having an affair with.

9. Midpoint (pages 137–161)

Victory! Kamal Abdic is arrested and evidence is found in his home and his car. It seems the police (thanks to Rachel's help) are getting closer to the truth about what happened to Megan.

A and B stories cross as Rachel is leaving Scott's house, after finding out about Kamal (A Story) and running smack into her past: Tom and Anna (B Story). This time, however, Rachel reacts differently. She's indifferent to them (or so she tells herself) because she's still on the high of her (false) victory.

But like so many **false victory** Midpoints, something bigger is coming. A tiny bomb is waiting to explode and send the story (and us) in a new direction. And, as is so often the case in Whydunits, by the Midpoint we *think* we know what this case is about. We may even think we know *who*dunit. But we don't. A **Midpoint twist** will prove that it's *much* bigger than we thought. And that's exactly what happens in this novel.

Soon the **stakes are raised**, when Kamal is released without being charged and Megan's body is found buried in the woods. This is no longer a disappearance. This is a murder. And our prime suspect just got away.

10. Bad Guys Close In (pages 161–244)

Rachel has already started drinking again . . . a lot. Which proves that her Fun and Games change wasn't a real change. It was just a Band-Aid. Her **internal bad guys** are still in there, and now they're about to come out in full force and drive her toward the All Is Lost, which is evident in the fact that she still won't talk to the red-haired man from the train. She knows he knows something about that fateful Saturday night, yet she's still too afraid of the truth (theme!).

Meanwhile, however, in the Megan flashbacks, Megan's life is improving. She's opened up to Kamal about the tragedy of her past (accidentally killing her own baby in the bathtub), and is starting to feel lighter and less burdened.

In the present, more details about Megan's death surface: she died of a head trauma, and she was pregnant. Scott becomes a prime suspect in the case, yet Rachel gets closer and closer to him, eventually even sleeping with him, proving that she still hasn't learned the theme. "I wanted it," Rachel tells us. "I wanted to be with Jason" (page 217). "Jason" doesn't exist. He's a character in her dream world.

Rachel goes to see Megan's therapist, Kamal Abdic, posing as a new patient. At first, she's pursuing her misguided goals of wanting to get involved in the case and to feel needed, but then, in a **shift from wants to needs**, Rachel finds the sessions helpful in confronting her past with Tom and her drinking.

More memories start to surface for Rachel. She now remembers someone hitting her and walking away. She thinks it might have been Anna.

Meanwhile, from Anna's point of view, we learn things are going downhill for her, too. Rachel is driving a wedge between Anna and Tom. They fight a lot, and Anna starts to suspect that Tom might be having an affair—again. She hits an all-time low when she essentially *becomes* Rachel: drinking heavily and snooping through Tom's stuff.

11. All Is Lost (pages 244–252)

The case (and Rachel's internal story) both hit rock bottom when Scott invites Rachel over to tell her that the baby wasn't his—or Kamal's. Which means there's another guy. This turning point reveals, to both Rachel and us readers, that things were never what they seemed. The "him" Megan kept referring to was not Kamal. It was someone else. But who?

Scott is drunk and irate when he delivers this news. He's also found out that Rachel lied to him about a lot of things. And when he finds out that Rachel was seeing Kamal as a patient, he thinks she's been out to get him from the start. He attacks her, grabbing her by the hair and locking her in a spare bedroom. Then he threatens to kill her (**whiff of death**). Rachel is more certain than ever that Scott killed Megan.

Now all is lost for Rachel. And it was her lying and meddling that brought her there. But not facing up to the truth (Rachel's theme) also played a huge part in bringing her to this low moment. Because if she had confronted her past earlier, she might have realized who the real bad guy is in this story.

12. Dark Night of the Soul (pages 252–269)

Scott lets Rachel go—and she drinks herself into a stupor. She tries calling the police to tell them that Scott threatened her and definitely killed his wife, but they don't believe her. As a drunk rubbernecker, she's lost all credibility. And then Rachel does what many heroes do during the Dark Night of the Soul: she gives up. "All this time, I've been thinking that there was something to remember, something I was missing. But there isn't" (page 254).

Rachel tried to get involved, thinking she was helping, but that wasn't the answer. The answer has been inside her this whole time: locked inside the black box of her memory, inside her own past.

Only when Rachel finally confronts the red-haired man and asks him about Saturday night does she start heading toward a real solution. The red-haired man tells Rachel that when he saw her on Saturday night, she was upset. There was a man walking away from her, and he was with someone. A woman.

Rachel assumes this must have been Tom and Anna, but when she asks Tom about it, the stories don't match up. Tom tells her Anna was at home with the baby. So who was with Tom?

Then Tom says something that triggers her memory: "I'm surprised you remember anything at all, Rachel. You were blind drunk" (page 261). Rachel remembers Tom saying this to her another time she blacked out from too much alcohol and then he claimed she did something horrible. Things start to become clear for Rachel when she realizes Tom was the one who hit her on Saturday night (Dark Night epiphany).

Meanwhile, Anna is having a Dark Night of the Soul of her own. As she drinks and snoops through Tom's things, she finds a cell phone hidden in his gym bag. It belongs to Megan Hipwell.

13. Break Into 3 (page 271)

Memories fill Rachel's head as she realizes the truth about Tom. He's been lying to her and manipulating her for a long time. Rachel learns the theme and confronts the past, leading her to take action and (appropriately) get on a train. Headed where? We will soon find out.

14. Finale (pages 271–318)

POINT 1: GATHERING THE TEAM. Rachel goes to Tom and Anna's house to "collect" Anna. She can't do this alone; they—the two wives of the lying, murdering Tom Watson—need to do this together, as a team.

POINT 2: EXECUTING THE PLAN. Rachel tries to convince Anna to come with her, but Anna doesn't believe that Tom is a murderer. She just thinks Tom had an affair with Megan. Anna hasn't learned the theme yet; she's still living in her own fantasy world, afraid to accept the truth.

POINT 3: HIGH TOWER SURPRISE. Tom comes home, and things get messy. Rachel is there and confronts Tom, and he, of course, lies to get out of it. It's a battle for Anna's loyalty, and Tom is winning. Rachel tries to convince Anna to call the police, but she won't. Tom reveals the truth about killing Megan. Rachel tries to run, but Tom hits her on the head with a bottle and she passes out.

POINT 4: DIG DEEP DOWN. Both Rachel and Anna prove that they've learned the theme and that they have what it takes to win this. First, Anna sneaks into the hallway to phone the police. Then Rachel plays right into Tom's hand, letting him think he has the same control over her he's always had. Now *she* is manipulating him.

Cat's Eye View

For quick reference, here's a brief overview of this novel's beat sheet.

1. **OPENING IMAGE:** Rachel rides the train, fantasizing about other people's lives.

2. **THEME STATED:** "My mother used to tell me that I had an overactive imagination; Tom said that, too" (page 1). Rachel, Megan, and Anna all need to learn how to face reality.

3. **SETUP:** Rachel has a drinking problem and often blacks out, making her an unreliable narrator. Megan's marriage is not as perfect as Rachel has dreamed it is.

4. **CATALYST:** Rachel blacks out and wakes up with bruises, unable to remember what happened the night before.

5. **DEBATE:** What happened on Saturday night and what will Rachel do about it? Rachel finds out that Megan Hipwell is missing.

6. **BREAK INTO 2:** Rachel inserts herself into the case, trying to help solve the mystery of the missing Megan Hipwell.

7. **B STORY:** Rachel meets Scott Hipwell, Megan's husband, and Anna's side of the story is introduced (twin B stories).

8. **FUN AND GAMES:** Rachel quits drinking and seems to make strides with the case (upward path).

POINT 5: THE EXECUTION OF THE NEW PLAN. As Rachel lets Tom kiss her, she slips her hand into a drawer in the kitchen and steals something. Then she runs. When Tom chases after her, Rachel plunges a corkscrew into his neck. The use of a corkscrew as the final weapon is not coincidental. It represents Rachel's drinking problem, her past, and, now, her triumph as she uses it to, once and for all, rid herself of her demons.

9. **MIDPOINT:** The main suspect, Kamal Abdic, is arrested (false victory), but stakes are raised when he's released and Megan's body is found, upgrading this case to a murder investigation.

10. **BAD GUYS CLOSE IN:** Rachel takes up drinking again, sees Megan's therapist (Kamal), sleeps with Megan's husband (Scott), and starts to remember things from Saturday night. Anna suspects Tom of having an affair.

11. **ALL IS LOST:** Scott finds out Rachel has been lying to him and locks her up, threatening to kill her (whiff of death). Rachel discovers Megan was pregnant when she died—and the baby wasn't Scott's or Kamal's.

12. **DARK NIGHT OF THE SOUL:** Rachel drinks herself into a stupor, is turned away by the police, and finally confronts the red-haired man who gives her a key piece of information about Saturday night (Dark Night epiphany).

13. **BREAK INTO 3:** Rachel realizes Tom has been lying to her and manipulating her for a long time. She gets on the train.

14. **FINALE:** Together with Anna, Rachel brings down Tom for the murder of Megan Hipwell and when he tries to kill her, stabs him to death with a corkscrew.

15. **FINAL IMAGE:** Sober, Rachel rides the train toward her new life.

15. Final Image (pages 318–323)

In a mirror image to the opening, Rachel is on the train again. But this time things are very different. This time, she's been sober for three weeks, and she's moving forward, leaving her old world and her past behind her.

WHY IS THIS A WHYDUNIT?

The Girl on the Train contains all three elements of a successful Whydunit story:

- **A DETECTIVE:** Our hero, Rachel, is the amateur sleuth of the story. She's never cracked a case before and is therefore wholly unprepared for what she's getting herself into.

- **A SECRET:** The relationship between Megan and Scott leads to the unraveling of the whole case. It's the card that author Paula Hawkins withholds until the very end, turning it over just in time for Rachel (and the reader) to put the final pieces together.

- **A DARK TURN:** When Rachel sleeps with Scott Hipwell, we know she's in too deep. Not only is she sleeping with one of the suspects, but she's sleeping with a husband whose wife has been murdered. It's the moment when her obsession with the case overpowers her ethics.

Rites of Passage
When Life Gets in the Way

When I was little, I used to get these dull pains in my legs at night. My parents told me they were "growing pains." The result of my body, bones, and muscles changing. But what happens when the growing and changing happens in our minds? Do we also feel mental and emotional "growing pains"?

You betcha.

And that's what the Rites of Passage genre is all about.

Death, puberty, separation, midlife crisis, adolescence. These are the roadblocks of life that stop us in our path and force us to reexamine who we are as human beings. They're also the building blocks of an incredible story that will resonate with readers because, hey, we've *all* been there. We've all been kicked in the butt by life at some point or other. We've all experienced some kind of "life problem" that required us to grow and change in order to overcome it.

Rites of passage stories span centuries, cultures, races, genders, and ages. They are universal because *life* is universal. Life doesn't always give us what we want. In fact, it often dumps on us. It treats us unkindly, unfairly, and seemingly without respect. That's why Rites of Passage stories are usually tales of pain, torment, disappointment, hard knocks, and agony.

Sounds uplifting, doesn't it?

But actually, there's many a comedy that fits inside this genre, as well as countless harrowing and introspective dramas. After all, when life throws you a curve ball, you can choose to handle it with either humor or solemnity.

Whether you're writing a novel that explores death (like *The Sky is Everywhere* by Jandy Nelson or *The Shack* by William P. Young), the pains of adolescence (like *The Perks of Being a Wallflower* by Stephen Chbosky or *The Catcher in the Rye* by J. D. Salinger), a midlife or quarterlife crisis (like *Something Borrowed* by Emily Giffin or *About a Boy* by Nick Hornby), or even problems that span decades (like *The Kite Runner* by Khaled Hosseini), your job remains the same: Tell us a tale about someone dealing with some kind of life transition.

And to do that, you'll need three essential ingredients: (1) a **life problem**, (2) a **wrong way** to attack the problem, and (3) a **solution** to the problem that involves *acceptance* of the hard truth the hero has been avoiding.

Let's break them down one by one.

It's true that all great stories involve some kind of problem for the hero to overcome (Act 1), a wrong way to fix the problem (Act 2), and a solution that involves some kind of acceptance of the hard truth (Act 3), but what makes Rites of Passage stories special is the fact that the initial problem originates from simply being alive.

The *life problem* in a Rites of Passage story is usually unavoidable. It's a natural bend in the road of what it means to be human. We all have to grow up, and we all encounter struggles along the way, often the exact same ones. This is why so many young adult contemporary novels fall into this genre: they explore such a tumultuous time in the human experience. In *The Summer I Turned Pretty* by Jenny Han, the life problem is written right into the title (adolescence); in *The Truth About Forever* by Sarah Dessen, the hero, Macy, must overcome both the loss of her father (death) *and* all of the other challenges being a teenager can bring (adolescence).

But you don't have to be a teenager to have a little growing up to do, as evidenced in Rites of Passage stories like *Emma* by Jane Austen, in which Emma is dealing with the marriage of her beloved governess (separation) and even further in the past, the loss of her mother (death). Or *Something Borrowed* by Emily Giffin, in which Rachel is dealing with turning thirty (quarterlife crisis).

But don't forget that heroes are infamous for trying to fix things the wrong way first, and nowhere is that more true than for heroes of this genre. Which is why our second ingredient for writing a compelling Rites of Passage is a *wrong way* to attack the life problem, which usually involves some kind of avoidance of the pain. Emma in *Emma* doesn't face her life problem head-on; instead, she vows that *she* will never marry, and she busies herself in matchmaking for her friends. Lennie in *The Sky Is Everywhere* doesn't deal with her sister's death in a healthy way (at least not at first!). Instead, she falls for two different boys, one of them her dead sister's boyfriend. And Will Freeman in *About a Boy* isn't dealing with his quarterlife crisis very well. His wrong way to attack the problem is to attend single parents' groups (even though he doesn't actually have a child) in order to pick up women. The point of the wrong way ingredient is twofold: it illustrates your hero's resistance to change and gives your story a purpose. If your hero approached their life problem with grace, humility, acceptance, and gratitude, what would be the point of the book?

But in the end, all Rites of Passage stories are about some kind of *acceptance*, the genre's third ingredient. Usually, this is an acceptance of the very truth the hero has been avoiding. Jane Austen's Emma realizes that she's lonely and that the only person whose love life actually *needs* to be meddled with is her own. Lennie in *The Sky Is Everywhere* finally comes to accept the grief that she will have to carry for the rest of her life, instead of trying to run from it. And Rachel in *Something Borrowed* finally accepts the hard truth that it's time to move on from her childhood best friend, Darcy.

These "growing pains" tales almost always end with the same realization: we can't expect life to change, so we'd better change instead. But the true beauty of the Rites of Passage story is that when your hero discovers something about themselves, we, the reader, ultimately discover a little something about ourselves too. Because regardless of age, we all have a little growing up to do.

To recap: If you're thinking about writing a Rites of Passage novel, make sure your story includes these three essential ingredients:

- **A LIFE PROBLEM:** a universal challenge that often results from nothing more than just being alive (such as puberty, adolescence, midlife, separation, death, and so on).

- **A WRONG WAY TO ATTACK THE PROBLEM:** Your hero can't face this challenge head-on (at least not at first!). There needs to be some level of avoidance happening, usually as an attempt to evade the pain.

- **AN ACCEPTANCE OF THE HARD TRUTH:** This is the real solution, and it usually comes with the understanding that it's the hero who must change, not life itself.

POPULAR RITES OF PASSAGE NOVELS THROUGH TIME:

Emma by Jane Austen
Great Expectations by Charles Dickens
Anne of Green Gables by Lucy Maud Montgomery
Their Eyes Were Watching God by Zora Neale Hurston
The Catcher in the Rye by J. D. Salinger
Are You There, God? It's Me, Margaret by Judy Blume
About a Boy by Nick Hornby
Speak by Laurie Halse Anderson
The Perks of Being a Wallflower by Stephen Chbosky
The Kite Runner by Khaled Hosseini (*beat sheet included on the following page*)
The Truth About Forever by Sarah Dessen
Something Borrowed by Emily Giffin
The Shack by William P. Young
The Summer I Turned Pretty by Jenny Han
The Last Song by Nicholas Sparks
Room by Emma Donoghue
The Sky Is Everywhere by Jandy Nelson
Fangirl by Rainbow Rowell
Every Last Word by Tamara Ireland Stone

THE KITE RUNNER

BY: Khaled Hosseini
STC GENRE: Rites of Passage
BOOK GENRE: General fiction
TOTAL PAGES: 371 (Riverhead Books Paperback, 2003)

This debut novel by Afghan-American author Khaled Hosseini took the literary world by storm when it was published in 2003. While the novel deals with themes of atonement and guilt, it is ultimately a coming of age tale (spanning from childhood to adulthood) about a son who has a very complicated relationship with his father. And it's this complicated relationship that makes the novel a shining example of a Rites of Passage story.

1. Opening Image (pages 1–2)

The Opening Image of our hero, Amir, is a bit cryptic, but it's an effective tease for the rest of the novel, as we get exactly enough to pull us into the story.

After only two pages, we know that something happened to Amir in the winter of 1975 that changed his life forever—a hint of the Catalyst to come. And we know that the memory of this life-changing event was dredged up because of a phone call from someone named Rahim Khan. Amir also tells us that it wasn't just Rahim calling; "It was my past of unatoned sins" (page 1). This is a hint of the theme (courage) that will fuel the hero's transformative arc.

2. Setup (pages 3–73)

We flash back to Amir's childhood, growing up in Kabul, Afghanistan. The most important two characters of this Setup (apart from Amir himself) are Hassan, his childhood best friend, and Baba ("Papa" in the Middle East), his father.

Amir has a complicated relationship with both.

His baba is a wealthy Pashtun (Sunni Muslim) who lives in a large house with a beloved long-time family servant, Ali, a Hazara (Shi'a Muslim, a group that has been oppressed by Pashtuns for years). Hassan is the son of Ali.

The boys grew up like brothers, but there's definitely an unbrotherly power dynamic between them. For instance, Hassan prepares meals for Amir, makes his bed, and polishes his shoes. Plus, Hassan usually takes the blame for any trouble Amir gets into and even stands up for him in fights. But when Hassan gets picked on by the neighborhood kids for being a Hazara, Amir doesn't really do the same for him. Actually, there are times when Amir is mean to Hassan, playing harmless pranks on him, but Hassan never seems to mind.

The boys are bonded because they're both motherless—Amir's mom died in childbirth, and Hassan's mother left the family shortly after he was born.

It seems Baba—who is always doing good things for the community, like building orphanages—is constantly disappointed in Amir, and Amir feels guilty because he feels that he killed his mother.

War comes to Afghanistan in the Setup. Although it's a huge deal for the future of the country, it's a mini Catalyst for Amir's story. It's not until page 73 that Amir's major Catalyst appears and changes everything.

Meanwhile, the kids deal with a bully named Assef who is constantly harassing Hassan and wants to cleanse the Hazara from Afghanistan. Hassan threatens Assef with a slingshot and a rock, and Assef leaves, promising retaliation.

Also in this Setup, we learn the source of the book's title, as Amir introduces us to the tradition of kite fighting—a winter event in which kids make and fight kites, trying to cut down the other kites in the sky. Kite runners then run after the fallen kites to collect them. Amir is an excellent kite fighter, and Hassan, his servant and best friend, is an excellent kite runner, making them a good team.

The big kite-fighting tournament of 1975 is here. Amir wins the tournament, and Hassan takes off after the second-place kite (the greatest prize of the tournament).

3. Theme Stated (page 23)

As a child, Amir overhears his father talking to Rahim Khan (the man referenced in the Opening Image). As Baba voices his disappointment in his son, he says to Rahim, "A boy who won't stand up for himself becomes a man who can't stand up to anything."

In this moment we feel sorry for Amir, feeling that his father is very hard on him. But as the story continues, we (and Amir) start to realize how right his father was in this statement. One of Amir's biggest flaws is that he's a coward. He won't stand up for anything he believes in—unlike Hassan, who constantly stands up for Amir, and unlike his father, who will risk death to defend someone's honor.

4. Catalyst (pages 73–79)

After running after the fallen kite, Hassan goes missing, and Amir sets off to try to find him. He eventually discovers him in an alley surrounded by Assef and his gang. Amir watches, unseen, as Assef rapes Hassan.

Instead of intervening and coming to Hassan's rescue, Amir runs away, showing his cowardly flaw. When he meets up with Hassan later, he doesn't tell him that he saw what happened.

This is the event that Amir mentioned in the Opening Image/first chapter. The guilt and shame he feels for failing to protect Hassan will haunt him for the rest of the novel. And it's not until he learns the theme and stands up for something that he can atone for his sins, grow up, and complete his coming of age—and his Rite of Passage.

5. Debate (pages 80–103)

The Debate question of this novel is: What will Amir do about what he saw? Or, as he puts it on page 93, "What am I going to do with you, Hassan?"

Amir is too cowardly to tell anyone, and the guilt eats him alive. He develops insomnia. He notices differences in Hassan, who stops smiling and becomes very withdrawn. Their relationship changes drastically. They grow distant, and their friendship falls apart. Amir tries all manner of wrong ways to alleviate the guilt.

First, he asks his father if they can get new servants, and his father yells at Amir for even suggesting such a thing. Then Amir tries to start a fight with Hassan, thinking it will make him feel better if Hassan fights back, but he won't. This frustrates Amir, who comes up with another wrong way to deal with his overwhelming emotions.

6. Break Into 2 (pages 104–109)

Amir hides his new wristwatch and a wad of cash under Hassan's mattress and then tells Baba that these items are missing. When they are found under Hassan's mattress, Baba asks Hassan if he stole them. Back-to-back shocks come to Amir as Hassan admits that he did; then right afterward, Baba says that he forgives Hassan, even though Baba has declared that stealing is the worst of all the sins.

Ali and Hassan decide to leave, despite Baba's begging them to stay. Amir almost confesses what really happened but changes his mind, remaining a coward.

This is definitely evidence of Amir **fixing things the wrong way**. His cowardice and the guilt that stems from it is what drives this Break Into 2 decision to try to get rid of Hassan. He believes that if he doesn't have to see him anymore, he won't feel this way. Obviously, this will turn out not to be true.

7. Fun and Games (pages 110–173)

Act 2 of this novel takes place in a whole new world: America.

The story jumps ahead five years. Afghanistan has become dangerous, and Amir and Baba are being smuggled to Pakistan in the back of a truck, thus beginning the steady **downward path** toward the Midpoint.

When they reach America, it's not what either of them was expecting. At first they're forced to go on welfare, and Baba, a rich man in Afghanistan, now works at a gas station in Fremont, California. Amir graduates from high school, which pleases Baba, but Baba doesn't approve of Amir's choice to study creative writing in college.

In America, Amir is still fixing things the wrong way, hoping that being this far away will help him forget his past and Hassan. On page 136, he says, "America was a river, roaring along, unmindful of the past. I could wade into this river, let my sins drown to the bottom, let the waters carry me someplace far. Someplace with no ghosts, no memories, and no sins." But the memory of Hassan follows him wherever he goes. Even all the way here in America, he's still haunted by his guilt.

Meanwhile, Baba's health is failing. He is diagnosed with cancer, and the outlook is not good.

8. B Story (pages 140–142)

In America, Amir meets Soraya at a swap meet and almost instantly falls in love with her, calling her his "swap meet princess" (page 142). He learns that Soraya has a scandalous past, which has kept her from having any suitors. But it's actually what Amir loves about her. He loves that she too carries baggage. She too has "sinned."

Amir courts Soraya, and they fall in love. It's Soraya who will eventually help Amir face his own past and his own sins—as any good B Story character should do.

In fact, later, before they're married, Soraya comes clean about her own past, making Amir wish he had the guts to do the same. But alas, he doesn't. Because he hasn't learned the theme . . . *yet.*

9. Midpoint (page 173)

A month after Amir and Soraya get married, Baba dies in his sleep. Not only is this a **false defeat** for Amir, it's also when the emotional **stakes are raised**, big time. With Baba's death, the pressure is on for Amir to atone for his sins. Life is short. He can't die with the Hassan incident on his conscience, can he?

10. Bad Guys Close In (pages 174–214)

Despite his father's death, Amir's life heads on a general **upward path**. Amir and Soraya both enroll in college, and Amir writes his first novel, gets an agent, and gets a book deal (if only it happened that fast in real life!).

Amir and Soraya try to have a child, but Soraya is unable to get pregnant.

We fast-forward ten years. Amir gets a call from Rahim Khan (this is the phone call from the Opening Image). Rahim is very sick and wants Amir to come to Pakistan to see him. Before he hangs up the phone, Rahim utters a nod to the theme: "Come. There is a way to be good again." Could Rahim know about the terrible things Amir did back in Afghanistan?

Amir boards a flight to Pakistan. In Pakistan, Rahim tells Amir that he's dying, and before he goes, he wants to tell Amir a story about Hassan. It appears Amir's past is about to catch up with him. No more hiding.

Rahim tells Amir about how he found Hassan years after Amir and Baba left Afghanistan. He was married, with a child on the way. His father had died after walking into a landmine. Rahim invited Hassan and his wife to come live in Baba's old house (where Rahim was living at the time) and help him take care of it. They agreed. Hassan's wife gave birth to a boy, and they named him after a character from a book Amir used to read to Hassan. As the fighting in Kabul got worse, Hassan took good care of his son, Sohrab, teaching him how to read, write, shoot a slingshot, and run a kite (just as Hassan used to do as a kid).

11. All Is Lost (pages 214–223)

Rahim gives Amir letters from Hassan and a Polaroid of him with Sohrab. In the letters, Hassan tells Amir that he still thinks about him.

Then Rahim breaks the news that Hassan and his wife were executed by the Taliban (**whiff of death**), leaving Sohrab alone in an orphanage in Kabul. Rahim wants Amir to go back to Kabul and get Sohrab from the orphanage. He knows of some people in Pakistan who will adopt him. On page 221, Rahim says, "I think we both know why it has to be you," revealing that Rahim knows what happened between Amir and Hassan.

At first, Amir refuses. He doesn't want to get involved. Then Rahim drops the *big* All Is Lost bomb: Hassan was actually Amir's half-brother. Apparently Ali, Hassan's "father," was sterile, and Baba slept with Hassan's mother. That's why Baba always showed such favoritism to Hassan, the same favoritism that made Amir jealous of Hassan.

Amir storms out of the apartment.

12. Dark Night of the Soul (pages 224-227)

What will Amir do with this information? Will he go to Kabul and get Sohrab, who is now revealed to be his nephew? Or will he be a coward, as he always has been?

Back in the apartment, Rahim reminded Amir of the theme: "A boy who won't stand up for himself becomes a man who can't stand up to anything. I wonder, is that what you've become?" (page 221).

Amir also remembers what Rahim said on the phone: "There is a way to be good again." And suddenly he knows what he must do.

13. Break Into 3 (page 227)

Amir agrees to go to Kabul to get Sohrab. This is his chance to redeem himself. This is his chance to stand up for something. He has learned the theme. He is finally ready to grow up and stop hiding from his mistakes.

14. Finale (pages 228-363)

POINT 1: GATHERING THE TEAM. Amir travels to Kabul. On the way there, he stays the night at his driver's house and witnesses how hungry his children are. His driver, Farid, upon learning that Amir is there to rescue a Hazara boy, offers to help. Amir now has his team. Before leaving for Kabul, Amir leaves a wad of cash under the mattress for Farid's family. This redemptive action directly counteracts the Break Into 2 beat (fixing things the wrong way) where he hid cash under Hassan's mattress to get rid of him.

POINT 2: EXECUTING THE PLAN. As they drive to Kabul, Amir sees evidence of the wars that have been going on since he and Baba left. They arrive at the orphanage, and after they convince the director that they are not Taliban, the director reveals that Sohrab is not there. He's been "sold" to a Taliban officer for reasons that seem very dark and sinister. The director tells Amir and Farid that the Taliban officer who "bought" Sohrab will be at the Ghazi Stadium the next day.

After they leave the orphanage, Farid tells Amir that it's probably better to just forget everything that happened here in Afghanistan. It's easier. But Amir proves, once again, that he's learned the theme and is now **fixing things the right way** when he says, "I don't want to forget anymore" (page 263).

The next day they go to the stadium for a soccer match. At halftime, two "adulterers" are stoned to death by a Taliban cleric.

POINT 3: HIGH TOWER SURPRISE. After the match, Amir goes to see the Taliban officer. The officer brings out Sohrab, and Amir is overwhelmed by his resemblance to Hassan. Amir soon figures out that the officer is actually Assef—the boy who raped Hassan. If ever there was a chance for Amir to redeem himself and his past mistakes, this is it!

POINT 4: DIG DEEP DOWN. Assef tells Amir he can have Sohrab, but he has to fight Assef first. Amir gets beaten up pretty badly in the subsequent fight, but he laughs, because ironically he feels at peace for the first time since that day in 1975 when he left Hassan in the alley. "My body was broken—just how badly I wouldn't find out until after—but I felt *healed*. Healed at last" (page 289).

Amir and Sohrab manage to escape Assef after Sohrab shoots him in the eye with his slingshot.

POINT 5: THE EXECUTION OF THE NEW PLAN. Amir recuperates from the beating in a hospital, and once he's regained consciousness he gets a letter from Rahim, admitting that he deceived Amir. There was no family in Pakistan ready to adopt Sohrab.

Amir asks Sohrab to come live in America with him and his wife. Sohrab eventually says yes, and the two visit the American embassy, only to discover that the chances of Amir being able to adopt Sohrab and bring him back to America are slim.

Upon hearing this news and knowing that he'll most likely land back in an orphanage, Sohrab attempts to commit suicide.

As Amir waits for news of Sohrab's condition in the hospital, he prays for the first time in over fifteen years. After Sohrab wakes up, Amir tells him that his wife has worked everything out with an American immigration lawyer and they can adopt him.

Sohrab is different now, though. He doesn't speak. He's sort of dead inside. Amir brings Sohrab to California, and his arc is completed when Soraya's father insults Sohrab by calling him a "Hazara boy," to which Amir stands up for himself and his nephew and says, "You will never again refer to him as 'Hazara boy' in my presence. He has a name and it's Sohrab" (page 361).

Time passes, and Sohrab still doesn't speak. He just sleeps and remains silent.

15. Final Image (pages 318–323)

One afternoon, Amir takes Soraya and Sohrab to a park and sees people flying kites. He buys a kite for Sohrab and tells him that his father was the best kite runner in all of Kabul.

He shows Sohrab how to fly the kite, and they cut another kite's string. Amir offers to run the kite for Sohrab. Sohrab smiles for the first time since arriving in America, and Amir takes off after the fallen kite, redeeming himself once and for all and becoming the kite runner.

WHY IS THIS A RITES OF PASSAGE?

The Kite Runner contains all three elements of a successful Rites of Passage story:

- **A LIFE PROBLEM:** Although this novel spans decades, it's essentially a coming of age story. Amir struggles with becoming an adult and dealing with the mistakes of his childhood. He also struggles with feeling unloved and underappreciated by his father, which leads to his life's biggest regret.

- **A WRONG WAY TO ATTACK THE PROBLEM:** By trying to kick Hassan out of the house, Amir begins a sequence of wrong way solutions. Until he returns home and learns the truth about Hassan, his strategy is consistently avoidance and diversion.

- **AN ACCEPTANCE OF THE HARD TRUTH:** Amir accepts the hard truth about his real relationship with Hassan when he agrees to go find Hassan's son and bring him back to Pakistan, and then even more so when he decides to bring him home to America.

Cat's Eye View

For quick reference, here's a brief overview of this novel's beat sheet.

1. **OPENING IMAGE:** Amir gets a call from Rahim, which Amir calls his "past of unatoned sins" (page 1). It's a cryptic reference to the Catalyst to come.

2. **SETUP:** Amir and Hassan are best friends but have a complicated relationship due to Hassan's position as a servant's son. They enjoy fighting kites together. Hassan is Amir's "kite runner." Amir also has a complicated relationship with his father, who seems to favor Hassan. A bully named Assef constantly picks on Hassan.

3. **THEME STATED:** Amir overhears his father say, "A boy who won't stand up for himself becomes a man who can't stand up to anything." Amir must learn how to stand up for himself (and others) and atone for his past sins.

4. **CATALYST:** Amir witnesses Hassan being raped by Assef but does nothing to stop it.

5. **DEBATE:** What will Amir do about the rape? His guilt eats him alive, yet he does not report it.

6. **BREAK INTO 2:** Amir approaches the problem the wrong way by framing Hassan for theft, causing Hassan and his father to move away.

7. **B STORY:** After moving to America, Amir meets Soraya, his future wife, who will help him learn his theme of courage and atonement.

8. **FUN AND GAMES:** Amir and his father move to America. His father gets a job as a gas station attendant; Amir attends college to study creative writing. Amir tries unsuccessfully to forget Hassan and his past.

9. **MIDPOINT:** Amir's father dies of cancer (false defeat).

10. **BAD GUYS CLOSE IN:** Amir writes and finishes his first novel, gets an agent, and sells his first book. Ten years later, he gets a call from Rahim (the call from the Opening Image), asking him to come to Pakistan. Rahim tells Amir what happened to Hassan after Amir left Afghanistan.

11. **ALL IS LOST:** Rahim reveals that Hassan was actually Amir's half brother and died, leaving behind a son, Sohrab, whom Amir must rescue from a Kabul orphanage.

12. **DARK NIGHT OF THE SOUL:** Amir struggles with the decision to go.

13. **BREAK INTO 3:** Amir decides to travel to Kabul to get Sohrab (his nephew), proving he's learned the theme.

14. **FINALE:** In Kabul, Amir rescues Sohrab, faces off with Assef (now a Taliban officer), and brings Sohrab back to America.

15. **FINAL IMAGE:** Amir teaches Sohrab how to fight kites and becomes the kite runner to the son of his former kite runner.

Institutionalized
Join 'Em, Leave 'Em, or Take 'Em Down!

It's your first day of middle school. You enter the cafeteria, gripping your tray like it's a life raft, searching for a place to sit. A place to *belong.* You see two options: an empty seat at the "cool" kids' table, or an entire table all to yourself. You know this is a choice that might define you for the rest of the year, maybe even the rest of your *life.* What do you do? Do you join the group, or do you forge a path alone?

Does this terrifying scenario sound familiar to anyone?

Just me?

Okay, moving on.

This question—to join or not to join—is at the heart of every Institutionalized story. These are the novels that spotlight groups of people and the ultimate choice whether to be a card-carrying member of the group or go it alone.

And the answer isn't always easy.

Institutions (or groups) come in every different size and shape. They can be as small as a family like the one in *Little Women* by Louisa May Alcott, or as large as a whole town or city, like the town of Maycomb, Alabama, in *To Kill a Mockingbird* by Harper Lee, or the city of Jackson, Mississippi, in the early 1960s in *The Help* by Kathryn

Stockett. They can even be subsections of society, like the world of the "greasers" and "socs" in *The Outsiders* by S. E. Hinton, the world of rich 1920s Long Islanders in *The Great Gatsby* by F. Scott Fitzgerald, or the world of the patriarchy in 1930s Georgia in *The Color Purple* by Alice Walker. Institutions can also be fictional, made-up establishments, like the theocratic society depicted in *The Handmaid's Tale* by Margaret Atwood, the deceivingly idyllic community in *The Giver* by Lois Lowry, or the dystopian world under the rule of the Party in *1984* by George Orwell. Finally, Institutionalized stories can even center around a unifying issue, event, or thematic element, like modern motherhood, as spotlighted by the three main characters of *Big Little Lies* by Liane Moriarty; life under the rule of Henry VIII, as spotlighted by the three main characters in *The Boleyn Inheritance* by Philippa Gregory; or the American Dream, as spotlighted by the eight featured characters in *The Joy Luck Club* by Amy Tan.

The number one indicator of an Institutionalized novel is that the story is about the *many*. Not necessarily the *one*. Even in the case of single narrators, as in *The Great Gatsby*, *The Outsiders*, or *The Handmaid's Tale*, these stories are more about the larger group the hero inhabits, and the hero's relationship with that group, than they are about the hero's solo journey.

In *The Great Gatsby*, we see the story through the eyes of a newcomer (Nick Carroway), but his life is far less interesting than the lives of the people he gets involved with, namely, Jay Gatsby and Daisy and Tom Buchanan. In *The Outsiders*, Ponyboy is our eyes into this fraught world between the "greasers" and the "socs" (and he's the character that changes the most), but there's a reason the title of the novel is plural.

No matter which institution you choose to highlight, the essential ingredients of a successful Institutionalized story are (1) a **group**, (2) a **choice**, and (3) a **sacrifice**.

Let's look at what we're dealing with.

The *groups* featured in Institutionalized stories are those we're either born into, brought into (often against our will!), or asked to join. Regardless of size, when done right these institutions can feel like the whole world to the characters inside them . . . and outside them. And the stories that fit into this wide-ranging genre usually present a centralized deliberation for the hero (or heroes) about the pros and cons of being "one of the gang." While at the same time, the author of an Institutionalized novel must explore the gang itself. What is this world about? Who are its members? What are its rules? And how easy is it to lose yourself inside this group?

We readers can relate easily to stories about groups. Human beings have been part of groups from the beginning. We're born into families, we join cliques at school, we get jobs at companies, we become members of communities. We're weighing the pros and cons of groups every day of our lives. Institutionalized stories are primal because biologically we're programmed to flock together. As primitive humans, we *died* if we tried to venture out to face the woolly mammoth alone. But as we evolved as a species, we began to wonder whether venturing out alone and forging our own path *is* the better option.

Which is why, when we read Institutionalized stories, we start asking ourselves questions that lie at the very heart of being human:

Can we really trust *others* to have our best interests at heart? Or does there come a point when we must rely on ourselves?

And which one is crazier? The group? Or me for leaving it?

Therein lies the origin of the name of this genre: Institutionalized. As we readers dive further into the world that you, the author, have set up for us, we should be seeing a little bit of the crazy that lies within *all* groups and families. Because the group dynamic *is* often crazy and sometimes even self-destructive. Herd mentality can defy all logic and reason. Being loyal to a group often contradicts common sense—sometimes even survival—but we still do it. And when we join the many we often lose a piece of ourselves.

So you, the author of an Institutionalized story, have a fairly tricky task on your hands: honoring the institution you've introduced to us, while at the same time exposing the problems of losing one's identity to it. As you peel back the layers of your "establishment" and reveal to us what makes it tick, we readers should be asking ourselves, *What would I do in the hero's shoes? Would I join or not? Would I stay or go?*

That is the **choice** at the heart of every Institutionalized story, and our second ingredient for succeeding in this genre.

To better understand this choice (and ingredient), let's take a look at three common character types that tend to appear in Institutionalized stories.

The primary hero of the story (or one of them, in the case of multiple heroes) is often a newcomer to the institution, endearingly dubbed the **naif**. When this is the case, the naif is usually introduced to the institution by someone more experienced. Someone to show them the ropes and introduce them to this new and unfamiliar world tucked within the great big world. In *Big Little Lies* by Liane Moriarty, for example, one of the heroes, Jane, is a naif who gets taken under the wing of Madeline as she steps into the institution of elementary school moms in a posh area of Sydney, Australia.

In *The Help* by Kathryn Stockett, Skeeter is our naif. Because even though she's lived in Jackson, Mississippi, her whole life, it's not until she teams up with Aibileen and Minny to tell the stories of "the help" that she truly realizes what kind of institution she's been living in.

Naifs are often used as the readers' "eyes" into the world. As they learn the rules, so do we. And it can be especially helpful to have a character like this to ease the reader into the world without the use of too much exposition, aka "info dumping."

But not all Institutionalized stories feature a naif character. Some novels are told through the point of view of another type of character called the **brando**. Named after the notoriously rebellious actor, Marlon Brando, these types of characters are existing members of the featured establishment. They're already entrenched in the system, but they're starting to doubt it. Or perhaps they've doubted it for years, but what can they do? They're stuck! This is *their* world, and the idea of leaving it seems crazy at first. These are characters like Winston in *1984*, Aibileen in *The Help*, Jonas in *The Giver*, Ponyboy in *The Outsiders*, Will in *Long Way Down* by Jason Reynolds, Montag in *Fahrenheit 451* by Ray Bradbury, and Celie in *The Color Purple*.

When the novel begins, there's already something different about these characters. They don't exactly fit in. They stand opposed to the system by their very nature. But it isn't until we get into the heart of the story that we see them actually acting on their doubts.

Naifs and brandos both have the important role of revealing the flaws of the institution you've chosen to write about, by being either an outsider (naif) or a rebellious insider (brando). But both ultimately accomplish this task by going up against the third character common in Institutionalized stories: the **company man**.

This character *embodies* the system or institution. They buy into it. They are rah-rah cheerleaders for it. They're not just a part of it; they will usually defend it to the death. As authors of Institutionalized tales, we rely on these characters to reveal the "crazy" of this world. This is what happens to you when you buy into this institution wholeheartedly and without any reservations. Memorable company man characters include O'Brien in *1984,* Aunt Lydia (or all the aunts, really) in *The Handmaid's Tale*, and Hilly Holbrook in *The Help.*

Because of their unwavering loyalty to the establishment, these kinds of characters tend to come off as insane or sometimes even strangely robotic. They've traded a little piece of their soul for the safety they craved within the system. They kind of *have* to feel a little off; otherwise, how else would they be able to cling so tightly to an institution that you, the author, are trying to poke holes in?

The company man represents one side of that fateful choice that all Institutionalized heroes must make: stick with the group or get the heck out of Dodge.

And that choice often gets more difficult as the novel progresses. Loyalty and resolve are tested as the brando or naif (or both!) gets more entrenched in the drama of the institution and its seemingly crazy rules.

But ultimately, all Institutionalized stories end with the third genre ingredient: a *sacrifice.*

Heroes either join the system (*1984),* "burn it down" (*The Help, The Outsiders, The Giver*), or escape from it *(The Handmaid's Tale, The Great Gatsby, The Color Purple).* The escape can also be a suicide (both literal or figurative).

Regardless of the ending, the hero's sacrifice serves as a cautionary tale about the dangers of entering into an institution. In the end, the deeper message is about listening to your inner voice. Yes, we all need to be part of some type of group to survive, but it's our individual human spirit—the thing that makes us who we are—that we ultimately must nurture and protect.

Beware the group!

Be yourself!

To recap: If you're thinking of writing an Institutionalized novel, make sure your story includes these three essential ingredients:

- **A GROUP:** a family, organization, business, community or uniting issue that is unique and interesting

- **A CHOICE:** an ongoing conflict between the naif and/or brando and the company man, usually revolving around the question to join or not to join (for a naif) or to stay or not to stay (for a brando)

- **A SACRIFICE LEADING TO ONE OF THREE POSSIBLE ENDINGS:** join, burn it down, or escape (including suicide)

POPULAR INSTITUTIONALIZED NOVELS THROUGH TIME:

The Scarlet Letter by Nathanial Hawthorne

Les Misérables by Victor Hugo

Little Women by Louisa May Alcott

The Great Gatsby by F. Scott Fitzgerald

Brave New World by Aldous Huxley

1984 by George Orwell

Fahrenheit 451 by Ray Bradbury

To Kill a Mockingbird by Harper Lee

The Outsiders by S. E. Hinton

The Handmaid's Tale by Margaret Atwood

The Color Purple by Alice Walker

The Joy Luck Club by Amy Tan

The Giver by Lois Lowry

Montana Sky by Nora Roberts

The Sisterhood of the Traveling Pants by Ann Brashares

My Sister's Keeper by Jodi Picoult

The Boleyn Inheritance by Philippa Gregory

The Help by Kathryn Stockett (*beat sheet included below*)

Big Little Lies by Liane Moriarty

Red Rising by Pierce Brown

Far from the Tree by Robin Benway

Long Way Down by Jason Reynolds

THE HELP

BY: Kathryn Stockett
STC GENRE: Institutionalized
BOOK GENRE: Historical fiction
TOTAL PAGES: 522 (Berkeley Paperback Edition, 2009)

This poignant historical fiction novel by Kathryn Stockett is a shining example of how an author can successfully balance multiple heroes in one story. *The Help* centers around three protagonists—Aibileen, Minny, and Skeeter—and, as you'll see from the beat sheet in the following pages, each character has her own set of beats (some overlapping and some unique to the character). If you're looking to write a novel with multiple perspectives, multiple main characters, or both, this is a great one to study. But, just as Kathryn Stockett has done, it's still important to decide up front who is *the* hero of the story. Who has the biggest transformative journey ahead of them? In *The Help*, while Minny and Skeeter play important roles and each experience their own emotional arcs, it is arguably Aibileen who changes the most, thereby making her the primary hero of this harrowing and heartwarming tale about three women who take on the segregated and racist institution of the "help" in Jackson, Mississippi, in the 1960s.

1. Opening Image/Aibileen (pages 1–2)

In the first chapter we're introduced to the first of our three heroes (and one of our brando characters), Aibileen, a black maid working for a white family in Jackson in 1962. We're given a glimpse of Aibileen's life and the institution of domestic "help" in 1960s Mississippi under the racial segregation laws of Jim Crow. Aibileen has raised seventeen white kids in her lifetime. Her current employer, Miss Elizabeth Leefolt, seems to want nothing to do with her own child, Mae Mobley, who Aibileen says is her "special baby."

2. Theme Stated/Aibileen (page 12)

While Skeeter (another of our three heroes and our naif character) is at Miss Leefolt's house for bridge club, she secretly asks Aibileen, "Do you ever wish you could . . . change things?" (page 12).

This is the primary theme of the novel: finding the courage to change an institution that is corrupt and unjust. And Aibileen is the furthest from learning that theme of any of the three heroes. Which is why, in her head, she responds, *"That's one of the stupidest questions I ever heard."* And then to Skeeter she says, "Oh no, ma'am, everything's fine" (page 12).

As we'll soon see, however, everything is not fine. But Aibileen is not prepared to do anything about it . . . yet.

3. Setup/Aibileen (pages 2–35)

We learn that Aibileen's son, Treelore, died on a lumber mill job site, getting crushed by a tractor—and she observes that "it weren't long before I seen something in me had changed. A bitter seed was planted inside a me. And I just didn't feel so accepting anymore" (page 35). This bitterness is a **stasis = death** moment for Aibileen. Something must change. *She* must change; otherwise, the bitterness might eat her alive.

As the ladies play bridge, we meet the novel's company man—Miss Hilly Holbrook, who won't use the bathroom in Miss Leefolt's house because it's the same bathroom that the help uses. Hilly mentions the bill she's working on: a "Home Help Sanitation Initiative," which requires every white home to have a separate bathroom for the help.

That evening, Aibileen goes home and talks to her best friend, Minny (our third hero and the other brando character). She warns her that Hilly has accused her of stealing (something she overheard at the bridge club meeting). We soon learn that Hilly fired Minny for reasons not revealed to the reader.

4. Catalyst/Minny (page 17)

When Aibileen warns Minny that Hilly might accuse her of stealing, this becomes Minny's Catalyst, even though it's still being told from Aibileen's point of view.

5. Debate/Minny (pages 17–35)

Can she get another job? That is the Debate question for Minny.

Minny starts asking around for more work, but no one will hire her, revealing another aspect of this institution: Once the company man accuses you of stealing, no one will trust you.

As Minny starts to worry that she may never find another job again, Celia Foote, a new woman in town, calls Miss Leefolt asking for a reference for a new maid. Aibileen answers the phone and gives her Minny's name and number, lying to Celia about the recommendation coming from Miss Leefolt.

6. Break Into 2/Minny (pages 36–45)

We switch to Minny's point of view just as she shows up for her job interview at Celia Foote's house. She really needs this job. Minny knows the real reason Hilly is spreading rumors about her is because of a "terrible awful" thing she did to Hilly, which Minny won't reveal to us yet.

Immediately, we realize that Celia Foote is the polar opposite of Hilly Holbrook and different from the other white women in the institution. For starters, she's *nice* to Minny, which Minny can't believe is genuine. She thinks Celia is playing with her. But she gets the job—at twice the pay of her last job. The only catch? Celia asks Minny to keep this a secret from her husband, Johnny, who thinks Celia can take care of the house herself. Minny agrees, but makes Celia promise to tell Johnny by Christmas.

7. B Story/Minny (pages 37–47)

The B Story character for Minny is Celia Foote, her new employer. Minny has been hardened by her work as a maid, and she's distanced herself from her employers. She doesn't trust them. Celia Foote is different, though. She will teach Minny that not all employers are the same, and eventually Minny will even grow to care about Celia Foote.

On page 45, Minny flashes back to the day she turned fourteen and was first put to work as a maid. Her mother told her the hard-and-fast rules for working in a "White Lady's house" (institution)—one being "White people are not your friends" (page 46). This is the paradigm Minny has believed all of her life. This is also a Theme Stated for Minny. She lives rigidly by the rules of this institution. She buys into the hard lines between black and white. But Celia Foote is different. She quickly proves to be color blind. She will show Minny that the lines exist only in her head.

8. Fun and Games/Minny (pages 45–226)

Minny starts work and is immediately suspicious of Celia who lives in this giant house by herself with no kids, lounges around a lot, and is always sneaking off upstairs. She tries to teach Celia to cook (at Celia's request), but it's a lost cause. She tries to get Celia out of the house so she can clean it, but Celia says none of the girls in town will return her calls.

3. Setup/Skeeter (pages 62–83)

We leave Minny and switch to Skeeter's perspective for a while as Skeeter drives home to her family's cotton plantation in Longleaf. She thinks about what went down at the bridge club that day and how she, Hilly, and Elizabeth (Miss Leefolt) have been friends since elementary school but now they're growing apart. She and Hilly went to University together, but Hilly left to get married while Skeeter stayed. Skeeter is stuck inside her own institution—the institution of young Southern white women in the 1960s. Everyone expects them to get married. No one expects them to work. But Skeeter wants to be a writer.

"I think about how things are different between Hilly and me, since I came home from school. But who is the different person, her or me?" (page 64). This is the kind of question posed in almost all Institutionalized stories: *Who's crazier? Them for joining or me for wanting to leave?*

When she gets home, she's immediately hounded by her mother about trying harder to find a husband and get married, and she has a stasis = death moment when she narrates, "I shudder with the same left-behind feeling I've had since I graduated from college, three months ago. I've been dropped off in a place I do not belong anymore" (page 65).

As Skeeter looks for a job in anything writing-related, she thinks about her own black maid, Constantine, who raised her and who Skeeter feels closer to than her own mother. Constantine left the family under mysterious circumstances while Skeeter was away at college.

Skeeter wants to try to track her down, but no one will give her any details about her new address.

In these pages, we learn more about Skeeter's status quo life: she wants to be a writer, she applied for a job at a publishing company but hasn't heard back, her mother doesn't know about her true life aspirations.

2. Theme Stated/Skeeter (page 73)

In a flashback, Skeeter remembers Constantine saying, "Ever morning, until you dead in the ground, you gone have to make this decision. You gone have to ask yourself, *Am I gone believe* what them fools say about me today?" The *choice* for Skeeter (and her theme) is whether to blaze her own trail and disregard what others think.

4. Catalyst/Skeeter (page 83)

Skeeter receives a letter from Elaine Stein at Harper & Row publishers, turning down Skeeter's application for an editor job because she has no experience. Elaine advises Skeeter to get an entry-level job at her local newspaper. But the best piece of advice Elaine gives her is to "Write about what disturbs you, particularly if it bothers no one else" (page 83). Elaine Stein is telling Skeeter to question the institution! Then Elaine adds a handwritten note offering to read Skeeter's *best* ideas and give feedback.

5. Debate/Skeeter (pages 84–142)

What will she do with this offer? That is Skeeter's Debate question. Skeeter immediately mails a letter to Elaine with some ideas and quickly realizes that they are ideas she *thinks* Elaine will find impressive, not ideas that really interest her. She then takes Elaine's advice and goes for an interview at the *Jackson Journal*, where she is offered a job writing the Miss Myrna column about house cleaning, which Skeeter knows nothing about.

Skeeter convinces Elizabeth Leefolt to let her interview Aibileen about cleaning advice. During their first interview, Skeeter asks Aibileen about Constantine, and Aibileen reveals that Constantine was fired but won't say more than that. Back home, Skeeter's mom admits that she *did* fire Constantine but won't say why.

Aibileen and Skeeter bond a little when Skeeter tells Aibileen about Ms. Stein's letter and Aibileen tells Skeeter about her son, who had wanted to be a writer before he died.

As predicted, Skeeter gets a response from Elaine Stein, saying her ideas are "flat" and asks her not to write again until she finds something more "original."

All of this talk about Constantine getting fired, separate bathrooms, and Aibileen's son who died inspires Skeeter with an idea. She knows it's a *dangerous* idea that crosses the line, but the idea won't leave her alone.

4. Catalyst/Aibileen (pages 105–119)

A series of mini Catalysts go off like little bombs in Aibileen's status quo world. First, Aibileen uses her newly built bathroom in the garage as a model for Mae Mobley, who's being potty trained. Mae Mobley won't go in the toilet in the house, but after seeing Aibileen using her bathroom, she goes in Aibileen's toilet. Miss Leefolt comes home and spanks Mae Mobley for using the help's bathroom, saying it's dirty in there and she'll catch diseases.

Then comes the three-year anniversary of Aibileen's son's death, followed by Robert Brown (the son of one of Aibileen's friends) getting beaten with a tire iron for using a white bathroom.

But the big Catalyst—the one that will finally push Aibileen to *do* something to change the status quo—comes when Skeeter shows up at Aibileen's house and asks to interview Aibileen for a book she wants to write about what it's like to work as a maid in Jackson, Mississippi.

She has an idea to interview other maids as well and write from a brand-new perspective. She swears they'll keep it a secret so no one gets in trouble.

5. Debate/Aibileen (pages 119–142)

Will Aibileen agree to participate in the book? A third Debate question is posed. Aibileen immediately shoots the idea down, saying it sounds too dangerous.

But previous events are playing in her subconscious. Aibileen knows the institution is wrong, but will *she* be brave enough to fix it?

5. Debate (cont'd)/Skeeter (pages 84–142)

Skeeter is in a tough place. Aibileen has turned her down for the interview, but she already wrote to Elaine Stein in New York, pitching the idea and lying that she had a maid interested in participating. Elaine Stein liked the idea and said she would read it, but now Skeeter has no one to interview.

At bridge club, Skeeter watches Hilly force Aibileen to thank her for her new bathroom. Skeeter is sickened by it and thinks, "*It's no wonder she doesn't want to talk to me*" (page 129). She's starting to get it, seeing the institution with new eyes.

Meanwhile, Hilly convinces Skeeter to go on a blind date with Stuart, a friend of Hilly's husband. The date goes horribly. Stuart is drunk and rude, insulting Skeeter every chance he gets. Skeeter's own institution (women and marriage) is looking pretty shoddy right now, too.

6. Break Into 2/Aibileen and Skeeter (pages 142–143)

Aibileen calls Skeeter and agrees to do the interview. She may even know a few other maids who might be willing to do it too. They agree to meet at Aibileen's house because it's safest. When Skeeter asks what changed Aibileen's mind, she replies simply, "Miss Hilly" (page 143).

8. Fun and Games (cont'd)/Minny (pages 45–226)

Minny is tired of being scared that Celia's husband is going to come home and kill her when he finds out Celia secretly hired a maid. She keeps trying to convince Celia to tell Johnny, reminding her of their agreed-upon deadline (December 25).

Minny finds out Aibileen agreed to tell her stories to Skeeter and thinks she's crazy. Minny vows she will never do it.

One day Minny shows up for work, and Celia is very upset and holed up in her bedroom. She sends Minny away without an explanation. Another day, while Minny is cleaning the bathroom, Johnny comes home, holding an axe. Minny is certain he's going to kill her. But actually he's very nice and tells Minny he knew Celia had hired help (Minny's awesome cooking gave her away). He says he's worried about Celia and just wants her to be happy. He tells Minny to let Celia keep pretending she hasn't hired help.

8. Fun and Games/Aibileen and Skeeter (pages 167–289)

Aibileen and Skeeter do the first interview. Aibileen tries to tell Skeeter about herself, but she's too nervous and constrained. It doesn't go well. She's so scared about what she's doing that she vomits.

Skeeter shows her qualities as a naif on the way home, feeling stupid for thinking she could just waltz in there and demand answers. This is clearly more dangerous and serious than she thought. The institution is becoming clearer to her.

Days later, they try again, and Aibileen says she wants to write the stories and read them to Skeeter. She thinks that will be easier. Skeeter isn't too thrilled about this, thinking she'll have to rewrite them all, but after hearing Aibileen read her first story, Skeeter realizes that Aibileen has serious talent and "this might actually work" (page 176).

For the next two weeks, Aibileen and Skeeter work on Aibileen's story, while pretending to be strangers at Miss Leefolt's home. As the interviews continue, Skeeter's eyes are opened to the institution and the world she's lived in but never really seen before. On page 183, she remarks, "Hilly raises her voice about three octaves higher when she talks to colored people. Elizabeth smiles like she's talking to a child, although certainly not her own. I am starting to notice things." This is definitely an upside-down world for Skeeter.

After they finish Aibileen's story, Skeeter sends it off to Elaine Stein. Elaine likes the story and wants her to do twelve more—by January. It seems impossible. She begs Aibileen to find more maids for them to talk to.

Minny finally agrees to join in and tell her story. The three women settle into a routine. Minny tells her story to Aibileen, and Skeeter tries to write it all down.

Meanwhile, Stuart comes by Skeeter's house, apologizes for his horrible behavior, and asks her out again. She agrees. The two have a much better date than the first and form a relationship.

At the library, Skeeter finds a copy of the Jim Crow laws of the South. She's surprised to see all of these "separation" laws in print. Her eyes are opened up even more about the institution that she's been practically blind to. She steals the pamphlet and puts it in her satchel, but then accidentally leaves her satchel at Hilly's house during a Junior League meeting. Skeeter freaks out, because the interviews with Aibileen and Minny are in there and Hilly loves to snoop. When she goes to get the bag, Hilly is pissed. Skeeter has no idea if Hilly saw the stories, but Aibileen says she doesn't want to stop working on the book, regardless. Thankfully, it's soon revealed that all Hilly saw in the satchel were the Jim Crow laws, so she thinks Skeeter is against segregation.

7. B Story/Aibileen and Skeeter (page 167)

Aibileen and Skeeter are each other's B Story characters. Through her stories, Aibileen teaches Skeeter what it's really like to be a maid and what the institution looks like from the inside, while Skeeter helps Aibileen find her voice and pushes her to tell her story, something she would never have done without Skeeter's book idea.

The more they work on the book together, the more they bond. Aibileen starts opening up more and more to Skeeter.

8. Fun and Games (cont'd)/Minny (pages 45–226)

Minny continues to clean Celia's home. Celia is still acting strangely, lying in bed all day. Celia keeps trying to get a hold of Hilly so she can hang out with her, but Hilly keeps snubbing her. Minny is relieved. If they ever connect, Hilly will tell Celia to fire Minny for what Minny did to her (the "terrible awful" thing that Minny still hasn't revealed).

Back at home, Minny's husband, Leroy, threatens Minny and the kids not to get involved with the civil rights movement, as it's too dangerous.

Minny realizes she's starting to care about Celia when she finds hidden alcohol and thinks Celia has been drinking. She gets mad (Minny's father and husband are both alcoholics). Minny and Celia argue, and Celia fires Minny.

Thanks to Aibileen, Minny also starts to realize how good she has it at Celia's house and goes to beg for her job back. When she gets there, she finds Celia in the bathroom, surrounded by blood. She's miscarried her baby (she was five months pregnant). This is the fourth baby she's lost. The "alcohol" that Minny thought she saw was actually a tonic intended to help Celia get and stay pregnant.

9. Midpoint/All (pages 290–298)

Skeeter finds out that Yule May, Hilly's maid, is interested in sharing her story. But then, soon after, she receives a letter from Yule May explaining why she *can't* share her story. She's in prison because of Hilly Holbrook. Yule May and her husband had only enough money to send one of their twin sons to college, so she stole a ring from Hilly (one that Skeeter claims Hilly didn't even like) to try to make up the difference. Hilly found out and had her arrested.

When Skeeter gets to Aibileen's house that night, there are maids lined up to tell their stories, all angry about what Hilly did to Yule May. Skeeter and Aibileen definitely have enough for their book.

On page 297, Skeeter says, "My relief is bitter, that it took Yule May's internment to bring us to this."

After everyone has signed up and left, Skeeter notes Minny standing in the corner. "But I see it, the flicker on her mouth, a hint of a softness beneath the anger. Minny has made this happen" (page 298).

All three characters' beat sheets merge at the Midpoint as their *goals* (to make this book happen) become aligned. They will now have enough stories to submit the book to Elaine Stein in New York.

It's definitely a false victory, however, because even though the women achieved their goal of getting the maids to tell their stories, the way in which the victory was achieved creates a **stakes-are-raised** moment, when they realize how dangerous Hilly Holbrook and her kind can be if they were ever to be caught.

10. Bad Guys Close In/All (pages 298–420)

Skeeter goes to Aibileen's house every night to collect the stories. She offers to pay each maid $40, and they all donate their shares to Yule May's sons' college fund.

Despite this, the Bad Guys Close In proves to be a **downward path** for all the women.

Stuart breaks up with Skeeter because he's still in love with his ex. Skeeter's mom has been sick lately, and her mysterious condition is getting worse. Hilly demands that Skeeter put her Home Health Sanitation initiative in the Junior League newsletter, which Skeeter edits. Skeeter refuses. Hilly threatens to get Skeeter kicked out of the league. Hilly also demands that Skeeter give back the Jim Crow laws that she stole from the library because people can't think Skeeter is an integrationist, otherwise no one will support the Junior League's cause: "the poor starving people of Africa" (page 331).

It's a highly ironic moment that eludes Hilly completely.

Skeeter narrates, "I wait for her to catch the irony of this, that she'll send money to colored people overseas, but not across town" (page 331). This is typical company man behavior. Hilly is so entrenched in the system, so brainwashed by its rules, any illogicality escapes her.

Skeeter gives in to Hilly and types up the initiative for the news-letter, wondering what Constantine, her former maid, would think of her, giving in to the pressures of others (theme). But she "accidentally" mixes up verbiage from the initiative and the league's coat drive, and the newspaper is printed with the words, "Drop off your old toilets at Hilly's address" (page 340). A few days later, Hilly's lawn is *full* of used toilets. The story gets written up in the *Jackson Journal* and the *New York Times*.

Hilly disowns Skeeter as a friend and tells all their mutual friends not to talk to her. Aibileen is really worried about what else Hilly (external bad guys) will do to get her revenge on Skeeter and how dangerous Hilly can be. And the anxiety is heightened when Hilly finds out that Minny (whom she fired) has been working for Celia Foote at the (fake) recommendation of Elizabeth Leefolt. Minny (and Aibileen) will both be in huge trouble if Hilly finds out Aibileen lied about the recommendation. When Hilly calls Celia's house, Minny answers and lies, telling Hilly that Minny quit and Celia is out of town.

11. All Is Lost/Minny (pages 344–365)

As each of the three women have to learn their own theme, the beat sheets diverge again. Minny hits rock bottom when Leroy beats her badly, this time while he's "cold-stone sober" (page 359).

Celia notices the cut above Minny's eye and questions her about it, not believing Minny's story about banging her head in the bathtub. She tries to get Minny to talk, treating her like a friend (Minny's theme), but their conversation is interrupted when a sex pervert intruder appears in Celia's backyard and the two women have to fight him off together.

As Minny washes her hands afterward, she wonders "how an awful day could turn even worse. It seems like at some point you'd just run out of awful" (page 365).

12. Dark Night of the Soul/Minny (pages 365–400)

Later that night, Minny speaks to Aibileen about what happened that day. As Minny talks about Celia, Aibileen points out to Minny that it "almost sounds like you care" (page 367). But Minny insists she's just upset because Celia doesn't see the lines between people. Aibileen repeats Minny's theme, assuring her that the lines don't exist. The institution has convinced Minny to believe in something that's not there.

On page 368, Aibileen says to Minny, "All I'm saying is, kindness don't have no boundaries."

Minny explains to Celia why Hilly doesn't like Celia (because Hilly used to date Johnny), and Celia decides she's going to try to talk to Hilly about it at the upcoming Junior League Benefit. Minny thinks that's a bad idea.

The annual benefit takes place, and everyone is there. Aibileen and Minny are serving and Skeeter is a guest, although she's still shunned by all of her friends, at Hilly's behest.

The auction winners for the baked goods are announced, and Hilly wins Minny's famous chocolate pie. For some reason, this angers Hilly, and she accuses a drunk Celia of signing her up for the pie. Celia is confused by the attack. She tries to explain that Johnny didn't cheat on Hilly with her, but in her drunken state, she accidentally tears Hilly's dress, then vomits on the carpet.

13. Break Into 3/Minny (pages 395–402)

Celia is upset about what happened at the benefit and doesn't understand why Hilly is mad at her. Minny proves she's learned her theme and, in a gesture of true friendship, tells Celia everything that happened between Hilly and her. She explains that after Hilly accused Minny of being a thief, Minny told her to "eat my sh*t" (page 398). Then she baked her a chocolate pie as a "peace offering," and only after Hilly had eaten two slices did she tell Hilly that she'd baked her own feces into the pie.

Celia thanks Minny for telling her the story, and the next day, she's feeling better and working in the garden. Celia writes a check to the Junior League, and in the memo line, she's written, "For Two-Slice Hilly" (page 402). Their friendship is sealed.

10. Bad Guys Close In (cont'd)/Skeeter (pages 298–420)

Elaine pushes up the deadline on the manuscript and tells Skeeter that she needs to have a section in the book about Skeeter's own maid, Constantine, which means Skeeter really has to find out what happened to her.

Meanwhile, Skeeter continues to feel the effects of Hilly's snub when she gets voted out as the editor of the Junior League newsletter.

Skeeter tries to convince herself she doesn't care and instead throws herself into working on the book.

When the book is nearly finished, the three women decide to title it *Help*.

11. All Is Lost/Skeeter (pages 420–430)

Thanks to Aibileen, Skeeter finds out the truth about Constantine: her mother fired her after her daughter talked back and spit in her face. Constantine and her daughter left, and Constantine died three weeks later (**whiff of death**).

12. Dark Night of the Soul/Skeeter (pages 430–447)

The book is now finished, but Aibileen, Skeeter, and Minny are worried about people figuring out the city in the stories is Jackson, even though they changed all the names and called the city Niceville. Minny decides they need to include the story about the chocolate pie, as insurance. Hilly will automatically know the book is about Jackson, but she'll work to keep it quiet so her secret is safe. It's a huge risk, but they have to take it.

Skeeter sends the manuscript to Elaine Stein, and they all wait.

Later, after Skeeter learns that her mother has stomach cancer (another whiff of death), she gets back together with Stuart (**return to the familiar**).

13. Break Into 3/Skeeter (pages 447–452)

Stuart proposes, and Skeeter knows she has to tell him the truth. She proves that she's learned her theme (about not caring what people think of her and blazing her own trail) when she tells Stuart about the book she's been working on—making sure to leave out any names.

Stuart is appalled: "Things are fine around here. Why would you want to go stirring up trouble?" (page 449). But Skeeter stands her ground, insisting that things are not fine. Stuart withdraws his proposal, takes the ring, and leaves.

13. Break Into 3/All (pages 452–455)

Elaine Stein calls and says she wants to publish the book. All three heroes join in this moment of celebration and this step into the synthesis world of Act 3. They are no longer separated by the invisible lines of the institution; they are in this together. And this book being published represents the "sacrifice" that all of them make in an effort to "burn down" the institution.

14. Finale/All (pages 456–516)

Months later, they're all wondering what's going to happen when the book is released and the people of Jackson start to read it. Aibileen narrates, "Feels like we been waiting for some invisible pot a water to boil for the past seven months" (page 459).

After the book is published, Aibileen and Minny go to church, and everyone applauds them. The reverend hands Aibileen a copy of the book, signed by every member of the church. "We know you couldn't put your name on it, so we all signed our own for you" (page 467). The reverend also has a wrapped book for "the white lady. You tell her we love her, like she's our family" (page 468).

The book gets featured on TV, and people start to wonder if it's about Jackson. Hilly now has a copy, and the three women wait for her to read the final chapter (about the chocolate pie).

Back at work, Johnny thanks Minny for everything she did for Celia. "You'll always have a job here with us, Minny. For the rest of your life if you want."

As Hilly reads the book, she starts to think that it's about Jackson and vows to figure out which maids wrote it. She tells everyone to fire their maids, but soon changes her tune and starts insisting that the book is *not* about Jackson. (This is when we know that she's read the pie chapter.) She confronts Skeeter, knowing she was the one who contributed to the book, and threatens revenge on all the maids involved. "They better watch out for what's coming to them" (page 497).

Skeeter gets offered a job at *Harper's* magazine in New York, but refuses to take it because she doesn't want to leave Minny and Aibileen to deal with the aftermath. But Aibileen and Minny insist she must go and live her life.

Five thousand more copies of the book are printed, and Aibileen gets the Miss Myrna column job, solidifying her new job as a professional writer.

Minny leaves Leroy for good, after he threatens to burn down the house with her in it.

15. Final Image/Aibileen (pages 516–522)

Aibileen proves she's learned her own theme when Hilly accuses her of stealing and threatens to send her to jail. Aibileen finally stands up for herself, which she never would have done at the beginning. "I know something about you and don't you forget that . . . And from what I hear, they's a lot of time to write a lot of letters in jail" (page 519).

She's fired from her job anyway, but we know she'll be all right, because she now has the Miss Myrna job and the book revenue. As she walks to the bus stop, she realizes that she can start over, even though she thought she was "finished with everything new" (page 522). Apparently, people can change.

WHY IS THIS AN INSTITUTIONALIZED?

The Help contains all three elements of a successful Institutionalized story:

- **A GROUP:** This story is about the institution of black maids working in white families in Jackson, Mississippi, in the early 1960s.

- **A CHOICE:** All three women face choices when it comes to the institution and what to do about its injustices. And all three women are pitted against the company man— Hilly Holbrook—in various ways.

- **A SACRIFICE LEADING TO ONE OF THREE POSSIBLE ENDINGS:** join, burn it down, or escape. As a whole, the three women "burn down" the institution in the way they expose the injustices with the book. Skeeter also chooses to leave in the end.

Cat's Eye View

For quick reference, here's a brief overview of this novel's beat sheet.

1. **OPENING IMAGE/AIBILEEN:** Our first glimpse of the institution of the "help" in 1960s Jackson, through the eyes of a black maid who has raised seventeen white children in her lifetime, including her current charge, Mae Mobley. Aibileen is the first of two brando characters.

2. **THEME STATED/AIBILEEN:** "Do you ever wish you could . . . change things?" (page 12) Skeeter asks Aibileen, who immediately replies, "Oh no, ma'am, everything's fine" (page 12). The theme of the novel for all three heroes is courage. For Aibileen, it's about finding the courage to do what's right.

3. **SETUP/AIBILEEN:** Aibileen overhears Hilly Holbrook (the *company man*) talk about the initiative she's working on that will require every white home to have a separate bathroom for the help.

4. **CATALYST/MINNY:** Aibileen warns Minny, Aibileen's best friend and a fellow maid, that she overheard Hilly accusing Minny of stealing from her (which is untrue). Minny is the second brando character.

5. **DEBATE/MINNY:** Will Minny be able to get another job with Hilly spreading rumors about her? She asks around, but it seems no one will hire her.

6. **BREAK INTO 2/MINNY:** Minny gets a new job, working for Celia Foote, a new woman in town who hasn't yet heard the rumors about Minny. Celia is the polar opposite of Hilly.

7. **B STORY/MINNY:** Celia Foote is Minny's B Story character. Minny has always bought into the hard lines between black and white (a result of the institution), but Celia, who seems to be color blind, will teach Minny that those lines can be blurred and that the paradigm Minny has operated

under all of her life—"white people are not your friends" (page 41)—is not always true.

8. **FUN AND GAMES/MINNY:** Minny starts work and tries to teach Celia to cook, but it's a lost cause. Celia lies around the house all day, which aggravates Minny. But she later learns why when she finds Celia has suffered another (secret) miscarriage.

3. **SETUP/SKEETER:** Skeeter, a white friend of Hilly Holbrook, is the naif of the story. Skeeter wants to be a writer but all her mother wants is for her to find a husband. Skeeter was raised by a black maid named Constantine whom she loved dearly but who recently disappeared.

2. **THEME STATED/SKEETER:** Constantine told her, "Ever morning, until you dead in the ground, you gone have to make this decision. You gone have to ask yourself, *Am I gone believe* what them fools say about me today?" (page 73). The choice for Skeeter (and her theme) is whether or not to blaze her own trail and disregard what others think.

4. **CATALYST/SKEETER:** Skeeter receives a response from a New York publishing house. Elaine Stein tells Skeeter to get more experience (if she wants a job as an editor) and to write about something that disturbs her.

5. **DEBATE/SKEETER:** Will Skeeter find something to write about that will impress Elaine Stein? She gets a job writing a housekeeping advice column for the local newspaper but has to interview Aibileen in order to answer the letters. But speaking to Aibileen gives her an idea . . .

4. **CATALYST/AIBILEEN:** Skeeter asks Aibileen if she can interview her for a book she wants to write about what it's like to work as a maid in Jackson (institution).

5. **DEBATE/AIBILEEN:** Will Aibileen do it? At first, no way. But the racial issues in Jackson are heating up, and Hilly

continued

Holbrook is more insufferable than ever, eventually pushing Aibileen to change her mind.

6. **BREAK INTO 2/AIBILEEN AND SKEETER:** Aibileen agrees to do the interview.

8. **FUN AND GAMES/AIBILEEN AND SKEETER:** At first, Aibileen is nervous and stiff in the interview. She finally decides she wants to write her story herself. The more time Skeeter spends with Aibileen, working on the story, the more her eyes are opened. Elaine Stein likes the story and wants twelve more stories from other maids—by January. Aibileen gets Minny to share next.

7. **B STORY/AIBILEEN AND SKEETER:** Aibileen and Skeeter are each other's B Story characters. Aibileen opens Skeeter's eyes about the other side of the institution, while Skeeter helps Aibileen find her voice.

9. **MIDPOINT/ALL:** One of the maids in the community gets arrested because of Hilly Holbrook. In a false victory moment, tons of maids volunteer to share their stories for the book, as a show of solidarity against Hilly. The goal of finding enough stories has been reached, but the stakes are raised as all three heroes realize what would happen if they are ever revealed as the authors.

10. **BAD GUYS CLOSE IN/ALL:** Skeeter, Aibileen, and Minny collect the maids' stories. Meanwhile, Skeeter's mom is getting sicker from a mysterious illness, and tensions heat up between Hilly and Skeeter, leading to a falling out. Also, Hilly finds out Minny has been working for Celia Foote and is not happy about it.

11. **ALL IS LOST/MINNY:** Minny's husband beats her badly. Celia sees the bruises and comforts her.

12. **DARK NIGHT OF THE SOUL/MINNY:** Aibileen points out to Minny that it seems like she really cares about Celia.

13. **BREAK INTO 3/MINNY:** Minny proves she's learned her theme and, in a gesture of true friendship, tells Celia all that happened between Hilly and her: after Hilly wrongfully accused Minny of stealing, Minny baked her a chocolate pie with her own feces in it, and Hilly unwittingly ate it.

11. **ALL IS LOST/SKEETER:** Aibileen finally tells Skeeter the truth about what happened to her maid Constantine: her mother fired her, and Constantine died shortly thereafter (whiff of death).

12. **DARK NIGHT OF THE SOUL/SKEETER:** Their book is now finished, and Skeeter sends it to Elaine Stein. Now they have to wait. In the meantime, Skeeter learns that her mother has stomach cancer (another whiff of death) and gets back together with her ex-boyfriend (return to the familiar).

13. **BREAK INTO 3/SKEETER:** When her boyfriend proposes, Skeeter proves she's learned her theme by telling him the truth about the book she wrote. Stuart is appalled that she would knowingly stir up trouble. He breaks up with her.

13. **BREAK INTO 3 /ALL:** Elaine Stein wants to publish the book. It's a cause for celebration and anxiety. Their stories and truths will be out there. The Institutionalized sacrifice for all three heroes is to burn it down.

14. **FINALE/ALL:** The book is published anonymously and becomes a success. Hilly (whose embarrassing story about the chocolate pie is in the book) spreads the word that the book is *not* about Jackson in order to save her own reputation. Skeeter gets a job offer in New York and gives her housekeeping column job to Aibileen.

15. **FINAL IMAGE/AIBILEEN:** As revenge for the book, Hilly accuses Aibileen of stealing and threatens to send her to jail. Aibileen finally stands up to Hilly, threatening to tell everyone that *she* is the woman in the book who ate the chocolate pie. Hilly backs down.

Superhero
Being Extraordinary in an Ordinary World

In every era of human history, in every culture, in every mythology, there can be found a story of a "chosen one." This is an individual who is, in some way, superior to the rest of us, whose job (and destiny) it is to rise up, overcome great obstacles, defeat the greatest evil, and maybe even save the world!

From Jesus to the Buddha to Hercules to Harry Potter, these are the heroes who are the least like the rest of us, but who still inspire us to become better versions of ourselves.

The stories that fall into the Save the Cat! genre called Superhero are about an extraordinary person who finds themselves in an ordinary world, among us mortals.

Now, before your mind starts to wander to men and women in capes and tights, let me just say that Superhero stories are not just about comic book superheroes (although those are certainly in there as well!). This genre embraces any hero who finds themselves destined for greatness—whether they like it or not.

But it's not easy being special, as all the great Superhero novels show us. Being different and bestowed with greatness often comes with a price. And that price is usually some variation of being misunderstood by the rest of the world. Because, let's face it, we don't always revere those who are different.

And *that* is what makes this genre relatable. Even if we ourselves haven't been endowed with magical powers, special abilities, an unrivaled mind, steadfast ambition, or even an unwavering faith in a certain mission or destiny, we've all experienced the curse of being different, feeling different, or being misunderstood.

The (super) heroes of this genre come in all shapes and sizes, and with all different kinds of "abilities." From the real-life superheroes of history, like Elizabeth of York in Philippa Gregory's massively successful historical fiction novel *The White Queen*, to the magically inclined superheroes of fantasy novels, like the Harry Potter series by J. K. Rowling and the Percy Jackson series by Rick Riordan, to the heroes who, by their very nature, break the accepted "mold" of society, as in the Divergent series by Veronica Roth, or even beloved children's novels like *Matilda* by Roald Dahl.

All of these stories are essentially the same. They all tell the tale of a chosen one who is misunderstood by the rest of society, gets very little respect (at least at first!), and ultimately is *different* from the rest of us.

That's why most Superhero stories are stories of triumph and sacrifice. These are characters destined for greatness, but greatness isn't always easy to achieve. These heroes must rise up and face great challenges and obstacles in order to fulfill their destinies. That is, after all, what makes them *super*. How many of us would simply give up when faced with those same odds? But not these heroes. On some level, they *know* in their hearts and souls that this is their path, and they will not stray.

Our three ingredients for mastering this genre are (1) a hero with a special **power**, (2) a **nemesis** who stands opposed to our hero, and (3) a **curse** that our hero must suffer as the price for their greatness.

Now, don't be fooled by the word *power*. Not all superheroes are magically inclined. A superhero's power can simply be a mission to do good or be great. Or possibly even an undying faith in a cause. It's either magic or *feels* like magic because the hero's faith and/or embedded destiny are so unnaturally strong.

Tris, the hero of *Divergent*, for example, has no magic to speak of, but her very nature of being "divergent" (fitting between the established factions of society) makes her special and therefore a danger to the status quo. And Day, one of the *two* superheroes in *Legend* by Marie Lu, is super in his ability to consistently evade the authorities, steal from the Republic, and generally make the government look foolish in their failed attempts to apprehend him.

On the other hand, you also have heroes like Harry Potter who are endowed with *actual* magic. But note, Harry's power is not that he has magic—everyone in his world has magic! Rather, it's that he's the chosen one to defeat Voldemort, because he's the only one, so far, who has faced Voldemort and lived to tell about it.

Regardless of your hero's mission or ability, this power is the thing that makes the hero more than human, more than the rest of us.

But with great power come great . . . enemies.

Enter the *nemesis*. This is the character directly opposing the hero. They have abilities that match the hero's, or sometimes even *greater* abilities, but the big difference is that their abilities are self-made. The nemesis lacks the one quality that makes for every great superhero:

Faith.

The superhero doesn't have to wonder if they are special. They *know* it (maybe not at first, but eventually). The nemesis, on the other hand, has to rely on themselves, their plots, and whoever else they've manipulated to their side. They must build a *façade* of being special and do whatever it takes to keep that façade from falling. Because the nemesis secretly knows (whether they accept it or not!) that they are the false hero. Otherwise they wouldn't have to try so dang hard!

Think about Lord Voldemort in Harry Potter and how much work he has to put in to be the evil villain that he is—creating Horcruxes, recruiting wizards, mastering dark magic.

Man, that guy must be tired!

Harry, on the other hand, doesn't really have to try to be special. He just is. Because he's the true chosen one. It's been his destiny since he was a baby. Does he always want that? No way! But that's the burden you bear when you're a superhero.

And what about Lord Warwick in *The White Queen* or Queen Levana in *Cinder* by Marissa Meyer? Those two nemeses are doing everything in their power to keep the world from realizing who the true superhero is. Fighting battles, sending in armies, brainwashing, and strategizing political marriages. It's a lot of work keeping up a façade of superiority.

It's that lack of *faith* in the mind of the nemesis that drives their need to kill the hero. This is what will prove (to themselves and the world!) that the *nemesis* is the "chosen one." Once Harry Potter is dead, Voldemort can stop trying. Once Cinder is "dealt with," Queen Levana will stand undisputed. Once Queen Elizabeth of York is knocked off her throne, Lord Warwick can finally rule the kingdom the way *he* wants to.

And there, in that very rationality, lies the nemesis's problem.

If they really *were* the rightful "chosen one," they wouldn't need to kill or prove it. The world would already know—just as they (usually) know with the superhero.

I must note, superheroes don't *always* survive the story. There's usually an ultimate showdown at the end of each Superhero novel (or series) in which the superhero and the nemesis finally have it out—mano a mano. And often, particularly when it comes to real-life superhero stories, the hero is destroyed. But that doesn't *really* matter, because we, the mortals—the readers—*we* have been changed by the journey. We have been touched by the universal lesson that the hero ultimately learned. *We* believe, and that is what makes the hero victorious . . . and immortal.

Finally, the third ingredient of every great Superhero story is a *curse*. And it might be the most important ingredient of all. Because the curse is what balances out the superhero's power so we don't completely despise the novel's protagonist.

Matilda would not have been as successful as a character had she not been born into a family of dimwits, constantly being picked on and ridiculed by her shortsighted parents and brother. Imagine if she had started out at the top of her game, living with a family who adored and worshiped her for the "genius" that she is. Yeah, kind of hard to get behind *that* Matilda. Most likely, we'd just end up wrinkling our noses at her, because doesn't *she* think she's all that!?

Taking our heroes down a peg—giving them a handicap, so to speak (especially at the beginning of the novel or series)—is what makes these stories work.

Remember, after all, this hero isn't like you or me. So it's naturally going to be harder for us to relate to them. That's why we must show the *down* side of being special: the curse.

It turns out being special is not always all it's cracked up to be. It comes with its fair share of headaches and problems. The curse is usually some variation of being misunderstood. We mere mortals have a hard time accepting those who are inherently different from (and better than!) us.

Cinder is a cyborg, and clever Marissa Meyer created a world in which cyborgs are considered inferior to the rest of society. Percy Jackson has been kicked out of every boarding school he's ever attended. Day in Marie Lu's *Legend* is a wanted criminal being hunted down by the Republic.

This is storytelling manipulation at its finest. All the greats have done it, and you have to do it too. Getting the reader on your super-hero's side is a constant balancing act. We can't pity them to the point where we just give up. And we can't dislike them to the point where we roll our eyes, shut the book, and go searching for something we can relate to. In the end, most of us will never *truly* understand what it's like to be a superhero, but we can understand what it's like to be singled out, ridiculed, and misunderstood. It's a curse that all human beings must overcome at some point in their lives. So make sure your superhero has to overcome it too.

In addition to the three essential ingredients of a Superhero story, there are also some other popular components that we often see in these types of novels.

First, a common "beat" that many Superhero novels contain (usually found in Act 2) is a **name change**. This is either for the superhero to disguise themselves or to fit in as they assume their new role in the Act 2 world. Elizabeth Woodville becomes Queen Elizabeth in *The White Queen*. Beatrice becomes Tris in *Divergent*. And June, a prodigy and the other superhero character in *Legend*, goes undercover in Act 2, dressed as a street beggar.

There's also a character type we see often in Superhero stories called the **mascot**. The mascot is usually a companion or sidekick to the hero, someone (or something!) that is always loyal to the superhero, despite the turmoil going on around them. In the Harry Potter series it's Harry's owl, Hedwig. In *Cinder* it's her quirky android, Iko. In *The White Queen,* it's Elizabeth's mother, Jacquetta. In *Legend* it's Tess (for Day) and Ollie, the dog (for June). These characters are not normally "super" themselves, not destined for the same exalted fate, but instead serve to show us just how different the superhero really is from the rest of us. Because these are the characters who have understood the superhero's greatness from the very start.

The Superhero genre is definitely popular among readers and moviegoers, but nowhere will you find it more prevalent than among books for teens and tweens. Just look at the list of Superhero novels that follows and count how many of them are best-selling young adult and children's books. Many of us have fantasies of being special, rising up and proving we are better than our peers, better than those who put us down. But at no time in our lives is this feeling more intoxicating than during our adolescent years. These are the years when we're figuring out who we are, what we're made of, how we can stand up without standing *out* too much. Which is why the lesson of the Superhero story resonates so well with us during this tumultuous time in our lives: See, even superheroes have problems. And those problems aren't much different from yours.

To recap: If you're thinking of writing a Superhero novel, make sure your story includes these three essential ingredients:

- **A POWER:** bestowed on your hero, even if it's just a mission to be or do good.

- **A NEMESIS:** who directly opposes your hero and who possesses equal (or even greater!) force, but who is the self-made version of the hero and lacks the faith to truly be "the one."

- **A CURSE:** for the hero to overcome (or succumb to) as the price for who they are, and which makes your hero relatable to us mere mortals.

POPULAR SUPERHERO NOVELS THROUGH TIME:

Dracula by Bram Stoker

Peter Pan by J. M. Barrie

Dune by Frank Herbert

The Bourne Identity by Robert Ludlum

The Lion, the Witch, and the Wardrobe by C. S. Lewis

Matilda by Roald Dahl

Parable of the Sower by Octavia Butler

Harry Potter and the Sorcerer's Stone by J. K. Rowling
  (*beat sheet included below*)

The Lightning Thief by Rick Riordan

Eragon by Christopher Paolini

City of Bones by Cassandra Clare

Mockingjay by Suzanne Collins

Divergent by Veronica Roth

Legend by Marie Lu

Miss Peregrine's Home for Peculiar Children by Ransom Riggs

Shadow and Bone by Leigh Bardugo

Cinder by Marissa Meyer

Origin by Jessica Khoury

Children of Blood and Bone by Tomi Adeyemi

HARRY POTTER AND THE SORCERER'S STONE

BY: J. K. Rowling
STC GENRE: Superhero
BOOK GENRE: Children's fiction/Fantasy
TOTAL PAGES: 309 (Scholastic US Paperback, 1997)

Spawning a box-office record-breaking film franchise, a stage play, merchandise, and even multiple theme parks, this first installment in the epic fantasy series by J. K. Rowling truly needs no introduction. But it's worth mentioning that it has one of the more perfect novel beat sheets I've found out there. Coincidence? I think not. Brilliant creativity, flawless worldbuilding, memorable characters, and a rock-solid story structure clearly contributes to this novel's astounding success.

Harry's struggle (throughout the series) to come to terms with the fact that he is the "chosen one" to defeat Voldemort (a power and a curse in one) makes this novel a winning example of a Superhero story.

1. Opening Image (pages 1–17)

A magical community is celebrating the retreat of the evil wizard, Voldemort. One boy has shockingly survived the battle. His name is Harry Potter. He is still a baby, and the encounter with Voldemort has left him with a lightning bolt–shaped scar on his forehead.

A mysterious wizard named Dumbledore drops baby Harry off on the doorstep of Number 4 Privet Drive—the home of Harry's aunt and uncle, the Dursleys.

In this chapter, we're introduced to J. K. Rowling's famous world of magic. We already start getting hints of what that world is like and who the key players are, but we won't truly come to understand it until Harry, the baby, is all grown up and presented with his destiny.

2. Theme Stated (page 13)

On page 13, Dumbledore says to Professor McGonagall (who has just morphed from a black cat): "Famous before he can walk and talk! Famous for something he won't remember! Can't you see how much better off he'll be, growing up away from all that until he's ready to take it?"

Like so many Superhero stories, this first installment in the Harry Potter series is about a hero who discovers how special they really are and has to learn to live with it. As "the boy who lived," Harry is marked as a chosen one, and this story, at its core, is about him coming to terms with that.

3. Setup (pages 18–45)

We fast-forward ten years; Harry is now eleven. He has a miserable life at the Dursleys with *lots* of **things that need fixing.** He has to sleep in a cupboard under the stairs. He's an orphan who knows very little about his real parents and never feels like he belongs. And the Dursleys treat him horribly. The **stasis = death** in this novel is clear: if Harry's life doesn't improve, he's going to wither away.

The problem is, Harry has no idea that he's special, or that he's even magical! Strange things do tend to happen when he's around, though. Like when Harry accidentally makes the glass in a snake cage vanish during a trip to the zoo, releasing the animal from its captivity.

4. Catalyst (pages 45–60)

Harry's Act 1 world is interrupted by the arrival of a mysterious letter in the post (Harry *never* gets mail!). His Uncle Vernon won't let him open it and burns the letter before Harry can read it. Then another letter arrives, and another. Soon the house is inundated with mysterious letters addressed to Harry Potter. The Dursleys try to escape the post by hiding in an isolated shack. That's when a loud knock comes at the door and a giant named Hagrid arrives to tell Harry that he's a wizard and he's been accepted to a wizarding school called Hogwarts.

Talk about a break in the status quo!

Harry also learns how his parents really died—at the hands of he-who-must-not-be-named—and about how he got the scar on his forehead. Hagrid wants to take Harry with him. The Dursleys protest. Who do you think wins that argument? Uncle Vernon or the giant?

Exactly.

5. Debate (pages 60–87)

The next morning Harry wakes up, thinking this has all been a dream. Until he realizes he's still with the magical giant. The rest of this novel's Debate is a transition from Muggle life to wizard life. Harry has to get ready for school and get ready for everything that goes with that.

Hagrid takes him to Diagon Alley—one of our first introductions to the wizarding world and its secret geography amidst the city of London.

Harry's transition includes physical preparations (buying spell books, cauldrons, robes, and so on) as well as mental preparations (learning about his past, his fame, and his importance in the wizarding world).

Harry has never felt like he ever fit in before. Will he finally fit in here? And can he ever live up to this epic reputation as "the boy who lived"?

6. Break Into 2 (pages 88–112)

The break from Act 1 to Act 2 is very clear-cut and well-defined. When Harry boards the train for Hogwarts, he's proactively leaving one world (the Muggle world) behind and decisively stepping into another (the upside-down wizarding world).

He's got the clothes, he's got the gear, he's even got the owl (Harry's mascot character)! The preparations are over. There's no mistaking it: Harry is a wizard now.

7. B Story (pages 90–106)

On the train, Harry meets the two people who will become his best friends, his helpers, and his confidants. Ron and Hermione are the **twin B Story** characters of the novel. They will both help Harry learn the theme of accepting his true destiny as "the boy who lived" and all the responsibility that comes with that.

8. Fun and Games (pages 113–179)

Everything about this novel's package—the cover, the description, the hook—promises us, the reader, the ultimate **premise**: a school for witches and wizards! *Cool!* And boy, does Rowling deliver on that promise.

As soon as Harry boards that train, he's in a whole other world, and it's a *fun* one. There's a hat that sorts you into houses; staircases that move; classes called "Defense Against the Dark Arts," "Potions," and "Charms"; flying lessons; a whole new sport, quidditch; and even fun magic candy!

This world is completely different from the one Harry knows. He's no longer a nobody who is ignored. Now he is famous and has friends!

But it doesn't take long to discover that Harry has enemies too. An instant rivalry sparks between Harry and Draco Malfoy (in Slytherin house). Also, Harry is extremely suspicious of a mean professor named Snape, who seems to have it in for Harry.

But despite his enemies, Harry's Fun and Games is definitely an **upward path**. He's loving his new world, and it seems as though Harry has finally found a place where he fits in. Plus, Harry makes the quidditch team, a huge accomplishment for a first-year student.

9. Midpoint (pages 180–191)

Harry's first quidditch match is his first **public outing** as his new self. He is now fully ensconced in this new world, and everyone in the stands can see it. His team wins the match (despite Harry's difficulties controlling his broom), and Harry is celebrated as a hero.

At this point, Harry believes he's found everything he wants: a place to belong, something he can excel at, and friends. But it's a **false victory**. The **stakes are raised** shortly after when Hermione announces that she believes it was Professor Snape who cursed Harry's broom during the match. It's no longer Fun and Games. Something bigger is going on at Hogwarts, and Harry and his friends are determined to get to the bottom of it.

10. Bad Guys Close In (pages 191–261)

During tea, Hagrid accidently slips up and tells Harry, Ron, and Hermione about someone named Nicholas Flammel who has something to do with a three-headed dog that the kids recently bumped into. They know the three-headed dog is guarding something. But what?

The plot thickens!

At Christmas, Harry receives a gift from an anonymous stranger: an invisibility cloak that used to belong to his father.

Soon after, Harry finds the Mirror of Erised, a looking glass that reveals your deepest desire. When Harry looks into the mirror, he sees his parents and feels lonely despite having found his place at Hogwarts. He starts to have nightmares about his parents dying (**internal bad guys**).

Later, Harry, Hermione, and Ron learn that Nicholas Flammel is the inventor of the Sorcerer's Stone, which has the power to make someone immortal. They rationalize that this must be what the three-headed dog is guarding.

Meanwhile, the external Bad Guys Close In when Harry suspects Snape of working for Voldemort, and Harry and his friends are caught sneaking around the castle after hours and get put in detention. During detention—served with Hagrid in the Forbidden Forest—Harry finds a wounded unicorn and a sinister hooded figure who has been drinking the unicorn's blood. The scar on Harry's forehead starts to burn. Harry is certain the hooded figure was Voldemort, who had been drinking the unicorn blood to stay alive long enough to get to the Sorcerer's Stone.

11. All Is Lost (pages 261–266)

Thanks to another slipup by Hagrid, Harry, Ron, and Hermione discover that Voldemort and Snape now know how to get past the three-headed dog guarding the Sorcerer's Stone. If nothing is done, Voldemort will soon have his hands on the stone and will become immortal (a reverse **whiff of death!**).

12. Dark Night of the Soul (pages 266–269)

What are they going to do?

Harry, Ron, and Hermione know they can't let Voldemort get his hands on the stone. Suspecting Snape is behind all of this, the kids go to tell Dumbledore, but the headmaster has left the school on business. And when they try to tell Professor McGonagall that the stone is in jeopardy, she dismisses them, avowing that the stone is safe.

13. Break Into 3 (pages 269–271)

They are left with no other choice. They *have* to go after the stone themselves. Harry, Ron, and Hermione make a plan to sneak out of their house after hours and try to stop Professor Snape from getting the stone for Voldemort.

14. Finale (pages 271–309)

POINT 1: GATHERING THE TEAM. In preparation of storming a real castle (the Hogwarts castle!), Harry, Ron, and Hermione meet in the common room after everyone has gone to sleep. They have to get past Peeves (the poultergeist) and Neville Longbottom, who tries to stop them from sneaking out and getting the house in trouble.

POINT 2: EXECUTING THE PLAN. The kids reach the third-floor corridor to find the three-headed dog has already been lulled to sleep and the trap door is open. Which means Snape has already been there and they might be too late! The kids head down the trap door after him, encountering a devil's snare, a wizard's chess, and a potion test. With each challenge, a member of Harry's team makes a **B Story sacrifice** (Ron with the wizard's chess and Hermione with the potion), so that Harry, the hero, can get to the end and face whatever is waiting there—alone.

POINT 3: HIGH TOWER SURPRISE. Expecting to find Professor Snape in the final room, Harry is shocked to find another professor, Professor Quirrel—whom no one suspected! It turns out *he* is the one working for Voldemort and plotting to get the stone. Quirrell binds Harry with magic rope, and Harry has no idea what to do! How will he defend himself against Quirrell?

POINT 4: DIG DEEP DOWN. The Mirror of Erised is in the room, and Quirrell makes him look in it, hoping Harry will help him find the stone. This time, when Harry looks into the mirror, he sees himself hiding the stone in his own pocket. He lies and tells Quirrell that all he sees is his own success at school.

A creepy voice calls Harry a liar and asks to speak to Harry directly. That's when Quirrell unravels the turban on his head and reveals that Voldemort is *part* of Quirrell. They have been sharing a body. When Quirrell/Voldemort reaches for Harry and touches him, Harry's scar burns in pain. But Voldemort also cries out. That's when Harry realizes what's going on: as "the boy who lived," he already has the ability to defend himself against Voldemort. Right inside of him.

POINT 5: THE EXECUTION OF THE NEW PLAN. Voldemort commands Quirrell to kill Harry. But Harry, now understanding his own power, reaches out and grabs Quirrell's face, which causes blinding pain to shoot through Harry's body. He passes out and wakes up in the school's infirmary. Dumbledore tells him that Quirrell is dead, Voldemort's location is unknown (but he'll surely be back), and the stone has been destroyed. When Harry asks how he was able to get the stone in the first place, Dumbledore explains that he spelled the stone so that only the one who wanted it for selfless purposes could find it. He also explains that Harry was able to protect himself against Voldemort because of the love his mother gave to him (when she died for him); Voldemort couldn't penetrate that.

Later, after Harry is released from the infirmary, Gryffindor is announced the winner of the house cup, and Harry celebrates with his friends.

15. Final Image (pages 307–309)

Harry, Hermione, and Ron board the Hogwarts express train back to London. At the train station, Harry is met by Uncle Vernon, who is as unpleasant as always. However, Harry is a completely different person now. He's not the shy, insecure orphan he was before. He's confident. He has friends. He no longer feels alone.

Harry says goodbye to his friends and tells them that he will use magic over the summer to get back at his cousin, Dudley, confirming that the tides have finally changed for Harry and he is a mirror image of the boy we first met.

WHY IS THIS A SUPERHERO?

Harry Potter and the Sorcerer's Stone contains all three elements of a successful Superhero story:

- **A POWER:** Harry is not only a wizard, but also destined to be one of the greatest wizards of all time. He is the boy who lived, the boy who defeated Voldemort, marking him as something greater than the rest of his kind.

- **A NEMESIS:** Harry has two primary nemeses: Malfoy (his peer nemesis) and Voldemort (his ultimate nemesis). Both are self-made.

- **A CURSE:** Being marked as "the boy who lived" from such a young age definitely has its drawbacks. As Dumbledore says in the Theme Stated beat, Harry was famous before he could even walk. That's a lot for a child to live up to.

Cat's Eye View

For quick reference, here's a brief overview of this novel's beat sheet.

1. **OPENING IMAGE:** Voldemort has been defeated (for now), and the baby who somehow managed to survive the attack ("the boy who lived") is dropped off at the Dursleys' house by Dumbledore.

2. **THEME STATED:** "Famous before he can walk and talk! Famous for something he won't remember! Can't you see how much better off he'll be, growing up away from all that until he's ready to take it?" The lesson Harry will have to learn in this novel (and the rest of the series) is how to deal with his status as "the chosen one."

3. **SETUP:** Harry has a horrible life with the Dursleys, who bully him and make him sleep in a cupboard under the stairs. He is shy, overlooked, and lonely.

4. **CATALYST:** Mysterious letters arrive that Harry is not allowed to open; finally a giant named Hagrid knocks on the door, informing Harry that he's a wizard and has been accepted to Hogwarts.

5. **DEBATE:** Harry goes to Diagon Alley with Hagrid in preparation for attending Hogwarts and learns that he is famous.

6. **BREAK INTO 2:** Harry boards the train for Hogwarts, officially leaving the Muggle world (Act 1) behind and entering the wizarding world (Act 2).

7. **B STORY:** On the train, Harry meets his new best friends, Ron and Hermione (twin B stories).

8. **FUN AND GAMES:** Harry enjoys life at Hogwarts, where he takes magical classes, learns to fly, and is recruited to play quidditch.

9. **MIDPOINT:** Harry wins his first quidditch match (false victory), but soon after learns that Professor Snape was (seemingly) trying to kill him during the game (stakes are raised).

10. **BAD GUYS CLOSE IN:** Harry, Ron, and Hermione learn about the Sorcerer's Stone (which gives eternal life) and discover that Voldemort is after it.

11. **ALL IS LOST:** Harry, Ron, and Hermione find out that Voldemort (via Snape) is about to get his hands on the Sorcerer's Stone, which is being kept in the Hogwarts castle.

12. **DARK NIGHT OF THE SOUL:** The kids try to go to Dumbledore for help, but he's gone, and Professor McGonagall doesn't seem to take their concerns seriously.

13. **BREAK INTO 3:** Harry and his friends decide to go after the stone themselves (to protect it from Voldemort).

14. **FINALE:** After passing multiple wizarding challenges, Harry discovers that Professor Quirrell (not Snape) is the one working with Voldemort. Harry defeats Voldemort (for now) by finding power within himself and touching Voldemort's face and saves the stone.

15. **FINAL IMAGE:** At the end of the school year, Harry arrives back home a changed person. He is now more confident and less lonely and has found where he belongs.

Dude with a Problem
Surviving the Ultimate Test

As much as we love our stories about "the chosen one" and those destined to save the world, sometimes, as readers, all we want to do is be inspired by an ordinary guy or gal who rises up to extraordinary challenges.

Enter the Dude with a Problem.

In other words, an ordinary guy or girl encounters extraordinary circumstances.

It's hard to find a more relatable genre because we are all ordinary dudes or dudettes. And we all know that any ordinary day can become extraordinary in the blink of an eye.

Unlike in Superhero stories, these dudes are not special and not destined to save the world (at least not when the story begins!). They're just average Joe Schmoes or Jane Schmanes, going about their daily lives, minding their own business, when BAM! Through no fault of their own, they find themselves dragged into a hot mess of trouble that they certainly did not expect nor invite.

And are they equipped to handle this world of hurt they suddenly find themselves in? *Seemingly* not. But that's what makes the Dude with a Problem stories so dang good. Eventually, our dudes and dudettes will rise to the occasion and accomplish things that they (and we!) never thought possible!

"Dudes" come in all shapes, sizes, genders, races, and occupations. From Mark Watney in *The Martian* by Andy Weir (a regular dude astronaut) to Stanley Yelnats in *Holes* by Louis Sachar (a regular dude kid) to Katniss Everdeen in *The Hunger Games* by Suzanne Collins (a regular dudette teen living in Panem) to Mitch McDeere in *The Firm* by John Grisham (a regular dude lawyer). Even Buck in *Call of the Wild* by Jack London is a regular dude dog!

All of the stories that fit into the Dude with a Problem genre are stories of a lone man, lone woman, or lone group (or lone dog!) who finds themselves facing incredible odds and whose survival often includes a struggle to hang onto their own sanity.

Our dudes usually don't ask for this trouble; sometimes they're not even sure how they got involved. But involved they are. They've got *big* problems on their hands. In fact, the bigger the problem, the better the story!

But remember, problems are relative. You gotta match your problem with the right dude (or dudette), taking into account your dude's given background, characteristics, and skill set. It's the relative size of the challenge that makes the stories work.

Mark Watney, for example, is a skilled astronaut and botanist. He would have no problem surviving in, let's say, the jungle. But that's not where Mark Watney finds himself, is it? He finds himself stranded and alone on freaking *Mars*. For most of us nonastronauts, what Mark accomplishes in *The Martian* would be literally impossible. But for Mark, it's only *nearly* impossible. And that makes all the difference. Because literally impossible makes for a very short and boring story, usually ending in death. But *nearly* impossible? That makes for some great fiction.

Another thing to note is that novels of this genre tend to work better if there are **external bad guys** in the mix. These are the forces working behind the scenes, throwing new and exciting challenges at our poor protagonist at every turn. Whether your bad guy is an individual like Annie Wilkes in *Misery* by Stephen King; an organization, group, or government like the firm of Bendini, Lambert, & Locke in *The Firm* or the Capitol in *The Hunger Games* or a force of nature like Mars in *The Martian* or the sea in *Life of Pi* by Yann Martel, the golden rule of villains remains the same:

The badder the bad guy, the greater the heroics, the better the story.

So make 'em bad. Better yet, make them *progressively* badder as the story goes on.

Think about Katniss Everdeen in *The Hunger Games*, facing harder and harder challenges from the Capitol Gamemakers as the competition goes on. Or even Mars itself, throwing more and more obstacles at poor Mark Watney the closer he gets to escaping the planet.

Regardless of who the bad guy or bad force is, the satisfaction of reading a Dude with a Problem novel comes when our dude uses his individuality to outsmart the enemy in the end. This is where that perfect pairing of dude and problem comes into play.

Mitch McDeere may not be able to survive on Mars, but he can survive a corrupt law firm, because he's a clever and ambitious lawyer. It's important to give your dude the abilities they'll need to conquer their problem up front, abilities baked right into their character DNA. But it's equally important that your dude (and your reader) not fully realize their potential and how they can use these skills until the time is right and the ultimate challenge is upon them.

The combinations of dudes and problems are endless, but the rules of the genre remain the same. You gotta have (1) an **innocent hero,** (2) a **sudden event,** and (3) a **life-or-death battle.**

First off, the *innocent hero.* They should have been dragged into the problem without asking for it. Wasn't Mark Watney just going about his day-to-day chores as the botanist aboard *Hermes 3* before a sudden freak Mars storm left him stranded on an uninhabitable planet? And wasn't Katniss Everdeen just going about her day-to-day life—hunting with Gale, trying to make ends meet for her family—when WHAM! Prim's name gets called at the reaping?

It's the hero's innocence that makes us readers love these stories so much. That dude could be us! We could find ourselves in the same situation and have to defy the same impossible odds. These are stories of survival, not punishment for a crime we committed (hence the *innocent* hero). Unlike Monster in the House stories (which we'll talk about in chapter 13), what the hero did to get into this mess is not what the dilemma is about. It's about *how* they're going to get themselves out of it.

Second, we need a *sudden event* that thrusts the hero into their world of hurt. "Sudden" being the operative word here. These Catalysts come seemingly from nowhere and force the hero to come to grips with what's happening, ASAP. Starr Carter in *The Hate U Give* by Angie Thomas is completely unsuspecting when her friend Khalil is shot by a police officer. Katniss Everdeen doesn't have time to think about her decision to volunteer for the Hunger Games in her sister's place. She just does it. And Mark Watney doesn't have time to hem and haw about his situation of being stuck on Mars. He's got to ACT FAST!

And finally, we need a problem worthy of this epic story. There must be a *life-or-death battle* involved in which the continued existence of an individual, group, or society is at stake.

If Mark Watney doesn't get off Mars, he dies. If Mitch McDeere doesn't find a way out of this firm, he dies. And if Katniss Everdeen doesn't kill twenty-three other tributes, she dies. Starr Carter in *The Hate U Give* also faces a life-or-death battle, but it's the battle for the continued existence of the community she grew up in. Khalil's death and the aftermath are tearing her neighborhood apart.

In other words, the problem must be BIG.

If you want to know whether your problem is big *enough*, try pitching your story to someone else. Their reaction should be something along the lines of "Dude, that's a *huge* problem." And hopefully their next thought is, *What would I do in that situation?*

If you've succeeded in this test, then congratulations: you've got yourself a killer Dude with a Problem story.

Another element you'll often see in Dude with a Problem stories is a **love interest**. They're not always there, but when they are, these characters are typically used as champions or cheerleaders for the hero. Isn't Peeta Mellark in *The Hunger Games* Katniss's biggest supporter and confidant? Isn't Chris in *The Hate U Give* on Starr's side through thick and thin? These B Story characters are the ones who will help the hero ultimately believe in themselves and find the strength they need to conquer this problem. These characters also often offer solace to our struggling dude or dudette in times of need.

Tender scenes between the hero and the love interest can often be found in what's called the **eye-of-the-storm** moment. This is the part of the novel where the action slows down for a minute and the hero (and reader!) get a chance to relax and reflect. And basically just *breathe*. When we have all action all the time, it can start to lose its potency and weary the reader. Think about the scene in the cave in *The Hunger Games* when Peeta and Katniss kiss. Or the prom scene in *The Hate U Give*. So much is going on in Starr's life at that moment, yet author Angie Thomas slows it down and gives us a welcome reprieve from all the drama with just a nice, normal high school prom.

Danger is still lurking, the storm still surrounds the hero, but in these moments, it's effective to take a break from the insanity and just be. These are also great opportunities to amp up love stories and friendships.

In the end, all Dude with a Problem novels are about the triumph of the human spirit. Our dude has survived! Or if he hasn't, there's a good, compelling reason for it. A reason that really makes us think. Dude with a Problem stories remind us that we, average humans, are actually a lot less average than we thought. We have hidden strengths. Hidden talents. And when put to the test, we persevere! We overcome! We triumph!

Reading these stories make us feel alive and inspired.

One lone teen defying an entire government? One lone astronaut defying an entire planet? One lone lawyer defying a firm run by the mob?

There's nothing more inspiring than that.

To recap: If you're thinking of writing a Dude with a Problem novel, make sure your story includes these three essential ingredients:

- **AN INNOCENT HERO**: who is dragged into the mess without asking for it—or possibly even aware of how they got involved, but in some way has the skills to overcome the problem (even if those skills are buried at first).

- **A SUDDEN EVENT:** that thrusts the innocent(s) into the problem. It should be definite and come without warning.

- **A LIFE-OR-DEATH BATTLE:** that threatens the continued existence of an individual, group, or society.

POPULAR DUDE WITH A PROBLEM NOVELS THROUGH TIME:

Robinson Crusoe by Daniel Defoe
The Call of the Wild by Jack London
The BFG by Roald Dahl
Misery by Stephen King (*beat sheet included below*)
The Firm by John Grisham
Holes by Louis Sachar
Life of Pi by Yann Martel
The Hunger Games by Suzanne Collins
The Martian by Andy Weir
The 5th Wave by Rick Yancey
Illuminae by Amie Kaufman and Jay Kristoff
The Hate U Give by Angie Thomas

MISERY

BY: Stephen King
STC GENRE: Dude with a Problem
BOOK GENRE: Psychological thriller
TOTAL PAGES: 351 (Scribner Paperback, 1987)

This book wouldn't be complete without a breakdown of a Stephen King novel. King is one of the most famous fiction writers of our time; his novels have sold more than 350 million copies around the world.

Although many classic Stephen King novels fit into another Save the Cat! genre, Monster in the House, I chose to analyze this psychological thriller—a shining example of a Dude with a Problem—because, well, it's about an author struggling to write the best novel of his career! (The opportunity was just too apropos to pass up.) But also because, according to King, he wrote this novel—about a fictional author feeling chained to his popular series of romance novels—as a metaphor for his own frustration at feeling chained to the popular horror novels that launched his career.

Not to mention, it's just one heck of a well-structured story!

Writing a novel can sometimes feel like you're trapped inside a house with a crazy psychopath who is threatening to kill you if you don't finish. But, on a less dismal (and more inspiring) note, in *Misery*, King depicts writing as a much-needed escape from our own miseries—and sometimes the very thing that can save our lives.

1. Opening Image (pages 1–6)

Our hero, Paul Sheldon, wakes up in a fog of pain. He's barely conscious, close to death. Someone is breathing into his mouth, trying to resuscitate him. When he comes to, he learns he's in Sidewinder, Colorado, with a woman named Annie Wilkes, who (according to her) is his number one fan.

2. Setup (pages 7–36)

As Paul slips in and out of consciousness, we learn more about him. Paul is the famous author of the Misery books, a series of Victorian-era romance novels. In the latest and last of the series, just released, Paul has killed off his main character, Misery, mostly because he hated writing the books and wanted to try his hand at a new genre. Paul had just finished his latest manuscript—*Fast Cars*—of which he's extremely proud. We also learn what happened to Paul to land him in this situation: his car crashed, and Annie (who used to be a nurse) found him, pulled him out, and splinted his broken legs. Annie has been giving Paul a pain-killer called Novril, and he's now addicted to it.

Paul soon surmises that Annie is crazy, dangerous, and unpredictable. She withholds drugs from him when he's in pain. She claims that they are a ways from town, and that's why she can't bring him to the hospital; the road conditions are too bad. But despite the fact that Annie saved him from that car wreck, Paul slowly starts to realize that Annie is keeping him prisoner here.

After Annie reads Paul's latest manuscript, she flies into a rage. Not only is it *not* a Misery novel (she's a huge fan), it's also full of swear words, which she highly disapproves of. As a punishment for his dirty mouth, she makes Paul take his pills with soapy water.

3. Theme Stated (page 19)

As Paul tries to piece together what happened to him and why he's here, Annie tells him: "You owe me your life, Paul. I hope you'll remember that. I hope you'll keep that in mind" (page 19).

There are many fascinating themes in this novel, but the Theme Stated, as it applies to Paul's life lesson, is about survival—and its ironic connection to his ghastly predicament. Despite the horror that befalls him in the next 332 pages, Annie did, in fact, save his life when she pulled him from the car wreckage. But more than that, Annie, through horrifying means, will ultimately push Paul to write his best novel to date: *Misery's Return*. The book that will end up saving his life, both literally and figuratively.

On page 7, King writes, "He was Paul Sheldon, who wrote novels of two kinds, good ones and best-sellers." This was Paul's view of himself at the start of the novel. He turned his nose up at the Misery novels, the ones that made him successful. But by the end, Paul will learn that best sellers *can* be good—if he puts in the effort to *make* them good. When Paul finally finds the inspiration for *Misery's Return*, he finds his escape from the misery of his situation. And he finds his will to live.

So, in a disturbing yet brilliant Stephen King–esque way, Annie Wilkes *does* save his life. In more ways than one.

4. Catalyst (pages 36–40)

Annie Wilkes is unstable. We're already starting to realize this. But it's not until page 36 that Paul (and we, the reader) see just how bad it can get. When Annie finishes *Misery's Child* to discover that Paul killed off the main character, putting an end to her favorite series, she goes ballistic, overturning the table by the bed. She then storms out of the room and tells Paul that she's leaving before she does something "unwise."

Paul is left alone and crippled in the house, without food, water, pills, or any indication of when (or if) Annie is coming back. This is the incident that finally pushes Paul to try to do something about his situation.

5. Debate (pages 40–70)

But *what* will he do? That is the Debate question.

After a day passes, he starts to wonder if Annie is dead. If she is, he will definitely die in this room. But Annie *does* return, and Paul immediately begs for his medicine. He's in a *lot* of pain. She agrees to give it to him *if* he agrees to burn his *Fast Cars* manuscript. She wheels in a charcoal grill. Paul is torn. He has no other copies. This is it. If he burns it, it's gone. But he needs his pills!

He burns it—and then secretly vows to kill her.

Later Annie brings him an old typewriter, the Royal, and tells him she wants him to write a new *Misery* novel—*Misery's Return*. It will be just for her—her payment for nursing him back to health. Will he do it?

He asks Annie if she'll let him go when he's done with the book. She *vaguely* says yes.

Paul knows she's lying but also knows that writing the book she wants might be the only thing that will keep him alive.

6. Break Into 2 (page 70)

Paul's answer to the Debate question is a proactive decision: he agrees to write *Misery's Return*. But he's also surprised to find that he is sort of looking forward to writing again.

7. B Story (page 109)

The B Story is Paul's relationship with the *Misery's Return* book. You might even say that Misery Chastain, the main character of the series, is the B Story character, as she is the one who will ultimately teach Paul the theme.

Before coming to Annie's house, Paul had already happily dismissed this character, this world, and this series. He was done with Misery Chastain. But the longer he writes the novel and the more

Annie pushes him to make it "fair" (meaning, not to "phone it in"), the more Paul finds himself drawn into the story, getting inspired by the plot and the character, and ultimately making it one of the best novels he's ever written.

"The irony was that the woman had coerced him into writing what was easily the best of the Misery novels" (page 209).

Misery's Return saves Paul's life. Both literally and figuratively. There are many instances when the ending of the novel is the one bargaining piece Paul has against the crazy, unstable Annie Wilkes. And, at the same time, the unfinished book gives him a will to live. (Something we novelists can definitely relate to!)

8. Fun and Games (pages 70–170)

The second act centers on the writing of *Misery's Return*. This is the Act 2 world for Paul. He hasn't gone anywhere new. There aren't any new characters introduced. But he's still *going* to an unexpected place: back into the series he thought he was done with.

The novel-within-a-novel format of King's book allows us to see some of Paul's efforts as he chugs away on the manuscript. But the writing gets off to a rough start. When Annie buys him the "wrong" kind of paper for the typewriter, she gets angry and punches him in his shattered knee before storming out of the house again.

Unsure of how long she'll be gone this time, Paul picks the lock on the door and wheels his wheelchair out of his room in an attempt to call for help. But the phone has been disconnected. He finds the stash of Novril painkillers in the bathroom and stocks up, just managing to get back into his room and hide the pills under his mattress before Annie returns.

Paul works on the first few chapters of the book, in which he has to figure out a way to bring Misery back to life, since he killed her at the end of the last novel. Annie doesn't approve of the first draft, saying that he "cheated" and the resurrection of Misery wasn't "fair." Paul realizes he can't just phone in this book in order to get it over with; Annie is too smart for that. He'll have to actually put some effort into this project (theme!).

On page 127, he has an idea, something that really inspires him. He begins to write, quickly losing himself in the writing.

On page 130, King writes, "Paul had no idea she was there—had no idea, in fact, that *he* was. He had finally escaped."

Annie reads the first six chapters of the novel and loves them.

"Shall I go on?" Paul asks on page 148, to which Annie responds, "I'll kill you if you don't!" It's dark and twisted but another nod to the theme that Annie Wilkes will ironically save his life, by pushing him to write his best novel yet.

For the next few weeks, Paul gets lost in his writing, averaging twelve pages a day. Paul and Annie establish a routine: he writes during the day, then, after dinner, they watch TV together. Strangely enough, despite his horrific situation, the Fun and Games takes on the feel of an **upward path** as Paul gets sucked deeper and deeper into the writing of his novel, losing himself in the story.

9. Midpoint (pages 170–180)

The book is going well. Paul is actually enjoying the writing. On page 170, King writes, "But it was also more richly plotted than any Misery novel since the first, and the characters were more lively."

This is turning out to be one of the best books he's written.

But obviously this is a **false victory**, because . . . well, um . . . he's still held captive in a psychopath's house. To remind us of this, the **stakes are raised** a few pages later when the rain comes and Annie falls into a deep depression. Paul always knew she was crazy and unstable, but this shift seems to reveal a whole new side of Annie.

"He realized he was seeing her with all her masks put aside—this was the real Annie, the inside Annie" (page 175). And after Annie suggests that they both kill themselves, Paul realizes, "*I'm closer to death than I've ever been in my life*" (page 177).

Annie finally says what neither of them had yet uttered aloud: that she's never going to let him leave. That she *will* eventually kill him. Paul buys himself time, though, by saying he doesn't want to die until he's finished the novel (**time clocks appear**). She agrees but says she has to leave for a while, and Misery Chastain saves Paul's life yet again.

10. Bad Guys Close In (pages 181–266)

Once Annie leaves, Paul ventures of out of his room again, searching for a means of escape. All the doors are bolted shut and even if he could get out, he realizes he's miles away from anything. How would he get anywhere in his condition?

Paul battles with his own sanity (**internal bad guys**) as a voice inside of him tells him to give up on ever getting out of here alive (a rejection of the theme). But Paul vows not to give up. He stocks up on food from the kitchen and then, on his way back to his room, catches sight of a scrapbook titled MEMORY LANE. This is when the **external bad guys** really start to close in. In flipping through the scrapbook, Paul realizes that Annie is even more dangerous and crazy than he thought. In fact, she's a serial killer who's killed countless people: family members, children, even babies! And somehow she keeps getting away with it. In her last trial, in Denver, there wasn't enough evidence to convict, and Annie walked again.

Paul realizes that if he's to have any hope of getting out of here alive, he'll have to kill Annie Wilkes. He starts to think of how he could do this, finally settling on stabbing her in the throat. He finds a knife in the kitchen and hides it under his mattress.

Annie returns and injects Paul with something. He loses consciousness, and when he awakes Annie reveals that she knows about every time Paul has picked the lock and gotten out. She even knows that he's been looking through her scrapbook—*and* she's taken the knife that he hid under the mattress, destroying Paul's hope of fighting back. Then Annie explains that the stuff she injected him with was a "pre-op shot" (page 227). Paul freaks out, wondering what she means by pre-op. Then Annie "hobbles" Paul by cutting off one of his feet and cauterizing the wound with a blowtorch, to ensure that he doesn't try to escape again.

As Paul deteriorates (also losing a thumb to Annie), so does the typewriter he's been writing on. It was already missing the N key, and it soon loses the R key and the E key, making it harder and harder to for him to finish the book and stay alive. He finally chooses to handwrite instead. This is not only another sign of his **downward path** but a nod to the metaphor of writing a book in general. The further you get, the harder it becomes.

As Annie's mental state gets worse, and Paul's sanity continues to falter, he realizes that he owes his life to Misery Chastain (the B Story character). "He was no longer sure. Not about anything. With one exception: his whole life had hinged and continued to hinge on Misery . . . He should have died . . . but couldn't. Not until he knew how it all came out" (page 246).

In fact, both Paul *and* Annie are hanging on, staying alive to find out how the book ends.

11. All Is Lost (pages 266–273)

A police car pulls onto Annie's property. At first Paul is paralyzed, unable to scream for fear of Annie's retribution. Then he finally calls out for help and throws an ashtray through the window of his room, shattering the glass and getting the cop's attention. But the moment the cop recognizes Paul as the missing writer, Annie kills the cop (**whiff of death**), stabbing him repeatedly and then running him over with the lawnmower.

Afterward, she turns to Paul and says, "I'll deal with you later" (page 273).

12. Dark Night of the Soul (pages 274–295)

Paul begs Annie to kill him and get it over with (all hope of surviving and finishing the novel is gone). Annie carries Paul down to the cellar, and Paul thinks she's going to amputate another body part. But instead, she locks him in while she goes to dispose of the cop's body.

Before Annie leaves, she restates the theme: "All I ever did was pull you out of your wrecked car before you could freeze to death and splint your poor broken legs and give you medicine to ease your pain and take care of you and talk you out of a bad book you'd written and into the best one you *ever* wrote. And if that's crazy, take me to the loony bin" (page 282).

It *is* crazy. And yet it's *so* true.

Paul knows that there is no escape. He will die after he finishes this book. He's sure of it. All hope of survival is lost. There's a literal Dark Night of the Soul as Annie leaves and locks Paul in the dark cellar with the rats.

13. Break Into 3 (pages 295–300)

But as Paul waits for Annie's return, dozing in and out of consciousness, he spots Annie's charcoal grill, the one she used to make him burn *Fast Cars*. As an idea starts to form, hope returns. Paul *finally* sees a way out of this.

He steals the can of lighter fluid from the grill before Annie comes back.

14. Finale (pages 300–348)

POINT 1: GATHERING THE TEAM. In preparation for his big Finale plan, Paul vows he'll finish the book in a week but makes Annie promise not to read any more until he's done. Then Paul hides the can of lighter fluid under the baseboard in his room.

POINT 2: EXECUTING THE PLAN. Paul writes, furiously trying to finish the novel. When another cop comes, Paul doesn't scream or alert him. He wants to be the one to finish Annie off. And he really does want to finish the book—for *himself* (theme).

Paul finishes the manuscript and asks Annie for a single cigarette, telling her he always has one after finishing a book. She agrees and brings him a single match. While she's in the other room, Paul pulls the lighter fluid out from under the floorboard. He douses the manuscript, and when Annie returns, excited to read the ending, he sets the book on fire. "And it's good Annie. You were right. The best of the *Misery* books, and maybe the best thing I ever wrote . . . too bad you'll never read it" (page 327).

As Annie reaches for the burning manuscript, Paul smashes the typewriter on her back and then stuffs burning pages into her mouth, choking her. She's able to get up, but trips over the typewriter and hits her head on the mantel, falling down dead.

POINT 3: HIGH TOWER SURPRISE. Except she's *not* dead! Annie opens her eyes and crawls toward Paul. She reaches him and strangles him, but passes out before she can kill him. Thinking she's dead again, Paul crawls out of the bedroom and shuts the door. Her fingers poke under the door, grabbing for him, before she finally lies still.

POINT 4: DIG DEEP DOWN. Paul pulls himself to the bathroom, finds the Novril, and downs three. As he sleeps, he struggles with his sanity again, still unable to believe that she's dead. He keeps thinking he hears something, but is it just his imagination?

He's terrified, but he knows he has to go back into that room. He has to get the *real* manuscript. (The one he burned turns out to be a fake.) He has to save the book that saved him.

Paul opens the door to the bedroom and thinks he sees Annie alive, but it turns out to be just his imagination. The cops show up, and Paul musters the strength to cry out to them.

POINT 5: EXECUTING THE NEW PLAN. The cops find Paul, and he tells them what happened and points them toward the bedroom. When they get there, there's no one inside.

Nine months later, Paul is mostly healed, with a prosthetic foot replacing the one Annie chopped off. *Misery's Return* is about to come out, and the publisher has scheduled a print run of one million copies, an unprecedented number. The novel is on track to be a massive success.

Despite all of that, Paul still sees Annie in the shadows, and he still misses his "Annie-dope." It seems he was addicted to her almost as much as to the Novril.

We learn that Annie had crawled to the barn and died there from the blow to her head she sustained after tripping on the typewriter. The very typewriter that had saved Paul's life, killed her. But in Paul's mind, she will never really be dead. He will continue to see her in his nightmares—and when he writes. Like it or not, Annie Wilkes will forever be his miserable muse.

Final Image (pages 349–351)

After "seeing" Annie coming at him with a chainsaw, Paul gets inspired to start writing a new idea. He feels terror as he writes, but also disturbing gratitude.

WHY IS THIS A DUDE WITH A PROBLEM?

Misery contains all three elements of a successful Dude with a Problem story:

- **AN INNOCENT HERO:** Apart from killing off his main character (a crime only in the eyes of psychopath fan Annie), Paul Sheldon did nothing to *deserve* the horror that befell him when Annie Wilkes brought him into her house and held him captive.

- **A SUDDEN EVENT:** The car crash that left Paul crippled and incapacitated is the sudden, unexpected event that thrusts him into this story.

- **A LIFE-OR-DEATH BATTLE:** Paul must fight (and *write*) for his life, aware that at any moment Annie might crack and kill them both.

Cat's Eye View

For quick reference, here's a brief overview of this novel's beat sheet.

1. **OPENING IMAGE:** Paul Sheldon wakes up in the house of Annie Wilkes in Sidewinder, Colorado. He's close to death and in excruciating pain.

2. **SETUP:** Paul is a romance novelist, famous for his series of books starring the character Misery, and Annie, a former nurse and definitely crazy, is his "number one fan." Paul was in a car accident and Annie saved him and brought him to her remote house to heal.

3. **THEME STATED:** "You owe me your life, Paul. I hope you'll remember that. I hope you'll keep that in mind" (page 19). The ghastly truth is, Paul's life is saved literally and figuratively by Annie Wilkes, who will force him to write *Misery Returns*, the best book of his career. The theme of this novel is thus survival—finding the will to live even in the most dire of circumstances.

4. **CATALYST:** Annie reads the latest book in Paul's best-selling series, *Misery's Child*, and freaks out when she discovers that Paul has killed off the main character. She storms out of the house, leaving him helpless and alone.

5. **DEBATE:** What will Paul do now? How will he possibly escape this psychopath? Annie returns with a typewriter and promises Paul she'll let him go if he writes a new Misery novel, bringing the character back to life.

6. **BREAK INTO 2:** Even though Paul doesn't believe that Annie will keep her promise, Paul agrees and starts work on *Misery's Return*.

7. **B STORY:** Misery Chastain, the heroine in Paul's best-selling book series, is the B Story character. Paul's relationship with Misery and the new book he's writing will ultimately teach him the theme of survival and save his life.

8. **FUN AND GAMES:** Paul takes an unexpected journey *back* into the world of Misery. We see snippets of the novel he's writing, interspersed with Paul's failed attempts to escape. When Paul shows Annie a few chapters of the book she makes him rewrite them, claiming they're not good enough.

9. **MIDPOINT:** Although Paul is still a prisoner, the Midpoint is a false victory. *Misery's Return* is actually going well. But the stakes are raised when Annie falls into a deep depression and Paul realizes that Annie will eventually kill him.

10. **BAD GUYS CLOSE IN:** While Annie is away, Paul finds a scrapbook documenting all of the people she's killed (external bad guys); meanwhile, he battles for his own sanity, losing his will to live (internal bad guys). When Annie discovers that he got out, she cuts off his foot.

11. **ALL IS LOST:** A police car shows up looking for the missing novelist, Paul Sheldon. Paul tries to call for help from the window and in a whiff of death, Annie kills the cop.

12. **DARK NIGHT OF THE SOUL:** Paul begs Annie to just kill him and get it over with, showing how far he is from learning the theme. She leaves to dispose of the cop's body, locking Paul in the dark cellar with the rats.

13. **BREAK INTO 3:** When Paul spots Annie's charcoal grill in the cellar, he gets an idea—and a renewed motivation to live.

14. **FINALE:** Paul finishes the novel—the best of his career—and then burns it in front of Annie. When she tries to stop him, he hits her with the typewriter. A fight ensues, and Paul finally crawls to safety, revealing that what he burned was a fake manuscript. The cops rescue him, and Annie is found dead. Nine months later, the book is on track to be his best-selling novel yet (thanks to Annie).

15. **FINAL IMAGE:** After hallucinating Annie coming at him with a chainsaw, Paul is inspired to start another book. She will forever be his miserable muse.

Fool Triumphant
Victory of the Underdog

I realize the title of this book references cats, but now it's time to switch gears for a moment and talk about dogs. Or rather, one very specific *type* of dog.

The *under*dog.

Who doesn't love a story about a victorious underdog? A poor, overlooked, cast-aside sap who rises up against those who have discounted them and proves to everyone (especially themselves) that they are worth something, dang it! They are valuable. They can and *will* make a difference.

That's what novels fitting into this next genre are all about.

Meet the Fool . . . Triumphant.

The hero of this type of story is a "fool" (an overlooked underdog) whose biggest disadvantage (and strength) is the fact that they are constantly disregarded, usually by some type of establishment or group of people.

Think about *Diary of a Wimpy Kid* by Jeff Kinney. No one expects *that* kid to excel in middle school—am I right? Or *Confessions of a Shopaholic* by Sophie Kinsella. Who would expect a woman who can't stop shopping to excel in the world of financial journalism? Or even Jane in *Jane Eyre* by Charlotte Brontë. The girl is cast aside and overlooked almost everywhere she goes. No one in society expects *her* to succeed and find happiness and independence.

And yet succeed she does.

They all do.

Because in the end, the fool in these stories is always triumphant. The underdog wins. And in that process, they end up (mostly by accident) exposing the establishment for the ridiculousness that it is. Essentially, it's the establishment that looks foolish in the end, if for no other reason than for daring to discount our hero.

To craft a successful novel in this genre, you'll need three important ingredients: (1) a **fool**, someone overlooked by society and often naïve to their own potential, (2) an **establishment** that the fool is in some way pitted against, and (3) a **transmutation** in which the hero becomes someone else, adopts a new name, or gets a new mission. Let's take a look at these in detail.

The *fool* can be anyone of any age. From a middle school boy like Greg Heffley in *The Diary of a Wimpy Kid*, to a teen girl like Mia Thermopolis in *The Princess Diaries* by Meg Cabot, to a grown woman like Becky Bloomwood in *Confessions of a Shopaholic*. The only criterion is that this hero start out disregarded and overlooked by those around them. But while being disregarded may seem like a weakness at first, it will ultimately prove to be the hero's greatest advantage.

The Fool Triumphant differs from a Superhero story in that no one seems to *know* that the hero is special (possibly even the hero themselves!). Unlike in Superhero stories, where almost *everyone* knows that this guy or gal is "the one," in Fool Triumphant stories no one seems to take our hero seriously at first, or consider them a threat.

Well, *almost* no one.

There's usually *one* person within the establishment who *does* see the fool's true potential and works hard to keep it hidden. This is a common character found in Fool Triumphant stories called the **jealous insider**. The person who can see the fool's true potential (possibly the only one!) and feels threatened by the fool, thus doing anything in their power to sabotage them.

The *establishment* is the group of people or subsection of society that the fool either is sent in to confront (like the beauty pageant world in *Dumplin'* by Julie Murphy, the fashion world in *The Devil Wears Prada* by Lauren Weisberger, or plain old middle school in *The Diary of a Wimpy Kid* by Jeff Kinney) or already exists within and naturally stands opposed to (like nineteenth-century society in *Jane Eyre* and *Oliver Twist* by Charles Dickens).

But don't let the Fool Triumphant *fool* you. This isn't like an Institutionalized story in which the fool sets out to join or destroy a certain group. The fool is usually just going about their business, living their life. They're not really looking to destroy anything. The fool's greatest strength and superpower (even if they don't realize it yet) is their innocence and their ability to just be themselves. The fool pokes holes and exposes the system that ridicules them by standing apart from what the system represents, thus exposing its flaws. And in the process, it's the fool who ends up getting the last laugh.

And finally, the *transmutation* is the moment in the Fool Triumphant story in which the fool *becomes* someone else, either by accident or as a disguise. While all stories have a metaphorical transformation, stories of this genre also contain this *physical* transformation, a moment where the hero changes their name, puts on a disguise, dresses up, changes their mission, or becomes a new person, if only for a few pages. Jane Eyre becomes a governess, Mia Thermopolis puts on the dress and the tiara and becomes Princess Mia in *The Princess Diaries*, Bridget Jones quits her job as a book publicist and becomes a TV journalist in *Bridget Jones's Diary* by Helen Fielding.

It's a key element in the story because it's the moment when the establishment starts to see the hero as someone a little less foolish than they once thought. It's the reverse of someone shedding their mask and revealing their true identity. The hero is essentially hiding their true identity in order to *fool* the people who have been disregarding them! But don't worry; the transmutation mask never stays on for long, because in the end, all Fool Triumphant stories celebrate the idea that regardless of what others think of us, we are our strongest when we are ourselves.

Fool Triumphant stories resonate with readers because we've all been there. We've all had to struggle to fit in, and we've all, at some point in our lives, been the victim of doubt. Someone or some group has told us "You can't do that!" But mostly, the Fool Triumphant story resonates with us because deep down, we all want to believe that one person can make a difference. We love our "foolish" heroes because they win for the underdog in all of us. And they teach us that believing in yourself is sometimes the only weapon you need.

To recap: If you're thinking of writing a Fool Triumphant novel, make sure your story includes these three essential ingredients:

* **A FOOL:** whose innocence is their strength and whose gentle manner makes them likely to be ignored by all but a jealous insider who knows too well.

* **AN ESTABLISHMENT:** the people or group the fool comes up against, either within their own environment, or after being sent to a new place in which they do not fit in—at first. Either way, the mismatch promises fireworks!

* **A TRANSMUTATION:** in which the fool becomes someone or something new, often including a name change that's taken on either by accident or as a disguise.

POPULAR FOOL TRIUMPHANT NOVELS THROUGH TIME:

Candide by Voltaire
Oliver Twist by Charles Dickens
Jane Eyre by Charlotte Brontë
Bridget Jones's Diary by Helen Fielding (*beat sheet included on the following page*)
The Princess Diaries by Meg Cabot
The Other Boleyn Girl by Philippa Gregory
Diary of a Wimpy Kid by Jeff Kinney
The Dork Diaries by Rachel Renée Russell
Wonder by R. J. Palacio
Dumplin' by Julie Murphy
The Season by Jonah Lisa Dyer and Stephen Dyer

BRIDGET JONES'S DIARY

BY: Helen Fielding
STC GENRE: Fool Triumphant
BOOK GENRE: General fiction
TOTAL PAGES: 271 (Penguin Books Paperback, 1996)

Although the classic novel on which it's loosely based (*Pride and Prejudice*) is a Buddy Love story, this hilarious runaway hit by Helen Fielding falls squarely in the Fool Triumphant category. Our fool, Bridget Jones, is a thirtysomething singleton who is pitted against the establishment of "Smug Marrieds" (as she calls them) who clearly look down on single women in their thirties. But Bridget's innocence (and thematic lesson of self-judgment) is what makes her triumphant in the end.

1. Opening Image (pages 1–2)

Meet our heroine, title character, and fool—Bridget Jones, who has just started a diary. The first two pages are the "before" snapshot of Bridget, in which she lists her New Year's resolutions. In this perfect first look at who Bridget is at the outset, we learn a lot about her flaws and the **things that need fixing** in her life, based on what Bridget wants to fix about herself: drink less, quit smoking, lose weight, be more confident, learn to program the VCR, and stop obsessing over not having a boyfriend. We also deduce that Bridget can be extremely self-critical, a flaw in and of itself.

But as we will soon see, by the end of the novel Bridget's real growth comes not from the things *she* thinks will improve her life but from learning to be content with exactly who she is.

2. Theme Stated (page 11)

At the annual New Year's Day turkey curry buffet (hosted by friends of Bridget's parents), a random party guest asks Bridget, "How does a woman manage to get to your age without being married?" (page 11).

This is both a statement of the theme and an introduction to the establishment that Bridget (the disregarded fool) is up against in this novel: being a lonely singleton in a world full of Smug Marrieds.

This question also represents the pressure that 1990s London society puts on a thirtysomething woman who is not yet married, while also implying that it's somehow Bridget's fault that she's single. *She* must be doing something wrong.

And this relates to the very lesson that Bridget must learn: self-acceptance. Bridget's neurotic quest for self-improvement (as evidenced in the Opening Image and at the start of every diary entry) shows that she buys into the view that she must be doing something wrong. Therefore, she's obsessed with changing herself—losing weight, quitting smoking, drinking less, buying fewer lottery tickets—all in hopes that it will help her find a boyfriend—and husband. But it's not until she learns to accept herself and be exactly who she is—essentially defying the establishment—that she actually does find love. And the man she does end up with will love her despite all of her self-perceived faults.

3. Setup (pages 4–19)

It's January, and Bridget isn't off to a great start with her resolutions, which tells us a lot about her as a hero: she's constantly trying (and failing) to better herself. Although self-improvement is always a good thing and usually a goal of any good plot, the twist on Bridget as a **flawed hero** is that she must learn that she doesn't *have* to change herself to find love. She's perfect the way she is. And *that* is how she will better herself.

Oh, the irony!

In the Setup, we meet the hilarious cast of characters that make up Bridget's **A Story**. First up, a neurotic and nagging mother who's always trying to get Bridget to change so she can meet a husband (no wonder she has the theme that she has!) We then meet Bridget's best friends: Jude, Sharon (aka "Shazzer"), and Tom. All three represent the establishment in different ways. Jude plays *into* the establishment, desperately clinging to a "vile" boyfriend who treats her horribly. Sharon consistently rejects the establishment by calling all men "emotional f*ckwits" and claiming that women will ultimately live in a world where men are not needed. And Tom is a *twist* on the establishment: he's a single *gay* man, who also struggles to find eligible men to date.

We also meet Daniel Cleaver, Bridget's boss and the "bad boy" she has a debilitating crush on. In fact, one of her New Year's resolutions is to stay away from Daniel, but I think we've established by now that sticking to resolutions is *not* Bridget's strong suit. As evidenced in the upcoming Catalyst.

4. B Story (page 9)

But before we reach the Catalyst, we briefly meet Mark Darcy, who will ultimately become a love interest and the B Story character of the novel (although his role as the B Story won't become evident until around page 87).

Just like the character in *Pride and Prejudice* who inspired him, Mark Darcy is immediately dismissed by Bridget as arrogant, conceited, and undatable. Little does Bridget know that Mark is more perfect for her than she thinks.

While Daniel Cleaver represents the A Story—Bridget desperately trying to change herself in order to get and keep a boyfriend—Mark represents the B Story: Bridget not even realizing that someone has fallen in love with the *real* her, because she was too distracted trying to be someone else.

The very fact that Mark eventually falls in love with Bridget without her even taking second notice of him just goes to show that Bridget didn't *need* to struggle so hard to be the "perfect person." She just needed to be herself.

But of course, all this doesn't happen for a while. First things first . . .

5. Catalyst (pages 19–20)

Bridget's life takes an interesting turn when Daniel sends her a flirty message at work. She immediately sends a message back, and the two initiate a hilarious and sexy office flirtation via email.

6. Debate (pages 20–52)

But what does it *mean*? That's what Bridget (and we, the readers!) desperately want to know. And it's also our Debate question.

What, if anything, will become of this flirtation?

Will this Cleaver chap turn out to be the future husband Bridget has been waiting (and dieting) for? Or will he turn out to be just another "emotional f*ckwit" who messes with Bridget's heart?

The question is not so easily answered. The signs point in all different directions as Daniel asks for her phone number and then doesn't call, then asks her on a date (for which she preps for hours!), only to stand her up.

When Daniel makes it pretty clear that he only wants Bridget for sex, Bridget turns him down. But Bridget's Debate over Daniel doesn't end there. The flirty messages continue, and although Bridget resolves not to engage, she does, vowing to stay "aloof" toward Daniel.

Meanwhile, Bridget's parents are going through marital problems and Bridget continues to play the fool at dinner parties with Smug Married couples who won't stop asking her why she's not married.

7. Break Into 2 (pages 52–53)

Bridget's aloofness seems to work when Daniel asks her out again. They go on a date and sleep together. The Debate of what will become of this flirtation is over. Bridget has made a choice to take the relationship to the next level. But was it a mistake? Does Daniel feel the same way about her as she feels about him? This will be the back-and-forth, push-and-pull dynamic of Act 2, which is the world of Bridget Jones *after* sleeping with Daniel Cleaver.

8. Fun and Games (pages 54–145)

The Fun and Games of this novel is Bridget struggling to create a relationship with Daniel Cleaver, who clearly doesn't want one. Is he or is he not her boyfriend? That's the big question that drives us to the Midpoint.

Helen Fielding does an excellent job of creating a **bouncing ball** narrative throughout the entirety of this novel, particularly in this beat. It's a constant battle of "He loves me! He loves me not!" Daniel doesn't call after they sleep together, so Bridget attempts to ignore Daniel, in hopes that he'll come around. It seems to work when Daniel asks her to go to Prague with him. But shortly afterward he cancels the trip.

Meanwhile, Mark Darcy (B Story character) still makes sporadic appearances in the story. Although Mark is introduced originally on page 9, it isn't until he reappears in the story on page 87 (and we get hints of the animosity between him and Daniel) that he really starts to slide into his role as the B Story character.

Also, the establishment is starting to show holes in its glossy façade. First, Bridget's mother leaves her father, claiming that she's fed up with being a wife. Then one of Bridget's Smug Married friends finds out her husband has been cheating on her. These are clear examples of the downside of the establishment that Bridget is up against. Not all marriages work out. Being married is not the "end all be all" happily-ever-after that the establishment wants you to think it is.

Despite this, Bridget is still diligently trying to obtain all of her goals of self-improvement (learning about the art of Zen and attempting to achieve "inner poise") and hopefully make Daniel her boyfriend. And it appears she's making excellent progress! By page 90, she has hit her goal weight (only to have her friends say she looked better before), she has mostly given up cigarettes (although she's replaced the addiction with scratch-out lottery tickets) and then, voilà! Daniel shows up at her door, drunk and professing his love. The relationship has officially begun!

But don't get too happy for Bridget. The bouncing ball hasn't stopped yet.

While Bridget thinks she might be pregnant, Daniel suddenly starts ignoring her again. She finds out she's not pregnant, and Daniel asks her out again. Daniel agrees to go on a mini break with Bridget (a huge deal for her), but the mini break turns out disastrous when they bump into a girl Daniel once slept with. Bounce! Bounce! Bounce!

What will become of this relationship? Will the ball of Daniel and Bridget continue to bounce up and down forever?

We'll soon have our answer.

9. Midpoint (pages 145–153)

Bridget and Daniel are invited to a Tarts and Vicars party (**Midpoint party**), but Daniel has to back out at the last minute for work. So Bridget goes stag, dressed as a sexy bunny, only to find that the Tarts and Vicars theme was canceled and no one told her. Now she's the *only* one dressed like a tart. (Let's all laugh at the fool!)

A and B stories cross when Mark shows up at the party with Natasha, a posh, stuffy colleague who is clearly trying to pursue Mark. She is the **jealous insider** who never fails to make snide comments about Bridget whenever the opportunity arises. During the party, Mark makes his negative feelings about Daniel clear, warning Bridget to take care of herself.

Mark turns out to be right a few pages later when the **false defeat** hits. Bridget goes back to Daniel's house after the party to surprise him and finds a naked woman on his rooftop balcony (**Midpoint twist**).

10. Bad Guys Close In (pages 153–237)

After you've been cheated on by a boyfriend (who probably wasn't really your boyfriend in the first place), there's really nowhere else to go but up, right?

And up Bridget goes!

She has a great night out with her friends, who cheer her up, and then her mother gets her a new job interview—in television!

Bridget gets the job (transmutation), which is good because it means she doesn't have to work alongside Daniel (who, by the way, is now engaged to the naked rooftop lady!). Despite a few hiccups, Bridget starts doing well at her new job.

But then Bridget gets invited to Mark Darcy's house for his parents' ruby wedding party, and Mark suddenly asks her out on a date! Bridget is confused. She never even gave Mark a second glance. On page 207, Mark says, "Bridget, all the other girls I know are so lacquered over. I don't know anyone else who would fasten a bunny tail to their pants . . ." One of her most embarrassing fool-ish moments of the year, and Mark actually liked her for it! Essentially, he likes the *real* Bridget, not the perfected glossy version of herself she's been trying (and failing) to be all year.

But when the date night comes, Mark seemingly stands her up. Thankfully, she's distracted by an important job assignment: a big legal case her boss wants her to cover. It turns out Mark Darcy is the barrister for the case, and he lets *her* have the exclusive interview. Plus, it's revealed that he *didn't* stand her up! He was banging on her door while she was drying her hair, and he thought *she* stood *him* up. Bounce! Bounce! Bounce!

Bridget throws a dinner party that goes horribly wrong, but Mark and her best friend Jude swoop in to save the day.

Finally, *finally* Bridget's life seems to be on track!

11. All Is Lost (pages 237–239)

Kaboom! Bridget's father calls to let Bridget know that her mother and her mother's new lover are wanted by the police. They've cheated a lot of people out of money on a time-share scam, and now they're nowhere to be found.

12. Dark Night of the Soul (pages 240–265)

Mark Darcy, the barrister, impressively takes action, flying to Portugal to find Bridget's mother, and helping the police sort out the mess and bring her home.

But then Mark stops calling.

It's December and still no word. Bridget wallows, proving that she has not yet learned the theme when, on page 250, she says, "Why? Why? Am going to be eaten by Alsatians despite all efforts to the contrary." Despite Mark's liking her for her, she still thinks her "failing" to better herself is the reason he's not calling her. She's so hard up in this Dark Night of the Soul that when Daniel calls her, drunk and blubbering, she actually rejoices and calls it a "Christmas miracle" (**return to the familiar**).

13. Break Into 3 (page 265)

On Christmas Day, Mark shows up at Bridget's house after dealing with an unseemly mess with mum's now ex-lover who's just been arrested by the police. Mark says he wants to take Bridget out to dinner.

Bridget accepts.

14. Finale (pages 265–267)

This book's Finale is admittedly short. When the book was adapted for film, one of the biggest changes the screenwriters made was bulking up the third act by adding some extra drama and suspense (essentially adding a Five-Point Finale!).

In the novel's Finale, Mark and Bridget have an excellent date. Mark admits that the reason he's been absent and not calling is that he's been busy trying to get the ex-lover of Bridget's mother to come back to England so the police could arrest him. When Bridget asks why he did all of this for her, he responds, "Isn't it obvious?"

But no, it wasn't. Not to Bridget. Not until now.

15. Final Image (pages 268–271)

In a mirror to the Opening Image, we now have reached the end of the year and Bridget's diary literally ends with a recap. She sums up all the alcohol units she drank, all the cigarettes she smoked, all the calories she consumed. And yet, despite all of that, she still calls it "an excellent year's progress."

Bridget has finally learned the theme: you can struggle and toil to change who you are, or you can just accept the fact that this is you and that's "excellent."

WHY IS THIS A FOOL TRIUMPHANT?

Bridget Jones's Diary contains all three elements of a successful Fool Triumphant story:

- **A FOOL:** As a thirtysomething single woman in London, Bridget is society's fool in every way. She's constantly laughed at, mocked, and asked why she's not yet married. She's an outcast and an underdog, and yet despite all of that, she still comes out triumphant at the end, by being herself.

- **AN ESTABLISHMENT:** The world of Smug Marrieds (as Bridget calls them). This is the group of people that Bridget is constantly pitted against as a thirty-year-old "spinster" (as the establishment calls her) and the reason Bridget feels the desperate need to change.

- **A TRANSMUTATION:** After being cheated on by her boyfriend, Bridget undergoes a huge transformation: she quits her job and takes a job in television, essentially reinventing herself as a new person.

Cat's Eye View

For quick reference, here's a brief overview of this novel's beat sheet.

1. **OPENING IMAGE:** In the first diary entry, Bridget lists her New Year's resolutions (aka everything she wants to change about herself).

2. **THEME STATED:** "How does a woman manage to get to your age without being married?" This is the question posed to Bridget at a party, implying that her single status is somehow her fault. This question introduces us to not only the establishment of this Fool Triumphant story, but also the lesson that Bridget will ultimately learn: she doesn't have to change herself just to get a husband.

3. **SETUP:** As Bridget gets off to a poor start with her resolutions, we meet the A Story characters: her friends and Daniel Cleaver, who is her boss and her "bad boy" crush.

4. **CATALYST:** Daniel Cleaver sends her a flirty message at work, instigating a sexy office flirtation.

5. **DEBATE:** What does it mean? Does Daniel want to be her boyfriend? Or does he just want to sleep with her?

6. **BREAK INTO 2:** Despite finding out that Daniel just wants to sleep with her (and probably doesn't want a relationship), Bridget makes the decision to sleep with him anyway.

7. **B STORY:** Mark Darcy (who is introduced in the Setup) embodies the theme in that he eventually falls in love with the *real* Bridget (without her even realizing it), proving that she doesn't have to change who she is to find love.

8. **FUN AND GAMES:** Bridget and Daniel's hilarious and dramatic on again, off again relationship delivers the promise of the premise as Bridget tries to determine whether or not Daniel is her boyfriend. Meanwhile, Bridget's parents split up.

9. **MIDPOINT:** Bridget catches Daniel with another woman. Obviously, he's *not* going to be her boyfriend (false defeat).

10. **BAD GUYS CLOSE IN:** Bridget picks herself back up by quitting her job and getting a job in television. Then, to her surprise, Mark Darcy asks her out, claiming that he likes her because she's not like the other girls he knows, but when the night of the date arrives, he (seemingly) stands her up. Bridget later learns it was a misunderstanding.

11. **ALL IS LOST:** Bridget's mother and her mother's new lover get arrested for running a financial scam.

12. **DARK NIGHT OF THE SOUL:** Mark Darcy flies to Portugal to try to bring Bridget's mother home but then stops calling. Bridget wallows, returning to the familiar, when Daniel calls her, drunk and blubbering apologies.

13. **BREAK INTO 3:** Mark shows up on Christmas Day and asks her out again. Bridget says yes.

14. **FINALE:** Bridget and Mark have a wonderful first date in which Bridget realizes that Mark really does love her just the way she is.

15. **FINAL IMAGE:** In a mirror to the Opening Image, Bridget sums up her year in her diary. Even though she didn't keep any of her New Year's resolutions to change herself, she still deems the year "excellent."

Buddy Love

The Transformative Power of Love (or Friendship)

Nothing is more primal than a love story. Don't believe me? Just take a look at the one *billion* dollars in revenue that romance novels bring in every year. They currently make up over 33 percent of the US book market. Why? Because nothing hits home more than our human desire for companionship.

But love stories don't always deal with romance. Yes, most romance novels do fit into this category, but our genre dubbed Buddy Love goes beyond just romantic love and, in fact, umbrellas every kind of love, from romance to friendship to even the love of a pet.

This genre is defined by its key characteristic: stories in which our hero is changed by someone else.

It's true, all stories are about transformation (or should be!). The plot is set into motion by a key moment or event (the Catalyst) that will eventually lead to the hero's ultimate change. But in Buddy Love novels, the plot that will bring about this change is usually set into motion by a *being* rather than an event.

That's why, in the majority of Buddy Love stories, the Catalyst *is* the meeting of that very special buddy. This being—whether it be a love interest, a new friend, a pet, or even an inanimate object!—comes into the hero's life and forever alters it.

Life doesn't start seriously changing for feisty Elizabeth Bennet in *Pride and Prejudice* until she meets the proud and disagreeable Mr. Darcy. Likewise, the world of Opal Buloni doesn't get turned upside down until she meets the scruffy mutt Winn-Dixie in *Because of Winn-Dixie*. And the lives of *both* Phoebe Summerville and Coach Calebow are turned upside down when Phoebe inherits the Chicago Stars NFL football team in *It Had to Be You* by Susan Elizabeth Phillips.

Regardless of *who* the buddies are, the dynamics of the story are the same: Buddy Love novels are about completion. One person being made whole by another. Or at the very least, one person (or dog!) who is the *Catalyst* for bringing about a certain change that the hero desperately needs.

In *Because of Winn-Dixie,* eleven-year-old motherless Opal is struggling with loneliness in her new town. She wants friends. Enter Winn-Dixie. The dog not only becomes her first friend, but also ends up leading Opal to meet a whole cast of interesting characters who eventually become her friends too. And in the end, Winn-Dixie also brings about the ultimate change that Opal needs in her life: to finally connect with her father and realize that *he* is enough for her.

In *Pride and Prejudice,* Elizabeth needs to learn how to get over her prejudices of others. Who better to eventually teach her to do that than the pompous Mr. Darcy, who turns out to be nothing like how she originally judged him to be!

Kissing scenes or no, these are essentially the *same* stories.

Both Elizabeth and Opal are made *better* because of another.

And even in the cases of stories where the buddies don't end up together (like *Eleanor and Park* by Rainbow Rowell or *The Fault in Our Stars* by John Green), the buddies of these stories still help change each other for the better.

Now, don't be fooled by the words "love story." Just because your novel includes a love story doesn't automatically kick it into the Buddy

Love camp. The question of whether your novel is *truly* a Buddy Love depends highly on how you define your A Story and your B Story.

Remember, the **A Story** is the primary story line, what's happening on the exterior, what the "hook" of the novel is, what's driving the action of the plot forward, whereas the **B Story** is often the side story, a character (or characters) who in some way represents your hero's spiritual or internal journey.

In Buddy Love novels, the A Story *is* the love story. It's the whole hook! We pick up *It Had to Be You* because we *want* to read how tenderhearted Phoebe Summerville (who is absolutely clueless about football) clashes with the macho, hardened coach of the Chicago Stars. That's the **promise of the premise**. Phoebe's relationship with the players and the team managers, and her learning curve as the owner of a pro football team—those are the side plot. It's the B Story that helps progress her arc.

Similarly, we pick up *Me Before You* by Jojo Moyes because the epic tale of ordinary Louisa Clark falling in love with extraordinary quadriplegic Will Traynor (A Story) touches our hearts. And even though, yes, Louisa's relationship with Will does eventually push Louisa to learn the theme of living well (the way that all A Stories push your hero toward change), that theme is *represented* by Louisa's tense relationship with Will's seemingly cold mother, Camilla Traynor (B Story), who, despite her wealth, has been stalled in her own life as well.

On the other hand, in novels of the non–Buddy Love variety, the love story or friendship story is usually found in the B Story. It's usually *not* the main focus of the plot.

But the ultimate test of whether your story is a Buddy Love is in the Catalyst beat. Is it the mere existence of *another* that sends your hero down the path to change? If the answer is yes, then you probably have a Buddy Love on your hands.

And if you do, then make sure you study the three elements of all great Buddy Love stories: (1) an **incomplete hero**, (2) a **counterpart**, and (3) a **complication**.

First off, let's take a look at the *incomplete hero*. Whose story is this, really? Even though Buddy Love stories are innately about *two* people, there's usually one half of the pair who will require the most work in order to get their life back on track. This is the person (or being) who has the biggest transformative arc ahead of them, who needs to change (and does change!) the most.

When studying Buddy Love novels, a hint is to look at who is narrating the story. If it's a first-person account like in *Me Before You* (narrated by Louisa Clark) or a close third-person account—meaning we see the perspective of only one character, like in *The Statistical Probability of Love at First Sight* by Jennifer E. Smith (narrated by Hailey Sullivan)—then chances are that's the primary hero the author has chosen because *that's* whose head the author wants you to get inside. Same goes for when you're writing your own novel. Who you pick as your narrator (or narrators) says a lot about whose story this really is.

Take a look at young adult best sellers like *The Fault in Our Stars* and *Twilight*. The female characters in these novels (Hazel Grace and Bella) are the heroes of the stories. The books are told through their points of view, while their love interests (Augustus and Edward) are the agents of change. Sure, Augustus and Edward have small arcs of their own, but it's nothing compared to the drastic way in which Hazel and Bella both change. After all, Augustus dies at the All Is Lost, leaving Hazel to finish her arc alone. And Edward has had several lifetimes as a vampire to do most of his changing. This particular novel is about Bella.

There are exceptions, however, where *both* buddies are equally changed by each other and therefore we end up with *two* heroes. These are called **two-handers**. In these situations, the author usually gives us *two* perspectives to match. Like in *It Had to Be You*, which features third-person narration from both Phoebe and Coach Calebow. Or in *Eleanor and Park*, another popular young adult novel. Rainbow Rowell chose to tell this tale of unlikely love from both Eleanor's *and* Park's points of view, which means she had to give them *both* equally compelling transformations. They even both got title credit!

Regardless of how many narrators or heroes you have, in all of these examples, our incomplete hero (or heroes) is in desperate need of some change in their life, and that change is going to come from our second Buddy Love element: the **counterpart**. This is the one person (or being) in the world who will (eventually) make our hero's life complete—or who will bring about the change our hero is so desperately needing.

Often the counterpart or buddy is a little quirky, a little unique. There has to be something about this exciting new person that's going to shake things up for our hero, which means they can't be dull or ordinary. They have to be *worth* an entire Catalyst! The introduction of this other has got to rip our hero right out of their stasis = death slump and into the second act!

Think about Augustus Waters, who shakes things up for Hazel Grace in *The Fault in Our Stars* with his witty dialogue and quirky views on life. Without him, Hazel would have never known love. She would have just continued to go on in her depressed state, essentially waiting to die.

Or think about the dog, Winn-Dixie, in *Because of Winn-Dixie*. This isn't a normal dog. Kate DiCamillo made sure of that. This dog has spunk. Character. He *smiles* at people. And without him, who knows if Opal and her preacher father would have ever found what they both needed in each other?

And finally, the third ingredient in every great Buddy Love story is a *complication*. This is what keeps the two buddies apart (at least for now!). The complication might involve another person, creating a love triangle, sometimes called a **three-hander**. The complication might be physical or emotional, like Will's condition in *Me Before You*. Or the complication could be a misunderstanding or a clash of character, which can often lead to the two buddies hating each other at the beginning (like in *Pride and Prejudice* or *It Had to Be You*). Other complication options include clashing personal or ethical viewpoints, an epic historical event, or even the general disapproval of society (like the star-crossed lovers of *The Notebook* by Nicholas Sparks). Or the complication could be that your counterpart isn't even human! Like in *Twilight*. Nothing complicates a good romance like finding out your one true love might kill you and drink your blood.

Regardless of what complication you choose to throw at your buddies, the element is crucial because it provides the primary conflict of the story. Without it, really, what's keeping the lovers from running off into the sunset together on page 10? That would be a pretty short novel.

Something must be keeping your lovers or buddies apart; otherwise, there'd be no story. The conflict in a Buddy Love story is what will make or break your novel. If you don't have enough of it, your reader will give up because the story is "too easy" and the love (or friendship) won't feel earned. The longer you can keep your "lovers" apart, the more gaps you can wedge between them, the better the story and the more engaged the reader. Even if your buddies get together early in the story, there has to be something precarious about their relationship. Why aren't they living happily ever after *yet*? The complication serves as a tiny bomb between the two counterparts, just waiting to go off and fling them apart.

Ironically, though, often the complication is *also* keeping the two buddies together. Hazel Grace and Augustus Waters in *The Fault in Our Stars* are bonded because they've both been through one of the worst things a person can go through: cancer. But that's also the thing that causes Hazel Grace to keep her distance at first. In *The Notebook*, Allie and Noah are kept apart by the prejudices of society and her family. And yet, that's the very thing that makes them *fight* to stay together. In *Me Before You*, Will's condition is the very reason Louisa met him in the first place (she was hired as his caretaker), yet it's also creating the main source of conflict between them (both physically and emotionally), right until the very end.

That complication can be a tricky thing. It can pull buddies together and drive them apart. And often the complication leads to an All Is Lost beat in which the two lovers or friends actually *do* break up, separate, or have some kind of huge fight. Since the All Is Lost is defined as the lowest point of the story, this separation beat is often found in Buddy Love novels, because what's lower than losing the one you've grown to love? Buddies *need* this beat so that they can realize what they truly have and figure out how to fix their flaws (that is, learn the theme!) in order to save the relationship (or themselves!).

In the end, almost all Buddy Love stories contain a similar message: My life changed for having known another. That's the hook of these stories, and that's how love stories (romantic or not) teach us about life. Funny how we keep turning to the same lesson over and over again.

I guess it must ring true.

To recap: If you're thinking of writing a Buddy Love novel, make sure your story includes these three essential ingredients:

- **AN INCOMPLETE HERO:** who is missing something physical, ethical, or spiritual. They need another to be whole.

- **A COUNTERPART:** who makes that completion come about or has qualities the hero(es) needs.

- **A COMPLICATION:** be it a misunderstanding, personal or ethical viewpoint, physical or emotional challenge, epic historical event, the prudish disapproval of society, or an other. This is the primary source of conflict in the novel, working to keep the buddies apart, but also to pull them together.

POPULAR BUDDY LOVE NOVELS THROUGH TIME:

Don Quixote by Miguel de Cervantes
Pride and Prejudice by Jane Austen
Wuthering Heights by Emily Brontë
Anna Karenina by Leo Tolstoy
The Yearling by Marjorie Kinnan Rawlings
It Had to Be You by Susan Elizabeth Phillips
The Notebook by Nicholas Sparks
Because of Winn-Dixie by Kate DiCamillo
Safe Harbor by Danielle Steele
Twilight by Stephanie Meyer
Irresistible Forces by Brenda Jackson
Vision in White by Nora Roberts

Anna and the French Kiss by Stephanie Perkins
Eleanor and Park by Rainbow Rowell
The Fault in Our Stars by John Green
Me Before You by Jojo Moyes
The Statistical Probability of Love at First Sight by Jennifer E. Smith
Aristotle and Dante Discover the Secrets of the Universe by
    Benjamin Alire Sáenz
Everything, Everything by Nicola Yoon (*beat sheet included below*)
When Dimple Met Rishi by Sandhya Menon

EVERYTHING, EVERYTHING

BY: Nicola Yoon
STC GENRE: Buddy Love
BOOK GENRE: Young adult romance
TOTAL PAGES: 306 (Delacorte Hardcover, 2015)

Author Nicola Yoon burst onto the young adult novel scene in 2015 with her stunning and beautiful debut, *Everything, Everything*, about a girl with "bubble boy disease" who has been confined to her house for most of her life. But when a boy moves in next door, it changes *everything* for both of them. The novel, which interweaves traditional narrative with graphics, charts, illustrations, emails, instant messages, and other creative devices, debuted at number one on the *New York Times* best-seller list and was also adapted for film in 2017 starring Amanda Stenberg and Nick Robinson.

1. Opening Image (pages 1–2)

Our hero, Madeline ("Maddy"), introduces us to her all-white room with "white shelves and glistening white bookshelves." Her books come "from Outside, decontaminated and vacuum-sealed in plastic wrap" (page 1).

What is the reason for all of this? We will soon see. But for now, all Madeline tells us is that she has read a *lot* of books.

2. Setup (pages 3–20)

By page 3, we learn about Madeline's condition: she's essentially allergic to the world. She has severe combined immunodeficiency (SCID). She can't go outside. *Ever.* Her Act 1 world is literally her house and nothing else. No wonder she reads so much!

The only people Madeline ever sees are her mother (who's a doctor) and her nurse, Carla, who tends to her during the day while her mom is at work.

In the Setup, we're further introduced to Maddy and her unique world. Maddy is highly creative, but also very bored and lonely (**things that need fixing**). Her biggest want is to see the outside world. "Really there's only one thing to wish for—a magical cure that will allow me to run free outside like a wild animal" (page 11). But because of her condition, she probably never will.

She spends her days attending school online, reading, and writing and posting "Spoiler Reviews" of books. She spends her nights with her mom, watching movies or playing board games. Basically, her life is predictable.

So what better buddy to disrupt her world and send her life spinning in a new direction than someone who is completely *unpredictable*?

3. Catalyst (pages 20–21)

A moving van pulls into the driveway of the house next door. From her bedroom window, Maddy watches a teenage boy, dressed in all black (a counterpart to her all-white world), jump out of the truck.

From the very moment she first sees Olly, he is in motion. Constantly moving, jumping and running "wild" through life. He is the polar opposite of Maddy, someone who is literally stuck in one place. But as is the case with all Buddy Love stories, he is exactly what she needs. Someone who can pull her out of her lonely, predictable existence and teach her how to really live.

When their eyes meet through the window, nothing will ever be the same again . . . for either of them.

4. Debate (pages 22–41)

Who is this boy and what (if anything) will become of this? That is the Debate question. And Maddy spends the next twenty pages obsessively spying on Olly through her bedroom window, trying to answer that question.

Fascinated with him, Maddy makes logs of his family's comings and goings, marking Olly's schedule as "unpredictable" (an opposing reference to her predictability, which was directly noted earlier on page 13).

In her "spying," Maddy discovers that Olly is into Parkour, another direct opposition to her lifestyle. She also notices that Olly's dad is a very angry person who is often abusive to Olly, his mother, and his sister.

When Olly and his sister come to the door with a bundt cake that their mother baked, Maddy's mother has to try to politely decline it. She can't bring anything in from the outside that might contaminate the house and make Maddy sick. The mystery of her mother's refusal intrigues Olly, inspiring him to make contact with Maddy through their facing bedroom windows. Unable to speak to one another, Olly constructs hilarious tableaus in his window that make Maddy laugh.

The Debate comes to an end when Olly writes his email address on the window. Maddy doesn't hesitate.

5. Break Into 2 (page 42)

Maddy emails Olly. Their relationship officially begins.

6. Theme Stated/B Story (page 68)

Maddy's nurse, Carla, states the theme when she tells Maddy, "Everything is a risk. Not doing anything is a risk. It's up to you" (page 68).

Maddy is extremely risk averse at the start of this novel. As well she should be, in her condition. But if she wants to really live—not just stay alive—she'll have to find the courage to take risks that she's never taken before, including risking her own life. *There's more to life than living* is essentially the lesson Maddy will learn by the end of the novel.

Carla, who states the theme, is also the B Story character. Even though meeting Olly is what pushes Maddy outside of her comfort zone, it's Carla who helps her every step of the way.

7. Fun and Games (pages 42–130)

The Act 2 world is Maddy's life with Olly in it. It's night and day different from her world without him.

A fun and witty email exchange begins, which quickly morphs into an instant message conversation. In this **upward path** Fun and Games, Maddy and Olly slowly get to know each other, talking about small stuff to start with (favorite books, movies, and food). But soon, as they begin to trust each other, they move to more serious topics (Maddy's disease and Olly's abusive father). Maddy is consistently able to make Olly smile, even during his darker moments, which proves that he's just as in need of her as she is of him.

After Carla reveals that she knows about Maddy's conversations with Olly, Maddy asks Carla if they can meet in person, promising to keep it a secret from her mother (who would never approve). Carla, of course, says no (it's way too dangerous), but then changes her mind, embodying the theme in her belief that some things are worth the risk.

Olly is decontaminated in the house's airlock system, and the two meet in the sunroom, where they are ordered *not* to ever touch. During their first meeting, it becomes obvious that Maddy and Olly are falling hard for each other.

But the **bouncing ball** narrative brings Maddy back down to earth as she realizes how dangerous this relationship is—not only to her health but also to her heart. "For the first time in a long time, I want more than I can have" (page 80). Maddy is worried about the wanting and the desire. Knowing that she can never really have Olly makes her immediately back off from the relationship.

But it's Carla—the B Story character—who convinces her not to break things off with Olly, once again bringing up the theme. "Do you really want to lose the only friend you've ever had over a little bit of heartache?" (page 86). Maddy quickly realizes Carla is right, and she takes another risk to see Olly again, vowing to just be friends.

But the more she sees him, the more convinced Maddy becomes that she will fall in love with Olly. It's inevitable. Olly and Maddy continue to open up to each other. Maddy tells Olly how her father and brother died: they were hit by a trucker who had fallen asleep at the wheel, shortly before Maddy was diagnosed with SCID.

Meanwhile, her mother is getting suspicious of her changed behavior. Maddy is more tired than usual and skipping their normal nightly activities (in order to IM with Olly).

Maddy feels guilty for lying to her mother. But she still continues to take bigger and bigger risks. In one of their secret meetings, Olly and Maddy touch for the first time, which immediately leads to a conversation about kissing. Maddy starts obsessing about the idea of kissing Olly. Could she *really* do it? The idea of her first kiss is exhilarating.

8. Midpoint (pages 130–138)

Olly and Maddy kiss for the first time in an epic **false victory** Midpoint. "And just like that, everything changes," Maddy notes on page 130.

But the **stakes are raised** a few pages later when Olly gets into a huge fight with his dad on the sidewalk outside. When Olly's dad punches Olly in the stomach, Maddy doesn't think. She just reacts. She runs out the front door of her house to get to Olly, her mother screaming at her to stop.

This is a definite **shift from wants to needs** as Maddy takes the biggest risk she's ever taken: going outside. Risking her *life*. For him.

After it's over, her mother realizes that Olly is not a stranger to Maddy. They know each other. Maddy lies and tells her that she and Olly are just online friends.

9. Bad Guys Close In (pages 139–235)

The **downward path** starts instantly when Maddy's mom finds the rubber band Olly wears around his wrist inside the house. She knows that the two have met in person. She immediately revokes Maddy's internet privileges, and fires Carla, replacing her with a horribly strict tyrant of a nurse named Janet.

Maddy can no longer talk to Olly, and she slips into despair.

Summer ends, Olly goes back to school, and the two see each other less and less. Then Olly comes home from school one day with a girl, and even though Maddy soon learns that it's just his lab partner, she quickly realizes that she'll never be able to compete with any other girl.

"It doesn't matter if she's pretty or not. It matters that she feels the sun on her skin. She breathes unfiltered air. It matters that she lives in the same world that Olly does, and I don't. I never will" (page 157).

After Maddy witnesses another fight between Olly and his father, she makes a decision: She books two tickets to Hawaii for her and Olly and sneaks out of the house, leaving her mother a goodbye letter that says, "Because of you I've survived this long and gotten a chance to know my small part of the world. But it's not enough" (page 168).

Maddy has tasted a piece of happiness with Olly and now she can't go back. She can't be happy again without him. "It's like I can't look at the world in the old way again" (page 168).

Maddy is able to convince Olly to go with her by lying about having obtained some experimental pills to keep her from getting sick. The two jet off to Hawaii for two days of bliss. Maddy sees and swims in the ocean for the first time, and the two dine on delicious food and spend a romantic night together. And throughout everything, Maddy gets closer and closer to learning the theme. On page 208, she notes, "I'm being reassured with every breath that I'm more than just alive. I'm living."

10. All Is Lost (pages 234–237)

But it all comes crashing to a halt when Maddy falls very sick and collapses in the hotel room. Then, in a **whiff of death**, Maddy's heart stops . . .

11. Dark Night of the Soul (pages 238–270)

. . . and starts again.

Maddy's mom arrives in Hawaii, discharges her from the hospital, and brings her home. Her bedroom has been turned into a hospital room, and Maddy's despair is deeper than ever as she realizes she will be trapped in her house forever. "How can I live the rest of my life in this bubble now that I know all that I'm missing?" (page 242).

Over IM, Maddy breaks up with Olly and rejects the theme when she says, "I've learned my lesson. Love *can* kill you, and I'd rather be alive than out there living" (page 247).

And in a very apropos Dark Night of the Soul moment, Maddy even draws a "Map of Despair" complete with "Mountains of Misery," a "Desert of Sorrow," and an "Ocean of Regret" (page 249). She stops responding to Olly's emails, and eventually his emails stop coming.

In attempt to cheer her up, Maddy's mom hires Carla back. Maddy and her mom slowly fall back into their old routine. Maddy even starts posting her Spoiler Reviews again (**return to the familiar**).

Olly, his mother, and his sister finally leave his father and hastily move out of the house while he's at work. As Olly looks up at Maddy's window, in a mirror to the Catalyst, their eyes meet for seemingly the last time.

Maddy finally reads Olly's emails and learns that Olly was able to convince his mother to leave his father only after he told his mother of Maddy's bravery in Hawaii. If nothing else, her risk-taking inspired someone else.

Then, Maddy's world shatters when she receives an email from the doctor who treated her in Hawaii, saying that she got Maddy's blood tests back and doesn't believe that Maddy has SCID—or has *ever* had SCID (**Dark Night epiphany**).

Her mom denies this, claiming that the doctor simply doesn't understand this rare and complicated disease. But Maddy is not 100 percent convinced. Especially after Carla tells her, "Sometimes I think maybe your mama's not quite right. Maybe she never recovered from what happened to your papa and brother" (page 270).

12. Break Into 3 (page 270)

Maddy takes the biggest risk of all when she vows to find out the truth about herself. She asks Carla (B Story) for help and Carla orders a blood test.

13. Finale (pages 271–305)

POINT 1: GATHERING THE TEAM. As Maddy waits for the blood test results, she decides to look through her mother's files. She finds records of almost everything *except* the official SCID diagnosis. "Where is the proof of the life I have lived?" (page 273). It seems there isn't any.

POINT 2: EXECUTING THE PLAN. She confronts her mother, who swears she has the diagnosis somewhere, but as she searches hopelessly for it, Maddy realizes that Carla is right. Her mother is not right in the head. "And that's when I know for sure. I am not sick and I never have been."

POINT 3: HIGH TOWER SURPRISE. Maddy quickly discovers that her mother never did recover from the death of her father and brother. And when Maddy got sick as a baby shortly after the car accident, her mother convinced herself Maddy had SCID. It was a way to literally protect her from the world—by hiding her away from it. Maddy's "entire life was a lie" (page 279).

Maddy gets the official word from her new doctor: She does not have SCID. But after living inside for her entire life, she has a very vulnerable immune system and has to take things slow.

Her relationship with her mother is forever altered, and she's not sure she can ever forgive her for what she did, despite B Story Carla's suggestion that she should.

POINT 4: DIG DEEP DOWN. Maddy eventually buys a ticket to New York City to find Olly. As she flies to New York, Maddy digs deep down and proves that she has finally learned the theme when she observes on page 300, "Anything can happen at any time. Safety is not everything. There's more to life than being alive"; and again on page 302 when she writes a Spoiler Review for *The Little Prince* that reads, "Love is worth everything. Everything."

Also, in her decision to seek out Olly, she starts to understand and forgive her mother. "Love makes people crazy. Loss of love makes people crazy" (page 300).

POINT 5: EXECUTING THE NEW PLAN. Maddy texts Olly and tells him to go to a used bookstore in NYC where there's a gift waiting for him. She hides in the stacks and watches him arrive. When he shows up, she notes that he's not wearing all black anymore (a nod to how much she has changed him as well).

14. FINAL IMAGE (PAGE 306)

A literal final "image" as we turn to the last page to find a visual representation (one of Maddy's drawings) of the gift Maddy left for Olly—a copy of *The Little Prince*. Inside, she has written, "Reward if Found: Me."

They have (re)found each other.

WHY IS THIS A BUDDY LOVE?

Everything, Everything contains all three elements of a successful Buddy Love story:

- **AN INCOMPLETE HERO:** Maddy is bored, lonely, and unable to safely leave her house. Despite the fact that she makes the most of her existence, she is still clearly lacking something.

- **A COUNTERPART:** From the moment he's described, Olly is Maddy's natural counterpart: a yang to her yin. A free spirit to her captive one.

- **A COMPLICATION:** Maddy's rare illness is the complication that is keeping them apart. It is the primary source of conflict between them throughout the novel.

Cat's Eye View

For quick reference, here's a brief overview of this novel's beat sheet.

1. **OPENING IMAGE:** A glimpse into Madeline's all-white bedroom, where the books are decontaminated and plastic wrapped.

2. **SETUP:** We learn that Madeline suffers from SCID (she's allergic to everything and completely vulnerable to infectious diseases), confining her to her house. She *wants* to be able to leave her house but probably never will. Her life has become boring and predictable.

3. **CATALYST:** A new boy named Olly moves in next door.

4. **DEBATE:** Who is this boy and what (if anything) will become of this? Maddy studies Olly, who in turn sets up hilarious tableaus in his window.

5. **BREAK INTO 2:** After Olly writes his email address on the window, Maddy makes the decision to email him, officially kicking off their relationship and moving Maddy into the world of Act 2 (her *unpredictable* life with Olly).

6-7. **THEME STATED/B STORY:** "Everything is a risk. Not doing anything is a risk. It's up to you" (page 68). Maddy's nurse, Carla (also the B Story character), states the theme, pushing Maddy to learn her life lesson of finding the courage to take risks and claim the life she wants.

8. **FUN AND GAMES:** Fun and witty emails and instant messages between Maddy and Olly lead to a secret meeting (facilitated by Carla). Maddy realizes how dangerous the relationship is, but she can't help falling in love with Olly.

9. **MIDPOINT:** A false victory when Maddy and Olly share their first (amazing) kiss. Soon afterward, Maddy witnesses a fight between Olly and his father and runs outside for the first time in years (stakes are raised).

10. **BAD GUYS CLOSE IN:** Maddy's mom finds out about the secret visits and cuts off Maddy's internet access and fires Carla, replacing her with a strict nurse. After another fight between Olly and his dad, Maddy buys airline tickets to Hawaii, and the two run away together.

11. **ALL IS LOST:** Their trip crashes to a halt when Maddy falls very sick and collapses. In a whiff of death, Maddy's heart momentarily stops.

12. **DARK NIGHT OF THE SOUL:** Maddy returns home to her "bubble" and is furthest from the theme when she breaks up with Olly and refuses to talk to him. Olly moves away, and soon afterward, Maddy receives an email from the doctor in Hawaii, claiming she doesn't have SCID.

13. **BREAK INTO 3:** Maddy takes the biggest risk of all: learning the truth about herself. She asks Carla (B Story) to help her order a blood test.

14. **FINALE:** Maddy snoops through her mother's files, finding no evidence that she was ever diagnosed with SCID, which the blood test confirms. Maddy realizes her mother convinced herself that Maddy had SCID so she could protect her from the same fate as Maddy's father and brother (who died in a car crash). Maddy buys a plane ticket for New York to find Olly. Through text messages, Maddy leads Olly to a used bookstore to find her—again.

15. **FINAL IMAGE:** A drawing of the book Maddy left Olly, which offers a "reward if found." The reward is Maddy.

11

Out of the Bottle
A Little Bit of Magic Goes a Long Way

> **WARNING! THIS CHAPTER CONTAINS SPOILERS**
> **FOR THE FOLLOWING BOOK:**
> *Twenties Girl* by Sophie Kinsella

Wishing. Whether it be on a shooting star, on a birthday cake glowing with candles, on a wishbone, or maybe even as we fall asleep, we've all wished for something at some point in our lives, and we've all wondered, *What if it actually came true?* That's why this genre, dubbed "Out of the Bottle" in honor of Aladdin and his magic wish-granting lamp, resonates so strongly with readers. It's a story that gets told over and over again. A hero wishes for something that will make all of their problems go away, and poof! It comes true!

But this magical genre isn't just about granting wishes. It's also about bestowing curses, sending guardian angels, swapping bodies, and even transporting your hero into strange dimensions and parallel universes.

Regardless of the type of nature-bending you choose to do, all of the stories in the Out of the Bottle genre boil down to the same thing: a guy or gal is bestowed with some sort of magic, realizes that "reality" isn't all that bad, and comes out in the end a changed person.

Presto!

The magic in Out of the Bottle tales is used as a vehicle—a convenient, clever, and thought-provoking way to illustrate a universal truth that we all could stand to learn: we are pretty dang great as we are. No magic required!

Because once the magic is bestowed upon our hero, they eventually have to learn that they didn't need it after all! Which is why you don't see a lot of "other world" fantasy or sci-fi novels in this genre. This genre isn't about exploring a new, fantastical world like in the Harry Potter series, the Lord of the Rings series, the Chronicles of Narnia, or a Song of Ice and Fire series (*A Game of Thrones*). Most of the heroes in the Out of the Bottle genre come from our world and are *temporarily* gifted (or cursed!) with magic. They're like us! And that's what makes them so much fun to read about.

Although this "touched by magic" genre is typically seen more in movies than in books (famous examples being *The Nutty Professor*; *Big*; *13 Going on 30*; *Freaky Friday*; *Bruce Almighty*; *The Mask*; *Liar, Liar*; *Shallow Hal*; and *Groundhog Day*), it's been done successfully in novels as well. And interestingly enough, the genre tends to be more popular in books for younger readers (like *The Indian in the Cupboard* by Lynne Reid Banks, *The Swap* by Megan Shull, *11 Birthdays* by Wendy Mass, *Before I Fall* by Lauren Oliver, and *If I Stay* by Gayle Forman), namely because magic and granted wishes tends to appeal particularly to kids and teens. But that doesn't mean adults can't join in the fun as well. Because who doesn't enjoy a little twist of magic, a little bending of the rules, or an answer to the universal question, "What if?"

Some favorites of this genre (of the nonkid variety) include *Twenties Girl* by Sophie Kinsella, *Landline* by Rainbow Rowell, and of course one of the most beloved classics of all time, *A Christmas Carol* by Charles Dickens. Even Oscar Wilde dabbled in some Out of the Bottle-ness of his own when he penned his famed classic novel *The Picture of Dorian Gray*.

Regardless of the intended audience, Out of the Bottle stories all share three commonalities: (1) a **hero deserving of the magic**, (2) a **spell** (or touch of magic), and (3) a **lesson**. Let's take a closer look at these.

Whether your hero is an underdog in desperate need of some magical intervention, like in *Twenties Girl,* or an unlikable grouch or arrogant jerk who needs to be taught a lesson with a nice little curse, like in *A Christmas Carol*, the hero must deserve this magic. And our Out of the Bottle hero must be properly matched with their bottle.

We readers need to immediately grasp and understand why *this* hero is getting *this* magic. And not only do we need to understand, we need to root for it! After the amazing job that Charles Dickens does setting up the awful miser Ebenezer Scrooge in *A Christmas Carol*, there's no way we're not totally on board when those three Christmas ghosts turn up and show that old grouch what's what. Conversely, when the poor, down-on-her-luck, recently dumped Lara Lington in *Twenties Girl* gets visited by the ghost of her 105-year-old Aunt Sadie, who helps Lara sort out her life, we get it. We're there, cheering her on. We *want* this for Lara just as much as she does.

So that's your first question when penning an Out of the Bottle: Why does this hero deserve this magic in their life? Are they a tread-upon Cinderella type who just can't catch a break (also called an **empowerment** story)? Or do they more resemble one of the wicked stepsisters who desperately needs a reality check (also called a **come-uppance** story)? Either way, make sure the reader *gets* it. Set up your hero so that when the magic strikes (usually at the Catalyst beat), we are saying, "Oh yeah, they *totally* deserve this!"

A word of caution, however: comeuppance stories can be harder to pull off than empowerment stories. When you have an unlikable hero, it's much easier for a reader to get prematurely turned off by the character and put the book down before the fun stuff even begins. Even though this meanie is eventually going to get what's coming to them, you don't want to lose your reader before you have a chance to give your character their much-needed kick in the booty. This is where a **save-the-cat** moment can really *save* your novel (see what I did there?). Give your hero *something* that is redeemable up front, ideally before the Catalyst beat and preferably within the first ten to twenty pages. Even the biggest nitwits on the planet have something about them that's worth saving. Show us why we should invest our precious time watching *this* hero transform. Prove to us early on that even though they don't look like much now, just you wait; they've got hidden depth. They're worth the pages.

Next up, in our Out of the Bottle checklist, you'll need a little bit of magic, of course! This is called the *spell* or the touch of magic. What exactly *is* the magic of this magical tale? Is it a flapper-dressed, Charleston-dancing ghost (*Twenties Girl*)? Is it an out-of-body experience (*If I Stay*)? Is it a magic landline phone that can call the past (*Landline*)? Or maybe it's a day that keeps repeating itself over and over (*11 Birthdays* and *Before I Fall*). Whatever it is, make sure it's front and center in Act 2 of your novel. After all, it's the whole premise of the story. This magical *thang* is probably going to be promised to readers on the back of the book or in the online description, so make sure you deliver on that promise!

Whether your hero wishes for the magic themselves or the magic is thrust upon them, make sure the spell itself is unique! Make it interesting, and fun, and exciting. This will be your novel's hook.

It's important to note that you don't have to spend a lot of time on *how* the magic works. The *why* is important (Why is this hero being bestowed with this magic?); the how (that is, the mechanics) less so. These stories are not really *about* the magic itself, but more what the hero gets out of that magic. So don't waste pages explaining the ins and outs of the spell or taking us down long-winded rabbit holes of explanation. In *Twenties Girl* the magic is simply introduced and dealt with quickly. "I don't know how it works!" says Lara's Great-Aunt Sadie. "I just think about where I want to be and I'm there" (page 73). And in *The Indian in the Cupboard*, we simply know that the cupboard is magic and it brings Little Bear, Omri's toy Indian figure, to life. Lynne Reid Banks doesn't go into much more detail than that!

More important than the how are the *rules* of the magic. Yes, even though it's magic, and even though it goes against the laws of nature, you still have to have rules. *And* you have stick to them, no matter how tempting it might be to play around and change things up at will to suit your plot. Remember that readers are going to have to willingly suspend disbelief in order to be pulled into your fantastical tale. They're going to have to say, "Well, that's impossible, but what the hey! Sounds like a good read!" But you only get one chance to do that. And if you cheat your readers by establishing the rules of the magic up front and then changing them further down the road, your readers will feel betrayed, and you will lose them. Readers of the Out of the Bottle genre dive into the novel knowing it's not going to follow the basic laws of nature, but they trust you to do it well. So don't betray that trust.

And finally, the third thing you'll need when crafting your out-of-this-world Out of the Bottle is a *lesson*. How is the hero transformed by this magic?

In the end, all heroes of this genre must realize something very important: that it's not the magic that will fix their lives for good. It's the heroes *themselves* who need to do that. The magic just showed them *what* needed to be fixed. That is the essence of the Out of the Bottle genre.

Although it's always nice to get a little shortcut in life—use magic to sweep all your problems under the rug—in the end, we all know it's *cheating*. And if the magic were the ultimate solution to the problems, what would we readers have to resonate with? We know that magic is never going to happen to *us*. Which is why most Out of the Bottle stories include some kind of moral or lesson about reality and humanity. Basically, that they're both pretty awesome. Being human has its advantages, too. And it turns out magic doesn't solve the *real* life problems. It was just a fun distraction for a while.

That's also why most Out of the Bottle heroes eventually have an Act 3 beat in which they have to **do it without the magic**. This is usually some big Finale moment when the hero proves, once and for all, that they didn't need that silly old magic to complete their transformation. They've got that part covered all on their own.

Because in the end, the true magic lies inside of *us*.

To recap: If you're thinking of writing an Out of the Bottle novel, make sure your story includes these three essential ingredients:

- **A HERO DESERVING OF THE MAGIC:** Whether you're empowering an underdog or delivering a comeuppance to a worthy recipient, make sure it's clear to the reader that this hero needs *this* specific supernatural boost.

- **A SPELL OR TOUCH OF MAGIC:** Regardless of how the magic comes to be (via a person, place, thing, or other), make sure you're setting up this illogical thing with logical rules that you stick to, lest you risk betraying your reader's trust.

- **A LESSON:** What does your hero learn from this magic and how do they ultimately fix things the right way (without the magic)?

POPULAR OUT OF THE BOTTLE NOVELS THROUGH TIME:

A Christmas Carol by Charles Dickens
The Picture of Dorian Gray by Oscar Wilde
Mary Poppins by P. L. Travers
Freaky Friday by Mary Rodgers
The Indian in the Cupboard by Lynne Reid Banks
Airhead by Meg Cabot
If I Stay by Gayle Forman
Twenties Girl by Sophie Kinsella (*beat sheet included below*)
11 Birthdays by Wendy Mass
IQ84 by Haruki Murakami
Before I Fall by Lauren Oliver
The Ocean at the End of the Lane by Neil Gaiman
Landline by Rainbow Rowell
The Swap by Megan Shull
Parallel by Lauren Miller

TWENTIES GIRL

BY: Sophie Kinsella
STC GENRE: Out of the Bottle
BOOK GENRE: General fiction
TOTAL PAGES: 435 (Dial Press Trade Paperback, 2009)

Made famous by her hilarious best-selling Shopaholic series, Sophie Kinsella is a modern queen of comedy in the book world. Her books have been translated into over thirty languages. *Twenties Girl*, about a twentysomething girl hilariously haunted by the twenties-girl ghost of her great-aunt Sadie, is (thus far) Kinsella's first novel to include a supernatural twist. The ghostly "curse" that hero Lara experiences and the unexpected life lessons acquired from said curse place this tale in the Out of the Bottle genre.

1. Opening Image (pages 1–10)

Twentysomething Lara Lington and her parents are preparing to go to a funeral for a 105-year-old great-aunt whom no one in the family really knew. But Lara is far more preoccupied by the list of lies she's recently told her parents. Like how her new start-up business is going extremely well and how her new business partner is super reliable and trustworthy. In reality, the opposite is true.

This list tells us a lot about Lara and the **things that need fixing** in her life. She also lies to her parents about being completely over her ex-boyfriend, Josh, who has just dumped her, when actually she's secretly praying they'll get back together (wants).

Lara's fibs tell us a lot about our hero and her flaws: she's the kind of girl who can't move on from her mistakes but instead tries to hide them from her family.

2. Theme Stated (page 8)

When Lara is talking (and lying) to her parents about her ex-boyfriend, her dad kindly tells her, "When you break up with someone, it's easy to look backward and think life would be perfect if you got back together" (page 8).

Lara's transformative journey is all about moving on. Rejecting the delusions she has about what her life *should* look like, and starting to enjoy what life *does* look like. To do that, she'll need more self-confidence. She'll need to become bolder and more courageous.

3. Setup (pages 10–25)

The family attends the funeral of Sadie Lancaster, Lara's 105-year-old great-aunt. Outside the funeral parlor, Lara bumps into her Uncle Bill, who is well known for founding Lington's Coffee, a massively successful company that he famously created from twenty pence he found in his pocket when he was broke. Now he does seminars called "Two Little Coins," teaching other entrepreneurs how to emulate his success.

Lara tries to ask him for help with her new head-hunting company (that's been failing miserably since her business partner, Natalie, left), but Bill shuts her down.

Then, after embarrassingly going into the wrong funeral, Lara finds her way into the right room, only to find there's hardly anyone there and no one even brought any photographs of Sadie. It seems no one knew Sadie Lancaster at all.

4. Catalyst (pages 25–28)

During the funeral, Lara hears an unfamiliar voice asking where her necklace is. Then she sees a girl, around the same age as Lara, sitting in the chair in front of her. Who is that?

When the girl tries to poke Lara, her finger goes *through* her. Freaky! The girl introduces herself as Sadie Lancaster, Lara's dead great-aunt.

5. Debate (pages 29–72)

Like most Out of the Bottle stories, the Debate is a reality check. *Am I dreaming? Is this real?* Lara is convinced she's hallucinating a twentysomething version of her great-aunt. But as hard as she tries to rid herself of the vision, Sadie just won't go away. In fact, she's *really* annoying. She keeps screaming for Lara to stop the funeral. She can't be buried until she finds a missing necklace. Lara finally complies, quickly making up an excuse to postpone the funeral: she has reason to believe Sadie was murdered and the police still need to investigate. Everyone thinks Lara has gone crazy—including Lara.

The next day, Lara convinces herself that Sadie is a figment of her subconscious. But then at lunch, Sadie teaches Lara how to properly eat an oyster, and Lara realizes her subconscious doesn't know how to eat an oyster. Sadie might actually be a real ghost!

6. Break Into 2 (pages 73–74)

Sadie continues to hound Lara about her missing necklace, claiming that she can't "rest" until she's found it and she needs Lara to help her look for it. Lara makes her a deal: "If I find your necklace for you, will you go away and leave me in peace?" (page 73).

Sadie agrees, and now we are officially in Act 2: the world of Lara and her magical twenties girl ghost.

7. Fun and Games (pages 75–211)

The search for the necklace brings Lara to Sadie's former nursing home, where the employees believe the necklace was accidentally sold in a fund-raising raffle. Lara goes home with a daunting list of names and phone numbers of people to contact who might have it.

While at the nursing home, Lara discovers that a mysterious man named Charles Reece came to visit Sadie before she died. Sadie doesn't remember Charles Reece, but Lara chalks it up to the stroke Sadie had years before her death, which severely affected her memory. They later learn that "Charles Reece" was actually Bill Lington, Lara's famous uncle, and that *he* took the necklace from Sadie. But what does rich Uncle Bill want with an old woman's worthless necklace?

The **promise of the premise** of this novel is the hilarious interludes of Sadie and Lara. Sadie is everything Lara is not: spunky, bold, and daring. In comparison to Sadie, Lara is a bit dull, and Sadie never misses an opportunity to tell her so. As most Out of the Bottle magic is intended to do, Sadie will help Lara realize her flaws so she can fix them herself.

As the two search for Sadie's necklace, they continue to ruffle each other's feathers, but ultimately form a friendship. Hilarity ensues as Sadie and Lara culture clash. They're both twentysomething girls but from very different eras with very different ideas about men, relationships, and living life.

Sadie points out that Lara shouldn't be lamenting her ex, Josh. She should be getting back out there and getting on with her life. In many ways Sadie is way more modern than Lara. On page 94, Sadie restates the theme when she says to Lara, "Darling, when things go wrong in life this is what you do. You lift your chin, put on a ravishing smile, mix yourself a little cocktail—and out you go."

During this Fun and Games, we also come to understand the rules of the magic, which Kinsella sets up effectively and uses to further the plot. For instance, we learn that no one else can see Sadie except Lara; Sadie can go wherever she wants and wear whatever she wants; and the most unique and creative rule in Kinsella's supernatural tale is Ghost Sadie's ability to subtly *persuade* people to do and say things by screaming comically loudly in their ear. Learning these rules gives Lara an idea. She sends Sadie to spy on her ex-boyfriend, Josh, to try to figure out why he dumped her so she can fix the relationship. Sadie doesn't approve, but she reluctantly agrees.

This is Lara **fixing things the wrong way**. She's using her magic "curse" to improve her life, instead of learning the theme, moving on, and fixing things the right way. Lara's wants are to get back together with Josh, so this drives the first half of Act 2 forward. Lara then convinces Sadie to use her powers of persuasion to give Josh a little nudge. She *knows* Josh still loves her, but she wants Sadie to prompt him a bit so he remembers. As we continue the **upward path** toward the Midpoint, Josh confesses that he loves Lara and made a huge mistake by breaking up with her. Lara is ecstatic. It's exactly what she wanted.

As she gets to know Sadie better, Lara learns that Sadie once had a special boy in her life too—the one who got away. He was a painter named Stephen Nettleton who died young, but not before painting a beautiful portrait of Sadie that was later lost in a house fire. Sadie hasn't really been in love since.

Lara also uses Sadie's help with her failing business, sending Sadie into an office building to solve a problem with a client. While inside the office building, however, Sadie spots a beautiful man named Ed whom she wants to date. Unfortunately, Ghost Sadie can't go on dates.

But Lara can . . .

8. B Story (pages 111–120)

Ed is the B Story character and the love interest of the novel. Sadie convinces Lara to ask Ed out on a date so she can third-wheel and live vicariously through Lara. Lara thinks she's crazy, but Sadie guilt-trips her into agreeing.

In a hilarious scene in Ed's office conference room, Lara asks Ed on a date in front of his entire staff. And with Sadie yelling in Ed's ear, Ed feels obliged to say yes, even though he has no idea why.

Later, for their date, Sadie makes Lara dress up like a 1920s flapper and act just like Sadie would, completely embarrassing Lara. She convinces herself she doesn't care though, since she's only doing this for Sadie and she's still in love with Josh.

But slowly Lara will come to fall for Ed (and Ed will fall for her too), helping her get over Josh and move on with her life (theme!)—just as Sadie said she should.

Ed represents the theme in that he, too, has had trouble getting over an ex. It's held him back significantly. In recognizing this flaw in Ed, Lara will eventually recognize this same flaw in herself.

9. Midpoint (pages 231–264)

Lara attends a huge business dinner with Ed, with lots of important guests (**Midpoint party**). She uses Sadie to successfully network and help her floundering business, and by the end of the night she has a promising new lead.

Lara now seems all-around victorious. She and Josh are back together (wants) and her business is on the verge of thriving. Of course, it's a **false victory** because Lara had to use magic to achieve all of it, particularly getting back together with Josh, whom she's clearly not meant to be with.

After the party, **A and B stories cross** and emotional **stakes are raised** as she has a heart-to-heart conversation with Ed and learns about his painful breakup.

Sadie persuades Ed to take Lara dancing. Even though Sadie is still pushing them together, it's Lara who, entirely on her own, asks Ed out again, this time to go sightseeing. It seems Lara is already starting to fall for Ed, even if she hasn't quite realized it yet.

10. Bad Guys Close In (pages 212–319)

Things start heading downhill for Lara after the party: Josh starts acting strangely toward her (is he changing his mind?). She comes close to getting Sadie's necklace back but loses it at the last minute. Lara's former business partner, Natalie (who had left Lara in the lurch), comes waltzing back into the office and starts taking credit for all the progress Lara has made with the business. And tensions are high between Sadie and Lara. Sadie is still highly disapproving of Lara's getting back together with Josh; Lara and Sadie fight, and Sadie declares that Josh got back together with Lara only because Sadie convinced him to do it.

Lara realizes Sadie is right after an awkward dinner with Josh where he can't come up with one good reason why they're back together. Lara breaks it off with Josh, proving that she's getting closer to learning the theme.

Meanwhile, Lara and Ed continue to bond during a fun sightseeing trip. Ed confesses that he likes her, but Lara can't bring herself to believe it. She guiltily thinks that Ed is still under Sadie's spell, just like Josh was. But during a romantic moment on the London Eye, Ed kisses Lara, and she realizes *she* has feelings for him.

Unfortunately, Sadie sees them kissing and becomes furious. Ed was supposed to be *hers*. Lara tries to apologize to Sadie, but only ends up looking crazy in front of Ed, who has no idea who she's talking to.

Sadie falls into a depression when she realizes she'll never fall in love again and no man will ever want her again because she's dead. She also laments that her life meant nothing. She left no mark. No one came to her funeral.

11. All Is Lost (pages 319–329)

The next morning, Natalie reveals that she spoke to Ed and told him that Lara was headhunting him—and not really interested in him. When Lara tries to call Ed to set the record straight, he's extremely cold and rebukes Lara for playing him to get ahead in the business world. Lara yells at Natalie for what she did and leaves the company.

Now, Lara has lost Sadie, Ed, and her business—all in less than twenty-four hours.

12. Dark Night of the Soul (pages 330–359)

Lara looks everywhere for Sadie, hoping to make amends with her. But the longer she searches, the more she falls into despair. In a mirror of the Debate, Lara again wonders whether Sadie really was real or Lara had made her up.

Lara's search leads her to Sadie's home town, where she visits an old vicarage and discovers something astonishing: a print of a painting depicting an "anonymous" young girl in her twenties, painted by a very famous painter whom she soon discovers was Sadie's lost lover. This is a print of the painting Sadie thought was lost in the fire! In the portrait, Sadie is her twentysomething self and is wearing the dragonfly necklace they've been searching for.

The woman guiding the tour of the vicarage explains that this is a copy of the famous painting called *Girl with the Necklace*. The original is hanging in the London Portrait Gallery, and no one knows who the subject was. But Lara does! (**Dark Night epiphany.**)

All of this time, Sadie felt like she'd left no mark on the world and died completely unnoticed and unloved. But the truth is quite the opposite: Sadie is famous, and her portrait is admired by millions!

13. Break Into 3 (pages 360–361)

After all Sadie's done for Lara, now it's time for Lara to help Sadie. But with Sadie still missing, she'll have to **do it without the magic**. To get Sadie acknowledged as the subject of the painting, Lara goes to the London Portrait Gallery to talk to the collections manager, Malcolm.

14. Finale (pages 362–425)

POINT 1: GATHERING THE TEAM. As a team of one, Lara gathers information. Malcolm tells her they purchased the painting in the 1980s from a contractually anonymous seller. He won't tell Lara who sold him the painting.

POINT 2: EXECUTING THE PLAN. Lara has to let Sadie know that her painting wasn't lost in the fire and that she died a famous woman. Lara finally finds Sadie at a jazz festival and they have an emotional reunion. But before Lara can tell Sadie about the painting, Sadie points out Ed (whom she persuaded to come there) and tells Lara to go talk to him (Sadie's way of apologizing for what happened at the London Eye).

As Ed and Lara reconcile, Sadie tries to convince Ed to do something by screaming in his ear. This time he rejects Sadie's influence, proving that he really loves Lara on his own. Without the magic.

Lara explains about the painting to both Sadie *and* Ed. She takes them both to the London Portrait Gallery to see it.

POINT 3: HIGH TOWER SURPRISE. While at the gallery, Lara and Ed bump into Malcolm, and Lara tricks him into pulling out the sales contract for the painting so Ghost Sadie can surreptitiously read it.

Sadie reveals that the seller was Bill Lington. Uncle Bill! He never told Sadie (his aunt) the painting was salvaged from the fire and he'd sold it to the National Portrait Gallery for 500,000 pounds!

POINT 4: DIG DEEP DOWN. Lara puts all the pieces together: Bill Lington didn't start Lington's Coffee with twenty pence. He started it with 500,000 pounds that he stole from his own aunt. The "Two Little Coins" seminar that has made him famous is a sham. And he wanted the necklace so badly because after Sadie lost her memory, it was the only thing linking Sadie to the portrait and revealing him as the fraud he is.

Lara vows to avenge Sadie and give Bill his comeuppance.

POINT 5: THE EXECUTION OF THE NEW PLAN. Because of her ghostly abilities to go wherever she wants, Sadie learns that Uncle Bill is on holiday in the south of France. Sadie and Lara set off.

Lara finally has to prove her newfound confidence and self-assurance when she confronts Bill about the necklace, forcing him to come clean to the public about how he really started the coffee company and giving Sadie and her painting credit for his success. Now everyone knows that the subject of *Girl with the Necklace* is Sadie Lancaster. She's left her mark on the world—just as she wanted.

(continued on page 226)

Cat's Eye View

For quick reference, here's a brief overview of this novel's beat sheet.

1. **OPENING IMAGE:** Twentysomething Lara lies to her parents about everything that's going wrong in her life, including a failing head-hunting business and relationship. Though she swears she's over her ex-boyfriend, she's clearly not.

2. **THEME STATED:** "When you break up with someone, it's easy to look backward and think life would be perfect if you got back together." Laura's internal story is about moving on from the past and embracing her life as it is, not as she *thinks* it should be.

3. **SETUP:** Lara attends the funeral of her 105-year-old great-aunt Sadie, a woman she never knew. The funeral parlor is depressingly empty. We meet Lara's uncle, Bill Lington, a famous businessman worth millions.

4. **CATALYST:** Sadie's ghost appears (as a twentysomething flapper girl) and starts talking to Lara.

5. **DEBATE:** Is it real? Is Lara going crazy? She convinces herself she must be hallucinating.

6. **BREAK INTO 2:** Finally admitting that Sadie is a real ghost, Lara agrees to help Sadie find a lost necklace.

7. **B STORY:** During her escapades to find the necklace, Lara meets Ed, a man whom Sadie falls in love with first and forces Lara to date so she can live vicariously through her.

8. **FUN AND GAMES:** Sadie and Lara (who are very different) butt heads about love and life as they try to track down the necklace. But Lara soon discovers she can use Sadie (the magic) to improve her life (fixing things the wrong way).

9. **MIDPOINT:** (false victory) Lara's life has drastically improved thanks to the magic (Sadie's ability to spy on people and persuade people to do things). Lara's business is on the upswing, and she's back together with her ex-boyfriend, Josh.

10. **BAD GUYS CLOSE IN:** Lara realizes that Josh isn't really that into her (Sadie just persuaded him to get back together with Lara). They still haven't found the necklace. And Lara's former business partner reappears, trying to take credit for all of Lara's recent successes. Then Sadie sees Lara kissing Ed (B Story) and storms off, furious.

11. **ALL IS LOST:** Lara's business partner tells Ed that Lara was only "headhunting" him and doesn't really care about him. Lara walks out on her new business. She's now lost Ed, her company, and Sadie.

12. **DARK NIGHT OF THE SOUL:** Lara searches unsuccessfully for Sadie. In Sadie's hometown, she discovers that Sadie is the unknown subject of a very famous (and valuable) portrait.

13. **BREAK INTO 3:** Lara vows to help Sadie discover how valuable she really is. But as Sadie is still missing, she'll have to do it without the magic.

14. **FINALE:** Lara tracks down the famous painting at the National Portrait Gallery and discovers they bought it from her Uncle Bill (who stole the painting from Sadie). After finding Sadie and reconciling with her (and Ed), Lara and Sadie together get revenge on Bill. They find the necklace, and now Sadie can finally rest.

15. **FINAL IMAGE:** Lara (now together with Ed) hosts another (better) funeral for Sadie, the famous woman from the painting. It's packed full of admirers. The two twenties girls have each helped each other move on.

Lara starts a new head-hunting business—all on her own—and later a large envelope arrives from Paris (the last known whereabouts of Sadie's necklace). Inside is the dragonfly necklace.

After a tearful goodbye with Ghost Sadie, Lara goes to the funeral parlor and puts the necklace around real Sadie's neck. When she reemerges from the funeral home, Ghost Sadie is gone.

Both twenties girls have moved on.

15. Final Image (pages 426–435)

A second (and much improved) funeral for Sadie is held. This one is elegant and packed with people, all admirers of Sadie and the painting, and all wearing 1920s outfits. Lara makes a touching speech about Sadie and the person she was in life. Unlike at the first funeral, Sadie is now known and understood.

WHY IS THIS AN OUT OF THE BOTTLE?

Twenties Girl contains all three elements of a successful Out of the Bottle story:

- **A HERO DESERVING OF THE MAGIC:** At the outset, Lara's life is a mess. She's hung up on an ex-boyfriend who wants nothing to do with her, her business is failing, and she completely lacks confidence. She's in desperate need of some magical intervention—and Ghost Sadie is just what the doctor ordered.

- **A SPELL OR TOUCH OF MAGIC:** The ghost of Sadie Lancaster is unique and entertaining. Sophie Kinsella takes a typical haunting story and turns it hilariously on its head, creating a whole new set of rules that give Lara the magical boost she so desperately needs.

- **A LESSON:** Sadie is everything Lara is not: free-spirited, bold, and adventurous. She teaches Lara an important lesson about life, love, and the power of a good flapper dress. Through Sadie, Lara learns to be confident in her own skin and move on from the things that are holding her back in life.

Golden Fleece
Road Trips and Quests and Heists, Oh My!

It's not the destination, it's the journey!

How many times have we heard this tired old cliché? Well, cliché or not, it's often the truth! And never more so than in the Golden Fleece genre, named after an ancient Greek myth—Jason, the Argonauts, and the Golden Fleece. It's basically about this guy, Jason, who goes on an adventurous journey with a bunch of other guys (including Hercules, because you *always* want him on your team) to capture the Golden Fleece, which will supposedly make Jason king. Obviously, along the way Jason and his crew encounter all sorts of obstacles and challenges, thus establishing one of the most beloved story types of all time: the road trip.

Because we all know road trips aren't about the final destination, whether that be a landmark, prize, trophy, or other physical thing. No, the road trip is about the great adventure! The quest! The pit stops, the detours, the *drama*!

But most of all, road trips are about what we discover along the way . . . about *ourselves*. At least that's what any great road trip novel *should* be about. But before you turn the page and continue to the next genre, thinking, *I'm not writing a road trip story*, you may want to hold on for a second. Sure, there are many great road trip novels that fall into this genre—like *The Grapes of Wrath* by John Steinbeck, *As I Lay Dying* by William Faulkner, *The Wonderful Wizard of Oz* by L. Frank Baum, and *The Adventures of Huckleberry Finn* by Mark Twain—but there are also several other non–road trip varieties that also fit into this adventurous genre. Under the Golden Fleece umbrella, we also get the pleasure of reading heist stories, in which the "road trip" is usually the road leading up to the great scheme and the third act is usually the heist itself. Some well-known examples include *Six of Crows* by Leigh Bardugo, *Heist Society* by Ally Carter, *The Great Train Robbery* by Michael Crichton, and *Prince of Thieves* (later adapted as the movie *The Town*) by Chuck Hogan.

The Golden Fleece genre also includes Epic Quest novels, where the "road trip" is a journey to some far-off treasure, prize, or birthright—like *The Fellowship of the Ring* by J. R. R. Tolkien and *A Game of Thrones* by George R. R. Martin. (Apparently, you need two Rs in your name to be successful in the quest genre.)

Basically, a Golden Fleece story features (1) a **road**, (2) a **team**, and (3) a **prize**.

The *road* is the setting for our journey. The hero and their team must traverse it to fulfill their quest or mission. But it doesn't have to be an actual road—it can be an ocean, like in *The Old Man and the Sea* by Ernest Hemingway. It can be a fantasy world, like in *The Fellowship of the Ring*, *A Game of Thrones*, *Alice's Adventures in Wonderland* by Lewis Carroll, and *The Wonderful Wizard of Oz*. The road can be another dimension or planetary system, or even a virtual world like in *Ready Player One* by Ernest Cline. It can even be the seven layers of hell, like in *Inferno*, the first part of Dante's epic poem *The Divine Comedy*. Or the road can be metaphorical.

As long as this road demarcates *growth*. Because that is the defining characteristic of a Golden Fleece: the ability to chart your hero's transformation along the journey. If you think you might be writing a Golden Fleece, ask yourself, Is my hero (or heroes) going somewhere definite, and can I track their progress in some way?

Novels that fall into the Golden Fleece genre sometimes employ clever devices to help the reader keep tabs on where the hero is over the course of the adventure. Like the scoreboard in *Ready Player One*, letting Wade (and the reader!) know when other players have found the keys and cleared the gates in Halliday's epic Easter egg hunt. Or the fun scrapbook element in Morgan Matson's young adult road trip novel, *Amy and Roger's Epic Detour*, which shows us where Amy and Roger have been and what they've been doing along the way.

Also common in Golden Fleece stories is a **road apple**—something that stops the journey cold, usually right when victory is in sight. It's a literal (or figurative) roadblock for the hero and their team to get around, forcing them to look more closely at their strategy, repair any bridges they've burned among themselves, and dig deep down to find their true skills and strengths.

The *team* that joins our hero on their quest can be as small or as big as you want. The Buddy Fleece is a popular subgenre of the Golden Fleece, in which the team consists of only two people, like in *Of Mice and Men* by John Steinbeck, *The Road* by Cormac McCarthy, and *The Adventures of Huckleberry Finn*.

The team can also consist of three or more members, like in *The Wonderful Wizard of Oz, Ready Player One*, and *The Grapes of Wrath*.

And in one Golden Fleece variant, dubbed the Solo Fleece, the team consists of only one person who usually ends up meeting several different helpers along the way. Like *Alice's Adventures in Wonderland, The Five People You Meet in Heaven* by Mitch Albom, or *Gulliver's Travels* by Jonathan Swift.

Regardless of team size, Golden Fleece stories often contain a B Story about friendship or love. Who the hero takes along on the journey (or is forced to travel with) is a big decision for the writer, because not only should one—or all—of these people play a role in your B Story (internal/spiritual story), but they also should bring to the table (or the road, as it were) a certain skill or talent that will be necessary along the journey. This can be a skill of either brains, brawn, or heart, but it should be something the hero lacks at the beginning of the novel, thus creating the need for this particular teammate. For example, the various team members who make up Kaz's crew in *Six of Crows* by Leigh Bardugo each help accomplish the heist with a specific skill (like acrobatics, demolition, even Grisha magic!).

Note too that when you set up a very large team (especially in heist novels), each member of the team should be introduced in a unique and interesting way. Many writers struggle to really get this right, but if you can do it well, your reader is in for a treat. And since getting all these people into the story can take up quite a few pages, it's important that those introductions be stellar and brilliant. Otherwise, you risk losing the reader before the quest for the fleece even begins!

Finally, the *prize*: the Golden Fleece itself. What are this hero and team after? What awaits them at the end of this long, daunting, and awesome journey? Although the prize must be compelling and appealing enough to kick-start the journey (and convincing enough for the reader to go along for the ride), in the end the prize doesn't really matter. It's not as important as the journey itself.

By the time Wade in *Ready Player One* actually finds the Easter egg hidden within the Oasis, he's already learned so much about himself and the world, he almost doesn't even care about winning the grand prize anymore. Of course, he still wants it, but it doesn't hold the same weight as it did at the start of the novel. Because it's not the most important element of Wade's journey.

Even so, the prize should be something *primal*. Something we can all relate to. Like going home (*The Wizard of Oz, Alice's Adventures in Wonderland*), securing a treasure (*Ready Player One, Six of Crows*), freedom (*The Adventures of Huckleberry Finn*), prosperity (*The Grapes of Wrath*), a crown (*The Selection* by Keira Cass), reaching an important destination (*Amy and Roger's Epic Detour, As I Lay Dying*), or gaining a birthright (*A Game of Thrones*).

The primal prize is what sets the story in motion—often tied in with the Catalyst beat—but it often has less value and meaning once it's actually achieved (or not achieved!). It's more of a device to get your team on the road and the story into action. In the end, your hero or heroes may not even get the prize, and that's OK! Because that's not what the story is really *about*.

One of the most resonating moments of this genre is when your hero (and readers) realizes that the treasure they're after pales in comparison to the real treasure they've gained along the way: love, friendship, teamwork, or whatever your theme/B Story might be.

For this reason, the Golden Fleece can be tricky to plot (there's a good reason there are so few heist novels out there). You must include milestones for your hero to reach along the way—usually represented in the form of people and incidents that the team encounters. And although these milestones may *seem* unconnected at first glance, in fact, in the grand scheme of the story, they *must* be connected. In *The Grapes of Wrath*, the Joads meet several people along their journey to find work in California: the Wilsons, Floyd Knowles, Timothy and Wilkie Wallace, and the Wainwrights, among others. Although these people are unrelated to each other, they are connected in the story as a whole. They all represent the theme of unification. People helping people. It's the very theme that Tom Joad will learn by the end of the story when he fulfills his destiny of unifying the migrant workers.

Each milestone of your Golden Fleece story must move your hero closer to their true end goal: Internal growth! Transformation! Real Change (with a capital C!). And how each milestone or incident affects the hero is not just plot, my friend. That is pure structure *gold*. It's the masterful interweaving of the A Story (the milestones) and B Story (the internal effect they have on the hero), until you reach a satisfying, transformational conclusion.

To recap: If you're thinking of writing a Golden Fleece novel, make sure your story includes these three essential ingredients:

- **A ROAD:** spanning oceans, miles, time, or even across the street, so long as it demarcates growth and tracks the progress of your story in some way. It often includes a road apple that stops the journey in its tracks.

- **A TEAM (OR BUDDY):** to guide the hero along the way. Usually, it's those who represent the things the hero lacks: skill, experience, or attitude. In the case of a Solo Fleece, the team usually consists of various helpers along the way.

- **A PRIZE:** something primal that's sought after—getting home, securing a treasure, freedom, reaching an important destination, or gaining a birthright.

POPULAR GOLDEN FLEECE NOVELS THROUGH TIME:

The Canterbury Tales by Chaucer
Gulliver's Travels by Jonathan Swift
Alice's Adventures in Wonderland by Lewis Carroll
The Adventures of Huckleberry Finn by Mark Twain
Heart of Darkness by Joseph Conrad
The Wonderful World of Oz by L. Frank Baum
As I Lay Dying by William Faulkner
The Grapes of Wrath by John Steinbeck
The Fellowship of the Ring by J. R. R. Tolkien
On the Road by Jack Kerouac
The Great Train Robbery by Michael Crichton
A Game of Thrones by George R. R. Martin
The Five People You Meet in Heaven by Mitch Albom
Prince of Thieves by Chuck Hogan
The Road by Cormac McCarthy
Amy and Roger's Epic Detour by Morgan Matson
Heist Society by Ally Carter
Ready Player One by Ernest Cline (*beat sheet included on the following page*)
The Selection by Kiera Cass
Six of Crows by Leigh Bardugo

READY PLAYER ONE

BY: Ernest Cline
STC GENRE: Golden Fleece
BOOK GENRE: Science fiction
TOTAL PAGES: 372 (Broadway Paperback Edition, 2011)

When this ode to 1980s pop culture hit bookstores in 2011, it took the world by storm, wowing gamers and nongamers alike with its taut plotting, creative world-building, and topical theme (reality versus virtual reality). It won multiple awards and received rave reviews from *Entertainment Weekly,* the *Boston Globe*, and *USA Today* (among others). No wonder Steven Spielberg agreed to direct the film adaptation.

In this Golden Fleece adventure novel, we join Wade and his team of fellow gamers on their quest to find a coveted Easter egg hidden inside a brilliantly imagined virtual reality world.

1. Opening Image (pages 1–9)

We meet Wade (aka "Parzival"), who explains that the world of 2045, in which this novel is set, is not a great place. A global energy crisis has brought about catastrophic climate change, famine, poverty, and disease. We learn that humanity's salvation—or at the very least, escape—is a massive multiplayer online virtual reality video game (the biggest in history) called the *Oasis*, which almost everyone on Earth plays religiously. In fact, most people spend all of their time inside the Oasis; some even work and go to school there.

We also learn about the prize of this Golden Fleece tale: an Easter egg hidden somewhere inside the Oasis by the founder himself— James Halliday—before his recent death. Whoever finds it will win $40 billion and ownership of the entire Oasis. Wade lays out the details of our Golden Fleece quest by explaining that there are three hidden keys (Copper, Jade, and Crystal) that open up three hidden gates, and that the Easter egg is behind the Third Gate. When the Easter egg was first announced, five years before the story begins, the world obviously went crazy trying to find the first key, but after years of no progress, the hype eventually dimmed. Until one player found the first key.

Our hero, Wade.

This first chapter is actually a hint at the Catalyst to come.

2. Setup (pages 10–69)

For the next fifty-nine pages we back up in time. The Setup tells the story of how Wade found the key, and the events leading up to that important moment, so that we can experience the discovery along with him. In these pages, we learn more about Wade and the rotten life he lives.

The following are among Wade's **things that need fixing** in real life:

- He lives in an overcrowded trailer park called the Portland Avenue Stacks.

- The world he inhabits is pretty much postapocalyptic.

- Orphaned, he lives with a horrible aunt who often steals his stuff and pawns it for money.

- Wade is overweight, acne-ridden, and socially awkward.

But in the Oasis, none of this matters. As his avatar, Parzival, Wade is much more confident and self-assured—and better looking. He can basically design his life however he wants. Which is why he spends most of his time in his hideout—an abandoned van near the stacks—where he's set up an Oasis console and can go about his virtual life undisturbed.

Also in the Setup, we see Wade at **home, work,** and **play.**

As we know, his home life is bleak. His work (for him, it's school) is done at a public school inside the Oasis. For play, Wade spends the majority of his time hunting for Halliday's Easter egg with his fellow "gunters" (egg hunters). In the Setup, we see Wade hanging out in a chat room with his best friend, Aech, where they talk about Wade's longtime crush, Art3mis (a gunter blogger he's never spoken to).

In the chat room, Wade and Aech get into yet another heated discussion about *Anorak's Almanac*, a journal left behind by Halliday that is believed to have clues to the whereabouts of the egg. And they talk about the novel's primary antagonist: an evil communications company called IOI, which pretty much runs everything in the world—except the Oasis. We learn that IOI has hired a huge team of gunters called "Sixers" to find the egg and secure the Oasis for IOI.

3. Theme Stated (page 45)

On page 45, one of Wade's gamer acquaintances, I-r0k, states the theme to Wade and his friend Aech: "you both obviously need to get a life." Even though this comes as a playful jab, it couldn't be more true for Wade. What's made very clear in this scene, as Wade shows off his knowledge of Halliday and '80s pop culture, is that Wade has no life outside of the Oasis and this Easter egg hunt. It's what's fueling him and giving him purpose. But by the end of the novel he'll learn that living in a video game is no way to live. At some point he has to face up to *reality* if he wants to truly be happy.

Wade's world marks a new era for humanity, in which almost everyone lives their lives inside a video game. With social media and the internet dominating our own lives, this premise is not too far-fetched for us to believe. So the theme of this novel hits home for any modern reader: Beware of the lure of false reality. Real life is always where it's at.

4. Catalyst (pages 69–70)

By page 69, we're almost caught up to the events described in the first chapter of the novel. Wade solves one of Halliday's riddles and figures out where the Copper Key is hidden. It's on the Oasis planet of Ludus, where Wade's public school is. Wade reasons that Halliday hid it there because he wanted a schoolkid to find it.

5. Debate (pages 70–76)

Immediately after Wade figures out where the key is hidden, the Debate question arises: *How do I get there?* The "tomb" where Wade suspects the key is hidden is on the other side of the planet, far away from where his public school is located, and he doesn't have enough money to teleport (walking would take too long). He gets the idea to use the public school system to get a teleportation voucher, by pretending to attend an "away" game for his school.

6. Break Into 2 (pages 77–86)

On page 77, Wade enters the Tomb of Horrors (a Dungeons and Dragons reference), where he believes the Copper Key to be, and effectively enters Act 2.

This is the upside-down world of Halliday's epic Easter egg hunt, filled with drama, intrigue, virtual battles, and '80s references galore!

In the tomb, Wade meets a virtual recording of Halliday's infamous avatar, Anorak, who tells him he has to defeat him at the '80s video game *Joust* in order to earn the Copper Key. In Wade's years of research trying to find the first key, he's practiced this game (and every other '80s video game), so he's prepared. He beats Halliday by finding the flaw in the artificial intelligence controlling Halliday's avatar and exploiting it (proving that Wade is a worthy contender for the prize). Wade is now the first person in the entire Oasis to have acquired the Copper Key, putting him at the top of the gunter scoreboard.

7. B Story (pages 87–99)

As Parzival leaves the Tomb of Horrors, victorious, he bumps into his longtime crush, Art3mis, the love interest and B Story of the novel. Although they start off as rival gunters, Art3mis will eventually teach Wade it's better to live in the real world than to hide in a virtual one. Because as Wade falls more and more in love with her throughout the course of the novel, he realizes that being with her avatar isn't enough. He wants to be with *her*.

Art3mis found the tomb weeks ago but has yet to beat Anorak at *Joust*. When Art3mis checks the scoreboard and sees Parzival's name at the top, she gets angry. She puts a barrier spell on him, trapping him for fifteen minutes. Even so, Wade can't help but give her some advice on how to win the game against Anorak, thus kicking off their tenuous relationship.

8. Fun and Games (pages 100–189)

The **promise of the premise** of this novel is the hunt for Halliday's Easter egg, and Ernest Cline definitely delivers on that promise. The Copper Key is engraved with a riddle that leads Wade to the First Gate, which Wade quickly clears by reenacting a scene from one of Halliday's favorite movies, *War Games*. At first it seems Wade is on an upward path, but his direction changes quickly as he struggles to solve the riddle leading to the Jade Key. And his Fun and Games quickly turns into a **downward path**. Art3mis clears the First Gate shortly after him, and, after a hint from Wade, his friend Aech's name jumps onto the scoreboard too. Meanwhile, Wade can't stop thinking about Art3mis (B Story), as the two exchange increasingly flirty messages.

Despite Wade's newfound fame as the first player to find the Copper Key, more players continue to clear the First Gate, and Wade soon finds himself back at square one, neck and neck with everyone else.

Things take a dive for Wade when he receives an invite to the IOI offices, where the evil head honcho, Sorrento, makes Wade an offer. If he leads a team of Sixers to Halliday's egg, they'll pay him a crapload of money. When he refuses, they threaten to kill him.

Scared, Wade logs out of the Oasis just as his trailer park explodes. If he weren't in his secret hideaway, he would be dead. That's when he realizes that IOI has access to confidential user information; otherwise they wouldn't have known where he lived.

Back inside the Oasis, Wade calls a meeting of the "high five" (the first five people to clear the gate) and warns them all to stay hidden. Even though they're each working separately to find the egg, this is Wade's Golden Fleece team: Art3mis, Aech, and two brothers from Japan, Daito and Shoto.

After IOI finds the Copper Key and the First Gate, Sorrento and other Sixers' names start appearing on the scoreboard. Wade knows he has to get out of Dodge and lay low. IOI can't know that he's still alive or they'll come after him again. He uses money from an endorsement offer to secure a fake identity and move into a new apartment, where he locks himself inside and vows to abandon the real world until he finds the egg. At this moment, with this vow, Wade is further than ever from learning his theme. But as he continues his flirtation with Art3mis inside the Oasis, and they reveal small pieces of *real* information about each other, we know not all hope is lost for Wade. Their romance blooms through chats and emails, and soon Wade loses focus on the hunt (A Story) because his motivation is being clouded by his blossoming feelings for Art3mis (B Story).

9. Midpoint (pages 180–189)

When a party (**Midpoint party**) is thrown by Ogden "Og" Morrow, the former partner and cocreator of the Oasis, Wade can't resist coming out of hiding to attend along with Art3mis and several other celebrities.

Wade's relationship with Art3mis reaches a peak, and the internal **stakes are raised** when he tells her he's in love with her. She freaks out and calls it off, saying they shouldn't speak until the hunt is over. This marks the start of Wade's **false defeat**, which is only made worse when, less than half a page later, IOI crashes the party and attacks the guests (**A and B stories cross**). There's an all-out war in the dance club. The external stakes are raised too when Wade realizes that IOI has come to the club specifically to kill him and Art3mis (they realized Wade did not die in the trailer park explosion).

10. Bad Guys Close In (pages 190–238)

After the catastrophe at Og's party, Wade vows to put his focus 100 percent on the hunt. No more messing around. He throws himself into the Oasis, getting further and further away from learning the theme (**internal bad guys**). He also has virtually zero contact with Art3mis, who has blocked all communication with him. It's now been half a year since Wade cleared the First Gate, and *finally* someone finds the Jade Key. It's Art3mis.

The Sixers (**external bad guys**) use an Oasis artifact to reveal that Art3mis was in Sector 7 when she found the key, and soon everyone converges on that sector. Wade follows a hunch that the key is on the planet of Archaide but soon realizes it's a false lead. He's about to leave when he stumbles upon a replica of a pizza place Halliday used to frequent as a kid. Inside, Wade decides to challenge himself to a game of *Pac-Man* to try to beat Halliday's top score on the game's scoreboard. After a few tries, he does it, playing a perfect game and earning himself a surprise reward: a strange quarter that he has no idea what to do with.

An alert that Aech has found the Jade Key jolts Wade back into the egg hunt. As thanks for his hint with the Copper Key, Aech sends Wade a hint of where to find the Jade Key. Things are finally looking up again for Wade as he obtains the key (by playing an old game called *Zork*). But the Sixers soon locate the Jade Key as well and a war breaks out, during which Daito's avatar dies and disappears from the scoreboard—our first **whiff-of-death** moment.

11. All Is Lost (pages 237–238)

As Wade struggles to decipher the next clue and find the location of the Second Gate, Sorrento successfully clears it, putting him at the top of the scoreboard. Two days later, Sorrento's score jumps again when he obtains the final Crystal Key. IOI is now only one gate away from finding the egg and having total control of the Oasis. All definitely seems lost. Or as Wade puts it on page 238: "This story was not going to have a happy ending. The bad guys were going to win."

12. Dark Night of the Soul (pages 239–266)

Wade wallows and laments as more Sixers acquire copies of the Crystal Key and move up the scoreboard. In reaction to the All Is Lost, Wade plans a virtual *and* real-life suicide, in a second whiff-of-death moment.

He's prevented from ending *both* of his lives when Shoto calls him, saying that Daito left Wade something in his will. The two decide to meet in Wade's Oasis stronghold, and in a third whiff of death, Shoto reveals that Daito is dead in real life too, at the hands of IOI.

This encourages Wade to take an important step toward learning the theme: he and Shoto exchange real names and talk about their real lives. Shoto says that he's giving up on the egg hunt and has a new quest: avenging Daito's death. He wishes Wade luck in finding the egg and gives him Daito's bequeathal: a Beta Capsule that turns you into a 156-foot-tall Ultraman superhero.

Wade figures out where the Second Gate is. He plays *Black Tiger* to clear it, and soon afterward finds the Crystal Key. He's warned by the accompanying riddle that the Third Gate cannot be unlocked alone—a hint that he'll have to get help if he wants to win this thing.

Wade figures out that the Third Gate is inside Castle Anorak, Halliday's impenetrable stronghold. When he gets there, the Sixers have already installed a force field over the entire castle, preventing anyone from getting in. Gunter clans are already trying to break down the shield, but to no avail. It seems hopeless. The end is certainly near, and soon IOI will have control of the Oasis.

Unless . . .

13. Break Into 3 (page 266)

Wade formulates a plan. Although he doesn't tell us what it is, he does hint that it's bold and incredibly dangerous. As he enters Act 3, he tells us, "I was going to reach the Third Gate or die trying" (page 266).

14. Finale (pages 266–368)

POINT 1: GATHERING THE TEAM. To kick off his secret plan, Wade emails Art3mis, Aech, and Shoto, telling them exactly where to find the Second Gate and how to obtain the Crystal Key.

POINT 2: EXECUTING THE PLAN. Although we still don't know exactly what the plan is, we're on the edge of our seats waiting to find out. It starts when IOI comes to arrest Wade for not paying his credit card bill. They take him into their indentured servitude program at IOI headquarters and give him a job in Oasis tech support, where he will work off his debt. Wade uses his new job to hack the IOI intranet to figure out how to bring down the Sixers' force field around Castle Anorak. He finds IOI's file on Art3mis and sees her *real* picture. Despite a birthmark covering half of her face, Wade still finds her beautiful (B Story). After copying data from the Sixers' database, he escapes the headquarters and logs back into the Oasis, sending a warning message to his team: Leave now. The Sixers know where you are.

Then Wade emails the major news feeds with proof (that he stole from the database) that IOI tried to kill him and did kill Daito.

He meets his team in a chat room and reveals that the Sixers haven't figured out how to open the Third Gate yet; the team quickly figures out it's because *three* copies of the Crystal Key are needed to open it. It's no longer every gunter for themselves; the four of them will have to work together! Wade reveals that he hacked the Sixer database and triggered the force field to drop the next day at noon. They'll be able to walk right into Castle Anorak. Then he emails every Oasis user and asks them to join in the fight against the Sixers.

Ogden Morrow suddenly appears, offering to help them in their quest by inviting them all to Oregon to launch their attack from there. Which means they're all going to meet . . . in *real* life! (Theme!)

Aech picks up Wade in his RV on his way to Oregon—and, surprise! Aech's gender and race are completely different from her avatar's! Wade proves he's already learned the theme when he says to her, on page 319, that it doesn't matter what she looks like or who she is in real life. "You're my best friend, Aech. My *only* friend, to be honest."

When they arrive at Og's house, they log in to the Oasis. It's go time!

The battle against the Sixers begins. And Wade's plan seems to be working. The force field comes down at noon, and everyone has shown up to fight, resulting in the largest battle in Oasis history. Shoto makes a sacrifice for the team when his avatar dies, and Wade uses his Beta Capsule to become Ultraman, destroying Sorrento's avatar, who disappears from the scoreboard.

Victory!

Or is it?

POINT 3: HIGH TOWER SURPRISE. As soon as Wade, Art3mis, and Aech step through the gate, a huge booming sound rings out, and all three of them die.

It's revealed that the Sixers have detonated a powerful weapon called a Cataclyst, killing *everyone* in the sector. But Wade is surprisingly given an "extra life" because of the quarter he won when he beat

Halliday's *Pac-Man* score. It's the first time in the history of the Oasis that anyone has ever received an extra life.

The rest of the team members are "dead," but Og patches them into Wade's feed so they can all talk to each other. Wade admits that he needs their help to finish this thing.

POINT 4: DIG DEEP DOWN. As proof that he's learned the theme and values his real-life friends more than the prize, Wade broadcasts a public message to the entire Oasis, revealing his true identity and vowing to split the prize money among his four friends.

POINT 5: THE EXECUTION OF THE NEW PLAN. To pass the Third Gate, Wade has to play *Tempest*, another '80s video game. Art3mis tells him about a bug in the game that gives him extra lives. Thanks to her help, he wins the game and enters stage 2 of the Third Gate, where he has to reenact another one of Halliday's favorite movies, this time *Monty Python and the Holy Grail*. Meanwhile, the Sixers are right behind him, playing *Tempest* and closing in. He successfully finishes the movie test and ends up in a replica of Halliday's office.

But where is the egg?

He tries to talk to his team, but there's no answer. As often happens at the end of the Finale, the hero is completely alone and must prove that he can do this on his own. Because of his extensive knowledge of Halliday, Wade passes the final test and reaches the egg. His avatar turns into Anorak, and his level and hit points max out at infinity. He is now immortal and all-powerful—in the game, that is.

But the game isn't real life.

A virtual Halliday appears to remind Wade of that and to restate the theme, which Wade has now learned: "I created the Oasis because I never felt at home in the real world. . . . as terrifying and painful as reality can be, it's also the only place where you can find true happiness. Because reality is *real*." Then he warns Wade, "Don't make the same mistake I did. Don't hide in here forever" (page 364).

With his new powers, Wade kills the surviving Sixers and resurrects his friends. It's soon revealed that Sorrento was arrested for murder.

15. Final Image (pages 369–372)

Back in Og's mansion, Wade logs out of the Oasis and goes to find Art3mis in the backyard. Outside, in the real world, he finally meets her in person. She introduces herself as Samantha, and Wade declares that he's in love with her. She kisses him, and Wade admits that, for the first time, he has no desire to log back into the Oasis. Not when real life is this good.

WHY IS THIS A GOLDEN FLEECE?

Ready Player One contains all three elements of a successful Golden Fleece story:

- **A ROAD:** Demarcated by the three keys and corresponding gates, the hunt for the egg across the universe of the Oasis is the road that Wade must travel to find what he's looking for.

- **A TEAM:** Even though they don't actually team up until the very end, Art3mis, Aech, Shoto, and even Daito form Wade's team. They each help him out in some way during his journey.

- **A PRIZE:** The Easter egg is the prize from page one. Wade spends the entire book trying to get to it, along with every other player in the Oasis.

Cat's Eye View

For quick reference, here's a brief overview of this novel's beat sheet.

1. **OPENING IMAGE:** Wade introduces us to the world of 2045 and the ultimate quest: the hunt for a billion-dollar "Easter egg" inside a virtual reality video game called the Oasis.

2. **THEME STATED:** "You both obviously need to get a life." I-r0k, Wade's nemesis, states the theme of "reality versus virtual reality." Reality is where true happiness is found.

3. **SETUP:** Wade (aka "Parzival") lives a crummy life in the stacks. He spends almost all his time in the Oasis with his BFF, Aech. His only purpose in life for the past five years has been searching for the Easter egg so he can win $40 billion and control of the Oasis.

4. **CATALYST:** Wade stumbles upon a clue that he believes will lead him to the first key in the hunt.

5. **DEBATE:** How will he get there? Wade quickly solves this problem by using his gift of ingenuity.

6. **BREAK INTO 2:** Wade enters the Tomb of Horrors and wins the Copper Key by playing *Joust* (an '80s video game).

7. **B STORY:** After winning, Wade meets Art3mis, his longtime crush, who is also close to finding the Copper Key. Art3mis will eventually teach Wade it's better to live in the real world than the virtual one he's been hiding in.

8. **FUN AND GAMES:** Wade becomes famous as the first player to find the Copper Key, but soon others catch up on the scoreboard, and IOI (the evil corporation that wants control of the Oasis) blows up Wade's trailer park.

9. **MIDPOINT:** (False defeat) During a Midpoint party, Wade confesses his love to Art3mis, who freaks out and breaks up with him. Then, shortly afterward, IOI crashes the party and a virtual war breaks out.

10. **BAD GUYS CLOSE IN:** Wade throws himself into the Easter egg hunt, but Art3mis and Aech find the second key first.

11. **ALL IS LOST:** Sorrento (the head of IOI) clears the Second Gate, putting him at the top of the scoreboard, and then finds the third key. It looks like IOI will win control of the Oasis.

12. **DARK NIGHT OF THE SOUL:** Wade wallows and plans a virtual (and real-life) suicide. But then he figures out where the Second Gate is, clears it, finds the third key, and discovers the location of the Third Gate. But IOI has built an impenetrable stronghold around it.

13. **BREAK INTO 3:** Wade formulates a plan, which he hides from the reader.

14. **FINALE:** Wade enacts his plan, which includes hacking into the IOI system, bringing down the stronghold, and joining forces with his team to clear the final gate and find the Easter egg.

15. **FINAL IMAGE:** Wade meets Art3mis (aka Samantha) in real life, claiming he has no interest in going back into the Oasis. Real life is good.

Monster in the House
More Than Just a Scary Story

There's nothing scarier than being trapped in an enclosed space with a monster who wants to kill you—and it might be your fault.

This describes the Setup of one of the most popular story genres of all time: the Monster in the House. This is where you'll find most of your favorite horror, slasher, and haunting novels, as well as some thrillers. The "scary story" is as primal as primal can be. Because even a caveperson (*especially* a caveperson!) can understand the concept "Kill the beast before the beast kills you!"

And the genre keeps expanding, with more successful novels being released each year, because there's always a new and exciting way to take the classic nightmare scenario of being stuck with a monster in the house and give it a fresh twist.

But as we study the three essential ingredients for this genre, we'll soon come to see that the key to cracking this frightening story archetype is not necessarily the scariness of the monster (although that helps!) or the claustrophobic nature of the confined space (also helps!), but the *reason* the monster is here. The beast's raison d'être (as the French would say) is what makes these tales truly scary and, more important, what makes them resonate with readers long after the final page is turned and the monster is destroyed (or not!).

This story type is *old*. You could easily say it's a classic. It dates all the way back to the myth of the Minotaur and the Maze. And authors have been successfully respinning this same template over and over again. From Mary Shelley's *Frankenstein* to William Peter Blatty's *The Exorcist* to Adam Nevill's *The Ritual*.

Stephen King and Dean Koontz have both made a "killing" in this genre. From *The Shining*, *Salem's Lot*, *It*, and *Pet Sematary* by King to *Watchers*, *Midnight*, and *Hideaway* by Koontz, many a classic novel by these two falls into this category.

And readers gobble them up! Why? Because the template works. It's a story blueprint that continues to haunt readers time and time again. The three essential ingredients of a successful Monster in the House tale are (1) a **monster**, (2) a **house**, and (3) a **sin**.

Let's take a look at the *monster* first. These come in all shapes and sizes. They can be as human as you and me (or at least *seem* to be on the outside!) or they can be as far out and as paranormal as our imaginations will allow. From serial killers to evil spirits to scientific experiments run amok, their common denominator is some sort of "supernatural" power. And I don't mean supernatural in the magical sense (although those monsters exist too). I mean it in the literal sense. These monsters function *outside* the realm of natural human behavior. For instance, a serial killer fueled by insanity has a supernatural power. They don't act like normal human beings. They are piloted by evil. Of course, there are also the monsters whose power really does come from something paranormal, magical, or science-fictional, like the spirits in *The Shining*, the demon in *The Exorcist*, the murderous nanoswarms in *Prey* by Michael Crichton, the mysterious mind-altering "ambrosia" found at the bottom of the ocean in *The Deep* by Nick Cutter, or the man-made creature in *Frankenstein*.

All monsters, by definition, are supernatural. They're driven by a motivation that goes against the laws of nature. Which is why, in so many of these types of novels, the characters (and the reader!) often don't just fear for their lives. They fear for their *souls*.

SO. MUCH. SCARIER.

Death is nothing. But the idea that something *worse* than death could happen to us? That's where the real fear comes in, because it goes beyond our comprehension as mere mortals. That's also why zombie stories are so successful. Those dudes aren't just dead. They're *un*dead. And that's so much worse, because of the fear that we, too, could lose our soul and become just like them.

Second, every great Monster in the House novel should have some kind of confined space in which the monster exists. We call this the *house*. And I'll give you a hint: the smaller the space (or the more isolated the heroes), the better the story. Houses can range from literal houses, like in *The Exorcist* or *The Haunting of Hill House* by Shirley Jackson, to an entire town, like in *Salem's Lot*; an isolated desert, like in *Prey*; a creepy lab stationed at the bottom of the ocean in *The Deep*; or even an entire country. As long as the monster's wrath is specific or targeted in some way. For instance, the monster in *Frankenstein* is free to roam about the entire world, but he attacks *only* Victor Frankenstein's closest friends and family. His beef is with his creator, no one else. Therefore, the "house" in that novel is Victor's family unit.

Whatever your choice may be, the key takeaway here is the idea of being *trapped*. If your heroes can just hop in the car and skedaddle right on out of there, where's the threat? What's the conflict? Where's the story? Being stuck somewhere or targeted for some reason is the whole point of the genre. Because what's scarier than a soul-destroying monster? A soul-destroying monster you can't escape from!

But more important than a monster and a house is the third genre ingredient: a *sin*.

The prey that the monster is stalking (often our hero or heroes!) cannot be completely innocent. Someone is responsible for bringing the monster into being, invading the monster's territory, or waking the monster up. And it's usually either the hero, a counterpart of the hero, or even all of humanity who has committed this sin. Either way, this catastrophe is somehow *our* fault.

In *Frankenstein*, the sin is Dr. Frankenstein's human arrogance in his attempt to play God and create human life. So it's only fitting that the very human life he created would turn against him.

In *Prey*, the sin is human greed (a popular sin among Monster in the House tales!). The company featured in the novel, Xymos, is so desperate to have their new scientific project succeed that they start messing with the laws of biology, letting technology run amok. And guess what happens? That very technology (in this case a swarm of nanoparticles) comes back to kill them. Crichton plays with this sin a lot in his novels. The same template can be found in his phenomenal best seller *Jurassic Park*, in which human greed leads, once again, to technology run amok. It's a warning to the rest of us about letting science go *too* far. And it's why these types of novels are so successful. We can heed that warning. It applies to *us*!

The sin is really what makes this genre work. It's what makes these stories resonate with readers. Because the sin almost always ties into the deeper theme, that universal lesson that we can all relate to. This sin is essentially a warning label to the rest of us.

Beware! This could happen to you, if you don't learn from these mistakes!

It's one thing to get eaten; it's another to get eaten because of something we did. The guilt of the sin adds to the horror of the situation. The sin is also important to the story because it usually holds a clue to destroying the monster itself. Let's figure out what we did wrong—fast—before we too succumb to the beast!

But more important, the sin raises a poignant underlying question: Who's the *real* monster here? It or us? It's a question certainly explored in the classic novel *Frankenstein* as well as many other Monster in the House tales.

The sin gives your story reason and meaning because it touches on the theme. Without it, what's the point? What are you trying to say?

There has to be a *reason* the monster is attacking this person, group, or society. What did these victims do to deserve the attack? What sin of humanity are they being punished for? Even if it's not the hero themselves who is responsible, someone, somewhere along the way decided to open Pandora's box and peek inside, and *this* story is the result.

The sin is also usually how we can tell the difference between a Monster in the House and a Dude with a Problem, two genres that often get confused. The question to ask yourself is, *Whose fault is this?* If the answer is *It's our fault!* or *It's the hero's fault!*, then you usually know you're looking at a Monster in the House.

Another popular (although not required) element that you'll often see in Monster in the House tales is a character called the half man. This is usually a mentor-type character, a survivor who has gone to battle with the monster before. They have prior knowledge of its evil and have possibly even come away damaged (or maimed) on account of it. In *The Deep*, our hero, Luke, finds the journals of Dr. Westlake, a scientist who has already perished at the hands of the mysterious "ambrosia" substance. In the journals, Dr. Westlake's ramblings grow more and more chaotic and insane, giving Luke a glimpse of what this terrifying substance can do.

The half man character can be an effective way to get mythology and background exposition into your story without it feeling like you're info dumping. This character is the literal embodiment of the threat the monster poses.

You might notice that the half man character (if he's still alive) will often die at the All Is Lost beat (where mentors often die), because in the end, the hero (or heroes) must face the monster alone. Killing off your mentor ups the stakes. Because once that help is gone, it's time to stop fooling around and come up with an Act 3 plan. Lest the monster come for you next!

To recap: If you're thinking of writing a Monster in the House novel, make sure your story includes these three essential ingredients:

- **A MONSTER**: supernatural in its powers, even if its strength derives from insanity—and *evil* at its core.
- **A HOUSE**: that is, an enclosed space, which could be a literal house, a family unit, an entire town, or the world.
- **A SIN**: meaning someone is guilty of bringing the monster into the house (or invading the monster's territory)—a transgression that can include ignorance and often relates to the theme the hero must learn.

POPULAR MONSTER IN THE HOUSE NOVELS THROUGH TIME:

Frankenstein by Mary Shelley
The Haunting of Hill House by Shirley Jackson
The Exorcist by William Peter Blatty
The Shining by Stephen King
Ghost Story by Peter Straub
The Keep by F. Paul Wilson
The Woman in Black by Susan Hill
Pet Sematary by Stephen King
Watchers by Dean Koontz
The Silence of the Lambs by Thomas Harris
Jurassic Park by Michael Crichton
Prey by Michael Crichton
The Ruins by Scott Smith
World War Z by Max Brooks
Heart-Shaped Box by Joe Hill (*beat sheet included below*)
The Ritual by Adam Nevill
Sweet by Emmy Laybourne
Kalahari by Jessica Khoury
The Deep by Nick Cutter
A Head Full of Ghosts by Paul Tremblay

HEART-SHAPED BOX

BY: Joe Hill
STC GENRE: Monster in the House
BOOK GENRE: Horror
TOTAL PAGES: 374 (William Morrow Paperback, 2007)

When aging rock star Judas Coyne buys a "ghost" from an online auction site, he gets much more than he bargained for after he discovers the ghost is irreversibly tied to him. This modern Monster in the House has chilled readers the world over, becoming a *New York Times* best seller and winning the coveted Bram Stoker award for Best First

Novel (a prestigious award in the horror genre) and earning Joe Hill (who is also the author of *Horns,* which was adapted as a film starring Daniel Radcliffe) a permanent place in the Horror Hall of Fame.

1. Opening Image (pages 1–8)

When Jude Coyne's assistant, Danny, asks Jude if he wants to buy a ghost off the internet, we're immediately thrown into this chilling, supernatural world of Joe Hill's creation. We learn quickly that Jude Coyne is a fifty-four-year-old, once-famous rock star living in upstate New York. He is still recognized everywhere but hasn't toured or recorded an album in years. Jude likes to collect disturbing things, so this ghost for sale seems right up his alley. The ghost is allegedly tied to a dead man's funeral suit that someone is selling on an online auction site. Jude chooses the equivalent of the "Buy Now" button, and *click!* Our Monster in the House tale begins.

2. Setup (pages 9–26)

The suit is delivered in a, you guessed it, heart-shaped box. As we wait for the ghost to make its first appearance, Joe Hill tells us more about his hero, Jude Coyne, and his world, showing us how deeply flawed Jude is in all aspects of his life.

On the family front (**home**), Jude hasn't spoken to his father in years, and we catch hints of an abusive past (**shard of glass**). His father is on his deathbed, and Jude essentially tells the nurse he doesn't care if his father lives or dies.

On the job front (**work**), again, Jude doesn't record or tour anymore. He lost two of his band mates (one to a car accident and one to AIDS), and he hasn't really gotten over it.

And on the relationship front (**play**), it seems Jude collects not only disturbing occult items but also goth girlfriends. He's had a string of them. But he never lets himself get too close, which is why he never calls them by their real name, but rather by the state they're from. His current live-in girlfriend is Georgia (aka Marybeth), a former stripper, and before her there was Florida (Anna), whom Jude kicked out when her depression became too much for Jude to handle.

Right away, we get the sense that Jude is insensitive, emotionally cut off (especially when it comes to women), and haunted by his past.

Before the *big* Catalyst comes and sets this adventure in motion, Joe Hill sets off mini Catalysts, letting us know that major change is coming soon. First, when the suit arrives, Georgia is pricked by what she thinks is a pin in it, but when Jude inspects the suit, he finds no pins. Next, Jude hears the radio playing in Danny's office, even though he knows the radio wasn't on in there before. When he goes to investigate, there's a strange voice on the radio saying creepy things like "The dead pull the living down" (page 19).

3. Theme Stated (page 26)

The puncture wound on Georgia's finger is looking bad (another mini Catalyst). But when Jude flippantly tells her to "Put something on that" because "there's less work for pole dancers with visible disfigurements" (page 26), Georgia lashes out at him. She says sarcastically, "You're a sympathetic son of a bitch, you know that?" To which Jude replies, "You want sympathy, go f*ck James Taylor."

Jude's blatant insensitivity to Georgia and his deeper-rooted inability to love will be revealed to be not only the reason the monster is in the house, but also the crucial flaw Jude must overcome by the end of the novel.

4. Catalyst (pages 27–30)

A noise wakes Jude; he thinks one of his two dogs (Angus and Bon) is in the house. But when he looks out the window, he sees them both in their pen. He ventures out into the hall, where he spots an old man sitting in an antique Shaker chair, wearing the suit that came in the heart-shaped box.

5. Debate (pages 31–69)

Like many stories that feature a brush with the supernatural, the question of this Debate is: Was it real? Is there really a ghost in Jude's house? Did he really buy a spirit off the internet? And if it *is* real, how does this supernatural magic work? To get answers, Jude tells Danny to track down the woman who sold him the ghost. Danny gets Jessica Price on the phone; she soon reveals that she's the sister of Jude's last girlfriend, Florida (aka Anna). Jessica explains that their stepfather, the ghost, blames Jude for Anna's death (she slit her wrists in the bathtub, apparently after Jude kicked her out of his house), and her stepfather is now haunting Jude seeking revenge. (It turns out Jessica purposefully targeted Jude online to make sure *he* was the one who bought the suit.) Jude vows to send the suit back to Jessica, assuming that the ghost is attached to it, but Jessica claims that it won't make her stepfather go away. She hints at the "house" (enclosed location) of this Monster in the House when she says, "Wherever you go, he'll be right there" (page 36). It seems the ghost is attached not to the suit but rather to Jude, and it won't stop until Jude is dead.

Jude then goes into research mode, trying to get to the bottom of this ghost business and the claim that Anna killed herself because of him. He tells Danny to dig up all the old letters Anna sent him after he kicked her out, and he starts reading old books about the occult. Georgia tells him to get rid of the suit because it smells bad, but Jude isn't convinced that will do anything.

Meanwhile, Georgia's wound is getting badly infected, and Jude keeps catching more glimpses of the ghost; he notices the ghost has black scribbles on his face where his eyes should be and holds a gold chain with a razor blade dangling from it—like a pendulum.

The ghost is becoming an increasing problem, and Jude is going to have to do something about it.

6. Break Into 2 (pages 70–72)

Jude finally decides to investigate the ghost. He does a web search for Anna's stepfather, uncovering an obituary for Craddock McDermott. The picture is of a younger version of the man he saw in the hallway. Jude discovers that Craddock was a skilled hypnotist.

Then a new email appears in his inbox. It's from Craddock. It's long and rambling, claiming that Jude will die. Jude smashes the computer.

7. Fun and Games (pages 72–165)

Joe Hill promises a ghostly adventure with this premise, and he delivers. The upside-down world for Jude and the creepy "fun" for us, the readers, is Jude's life with Craddock's ghost. As the day goes on, the threat of this ghost in Jude's life grows more and more dangerous. Georgia finds Jude in the closed barn with his car's motor running. She thinks he was trying to kill himself, but he swears he never started the engine. It must have been Craddock. After restless, disturbing dreams, Jude decides to sell the suit, only to find that Georgia burned it. Yet the ghost is still there.

The **downward** path continues when it's discovered that Craddock, as a hypnotist, seems to be able to persuade people to do things by listening to the sound of his voice. He persuades Jude's assistant, Danny, to hang himself, and he nearly convinces Georgia to shoot herself. Then he tries to hypnotize Jude to kill Georgia himself. Jude is able to stop himself just in time by cutting his palm and focusing on the pain.

Meanwhile, we get more information about Jude's relationship with his father. He was very abusive to Jude and his mother. One time he slammed Jude's chord-making hand in the door, hindering his ability to play the guitar.

As Craddock pursues him, Jude makes an important discovery about his dogs. Because they are "familiars" to him, they can help protect him against the ghost. The dogs' shadows are able to hold Craddock back.

Soon after that, Jude decides it's time for him, Georgia, and the dogs to leave. He wants to drive south to Florida to visit Jessica Price, the woman who sold him the suit/ghost.

8. B Story (page 78)

The B Story character of this novel is Anna McDermott, the ex-girlfriend whom Jude cast aside nine months ago and the stepdaughter of the ghost. Not only does she represent the theme (Jude's insensitivity and inability to love), because her gruesome fate was a direct result of his flaws, but she will eventually help Jude and Georgia chase the ghost of her stepfather away.

Although Anna is mentioned prior to this, page 78 is when we start to learn more about Anna through Jude's memories. He tells us about their relationship and how good it was at one point. Anna will continue to make more frequent appearances throughout the novel (first in memories, dreams, and flashbacks, and then as a ghost) as her role in Jude's transformation builds. We soon start to realize that Jude did love Anna; his flaws just kept him from showing it or acting on it, thus landing him in his current position.

9. Midpoint (pages 166–178)

The morning after Jude and Georgia leave for their road trip, they stop at a Denny's for breakfast. It's their first **public outing** since the ghost came into their lives, and it doesn't go well. In this **false defeat** Midpoint, after a waitress spills hot coffee on Georgia's still infected finger, Georgia runs to the bathroom to tend to it. When Jude sees Craddock's truck idling outside, he runs into the women's bathroom and is just in time to stop Georgia from killing herself (she smashes the mirror and tries to use one of the shards of glass to slit her throat). They escape the Denny's only to be chased by Craddock's pickup truck through a tunnel under an overpass. The truck barrels toward them, just missing and hitting a wall. When Jude looks at the truck again, he sees it's a Jeep with a dazed (hypnotized) man behind the wheel. The **stakes are raised** as Jude realizes that Craddock is powerful enough to manipulate strangers to try to kill them (**Midpoint twist**).

10. Bad Guys Close In (pages 179–265)

As they get back on the road, Georgia starts to ask Jude a ton of questions (something Anna used to do). **A and B stories cross** when Jude gets fed up and accidentally calls Georgia "Anna," which makes her cry. Afterward, Jude recalls the night he broke up with Anna and sent her home. That same night, he'd gone to a strip club and met Georgia.

After the false defeat Midpoint, the Bad Guys Close In is an **upward path** as Jude and Georgia get closer to the truth about Anna's death and an answer about how to defeat Craddock. They make a stop at the house of Georgia's grandma, "Bammy." There, Georgia gets out her old Ouija board and the two attempt to contact the ghost of Anna.

Through the Ouija board, Anna reveals that she didn't kill herself. Craddock killed her! They ask if Anna can help them; she replies yes and asks Georgia if she will be "the golden door" (page 219). Georgia and Jude don't yet know what this is (and neither do we!), but Georgia replies yes.

Later, Jude gets a message from his father's nurse: Jude's father (whom he hasn't spoken to in years) has been unconscious for the past thirty-six hours, and he's not going to last much longer (**internal bad guys**).

After leaving Bammy's house, Jude pulls over at a used car dealership and beats up a man named Ruger. He remembered Georgia telling him once that Ruger had molested her when she was thirteen. This is one of the many signs that Jude is changing. He's standing up for Georgia, protecting her instead of mistreating her. He's becoming more sympathetic, which is evident in the growing closeness with her he's been feeling ever since the Break Into 2. After this incident, Jude starts calling Georgia by her real name, Marybeth.

The two arrive at Jessica Price's in Florida and break into the house. A fight breaks out, during which the truth about what happened to Anna is fully revealed: Craddock had been molesting both sisters since they were children. He'd been able to hypnotize them to make them forget. After Jude sent Anna home, Anna threatened to turn Craddock in. He killed her (with Jessica's help) and made it look like a suicide. Craddock blamed Jude for changing Anna (after she'd been with Jude, Craddock could no longer hypnotize her), and that's why Craddock is haunting Jude.

Jude realizes that the signs of Anna's sexual abuse had been right in front of him but he never saw them (theme). It's also revealed that Jessica, who worships Craddock, was letting him molest her own daughter.

Jude is about to strangle Jessica by pressing a tire iron against her throat when suddenly Jessica's daughter, Reese, appears with a gun.

11. All Is Lost (pages 266–278)

A struggle ensues, and in a **whiff-of-death** moment, one of Jude's dogs (his protection against Craddock) is shot and killed. Craddock persuades Reese to aim the gun at Jude; she does, and blows off Jude's finger. As Jude and Marybeth (Georgia) try to get away, Jude's other dog is hit by Jessica's car (Craddock was manipulating her too). The dog is in bad shape, and Jude's finger is bleeding profusely as the two finally manage to get away. Marybeth wants to take Jude to the hospital but he refuses. Instead, he tells her they're going to Louisiana (Jude's childhood home).

12. Dark Night of the Soul (pages 279–309)

At the very end of the All Is Lost, Marybeth asks Jude, "How do you see this all endin'?" (page 278). Jude doesn't have an answer. That's what this Dark Night of the Soul is all about. It's a preparation for the end. As they head back to Jude's childhood home, Jude knows he will have to confront more than his current ghost. He'll have to confront his past ghosts as well—namely, his father.

As Marybeth drives, Jude has more dreams (visions) about Anna. He sees the night of her death play out (**Dark Night epiphany**). Anna threatened to turn Jessica in after finding out that Jessica was letting her own daughter be molested by Craddock. Then Jessica helped Craddock kill Anna by drugging her. In Jude's dream, right before Craddock slits Anna's wrists with a razor, Jude tells Anna that he loves her, and she says she loves him. Jude's transformation is nearly complete.

By the time they reach Jude's childhood home, the other dog is dead in the back seat. Which means Jude has nothing left to protect him against Craddock.

Arlene, the nurse, leads Jude to his childhood bedroom, where his unconscious father sleeps, and gives him morphine for the pain in his finger.

13. Break Into 3 (pages 310–314)

Arlene is scared off by the ghost, leaving Jude alone in the house with Georgia, Craddock (the real ghost), and his father (the metaphorical ghost of his past). Jude watches as Craddock climbs out of the heart-shaped box on the floor, and Jude greets him: "What kept you?" (page 314). Jude is finally ready to face his ghosts.

14. Finale (pages 315–354)

Craddock tries to manipulate Jude to strangle Marybeth, but Jude finds he's able to resist by humming a song he'd written earlier. Craddock is able to take over Jude's father's body, and Jude's two ghosts are now one.

A ghastly fight between Jude and Jude's father/Craddock follows, in which Craddock tries to cut Jude with his razor blade. Marybeth enters in the nick of time and stabs Jude's father in the neck and back. But then Marybeth slips in his blood and falls, and Craddock is able to cut her throat with his razor. As she bleeds out, she tells Jude that Anna is calling to her and asks him to make the golden door (referenced earlier). As Craddock pulls himself out of Jude's father's body and rises again, Jude uses Marybeth's blood to paint a door on the floor. Marybeth manages to roll over the door just as it falls open. She floats over it in a bright light and soon transforms into Anna. Anna grabs Craddock and pulls him through the door with her. He is gone for good.

Jude crawls to the door, looking for Marybeth, and falls through it.

Jude finds himself in his restored Mustang with Anna, who quickly transforms into Marybeth. Marybeth explains to Jude that they are on the "night road" where the dead travel. It's nice and bright, and Marybeth speculates that "maybe it's only night here for some people" (page 334).

When Marybeth tells Jude she has to go and it's time for him to get out of the car, he won't let go of her hand. He doesn't want to leave. He says, "We. Where we get out. We. *We*" (page 336).

Jude's transformation is now complete. He's no longer selfish and emotionally disconnected. He's now capable of love, and he's proving it. He's grabbing hold of that shard of glass that was planted by his father way back when he was a child and removing it for good.

When Jude wakes up in the hospital, he discovers that Marybeth was dead for a few minutes but came back to life. He saved her.

15. Final Images (pages 355–374)

Joe Hill ends his story with several quick "after" snapshots to sum up how life has changed for his hero, Jude Coyne. In a series of short, paragraph-long chapters we see Jude and Marybeth attending Danny's memorial, Jude finally recording a new album, Jude restoring another old car, and Jude and Marybeth getting married. Then we learn that the police found photo evidence that Craddock was molesting Jessica Price's daughter, Reese, and that Jessica, who allowed it to happen, was arrested for child endangerment. In the final chapter, five years later, Reese comes to visit Jude and Marybeth, apologizing for shooting him. When Jude looks at Reese, he sees Anna in her. He helps Reese, giving her money and buying her a bus ticket, redeeming himself as best he can for what he did to Anna.

WHY IS THIS A MONSTER IN THE HOUSE?

Heart-Shaped Box contains all three elements of a successful Monster in the House story:

- **A MONSTER:** Craddock McDermott, the evil hypnotist ghost who can persuade people to kill themselves and others, is Joe Hill's creepy invention and a worthy advocate for arrogant rock star Jude Coyne.

- **A HOUSE:** Although the monster can technically go wherever he wants, he is tied to Jude because Jude purchased his suit on the internet, and because Craddock, who practiced dark occult arts in life, linked his spirit to Jude before he died, thus making *Jude* the house in which the monster is enclosed.

- **A SIN:** Jude is responsible for bringing this monster into existence. His flaws of insensitivity, arrogance, and inability to love are the sins that created Craddock's ghost. When he kicked Anna (aka Florida) out of his house and sent her home, it directly led to Anna's death and Craddock's plan to haunt Jude from beyond the grave. And only in dealing with this sin is Jude able to rid himself of the monster.

Cat's Eye View

For quick reference, here's a brief overview of this novel's beat sheet.

1. **OPENING IMAGE:** Aging rock star Jude Coyne buys a ghost on the internet, introducing us to his obsession with the macabre.

2. **THEME STATED:** "You're a sympathetic son of a bitch, you know that?" Georgia, Jude's current girlfriend (in a long string of brief relationships), asks sarcastically, hinting at Jude's ultimate transformation journey: to become more sympathetic, learn to connect, and become capable of loving someone.

3. **SETUP:** After the purchased ghost arrives (linked to a funeral suit shipped in a heart-shaped box), strange things start to happen around Jude's house. We learn about Jude's relationship with his abusive father, his past as a rock star, and that he hasn't recorded an album in years.

4. **CATALYST:** Jude sees the ghost for the first time, sitting in a chair in his hallway.

5. **DEBATE:** Is the ghost real? Jude goes into research mode, contacting the seller, Jessica Price, who tells him the ghost is stepfather to her and to Jude's previous girlfriend, Anna, who killed herself after Jude cast her aside. Jessica claims the ghost is haunting him to avenge his stepdaughter.

6. **BREAK INTO 2:** Jude accepts that the ghost exists and decides to investigate. He learns the ghost is Craddock McDermott, a skilled hypnotist.

continued

7. **B STORY:** The dead Anna McDermott represents the B Story and the theme (Jude's inability to love). Resolving his past with Anna (and the callous way he dismissed her when she needed him most) will eventually also resolve the A Story—being haunted by Craddock's ghost.

8. **FUN AND GAMES:** In Jude's new, upside-down world of living with a ghost, we learn that Craddock can hypnotize people and persuade them to kill themselves. He's trying to get Jude to kill Georgia and himself. Jude's dogs seem to be his only protection.

9. **MIDPOINT:** The stakes are raised when, after leaving to confront Jessica Price in person, Jude and Georgia are almost killed by a stranger under Craddock's control. He can now manipulate almost anyone to do almost anything.

10. **BAD GUYS CLOSE IN:** Jude and Georgia (now referred to as Marybeth) stop at her grandma's house; they contact Anna with a Ouija board and learn that Anna didn't really kill herself.

11. **ALL IS LOST:** In a fight with Jessica Price and her daughter, one of the dogs is shot and killed, and the other is badly injured. Jude's protection against Craddock is almost gone. Jude decides to go to his childhood home, where his father is dying.

12. **DARK NIGHT OF THE SOUL:** On the drive, Jude "sees" a memory of the night Anna died and realizes that Craddock killed Anna after she threatened to turn him in for sexually abusing her, her sister Jessica, and Jessica's daughter, Reese. He's coming after Jude because he believes Jude turned Anna against him. Jude's other dog dies.

13. **BREAK INTO 3:** Finally ready to confront the ghost (of his present and past), Jude asks Craddock, "What kept you?" (page 314), signaling he's ready for the final showdown.

14. **FINALE:** Craddock takes over Jude's father's body; now Jude has to fight the father who abused him (directly facing his past). A bloody battle ensues, in which Marybeth is mortally wounded. Marybeth opens the "golden door" so that Anna can come through and take Craddock back to the "night road" (where the dead go). Jude and Marybeth fall through the door as well, but Jude pulls Marybeth out, saving her and proving that he's learned the theme and is capable of love.

15. **FINAL IMAGES:** Jude records a new album and marries Marybeth. The two are visited by Jessica Price's daughter, who looks a lot like Anna. Jude's final act of redemption for what he did to Anna is helping her niece.

Pitch It to Me!

How to Write Killer Loglines and Dazzling Synopses

If you can't explain it simply, you don't understand it well enough.
—ALBERT EINSTEIN

Regardless of what stage of the novel-writing process you're in—writing, revising, outlining, banging your head against the wall trying to come up with a great title—I can guarantee you that at some point along the way, someone is going to ask you the dreaded question:

What's your book about?

Whether your goal is to traditionally publish your novel (get represented by a literary agent and sell your novel to a major publisher) or self-publish it (either online or in print) or perhaps just to post it on Wattpad to see what happens, you still face the same challenge: you have to *sell* it. You have to tell someone (a literary agent, a publisher, a potential reader browsing through Amazon eBooks, or even the meandering Wattpad user!) what your book is about.

In short, you have to be able to *pitch* it.

What Is a Pitch, and Why Is It Important?

Think about the summary on the back cover or online sales page of your favorite novel. That summary is the book's written pitch. If you meet your favorite author and ask them what they're working on next, they'll most likely give you a verbal pitch, summarizing their new project in a few short sentences. A pitch doesn't tell you the whole story (because then what would be the point of reading the book?); it tells you just enough of the story to lure you in and leave you wanting more.

And *that* right there is why it's important.

If you want someone to read your novel—whether that be agents, editors, movie producers, or readers—you first have to hook them. You have to paint a picture of this story that is so compelling, so interesting, so *primal* that they can't wait to rip it out of your hands, shouting "GIMME! I NEED! I NEED!"

A pitch is your bait. And here's the *good* news: if you've already crafted your Save the Cat! fifteen beats, then your pitch will be a cakewalk (cat walk?).

The reason most authors struggle with pitching their novel is that it's not typically in our nature to take a step back and try to see our novels from a high-level, more sales-oriented point of view. *However*, I'm happy to report that the process I've been guiding you through in this book is, by its very nature, designed to force you to think about your story from this macro level.

In this chapter, I'm going to walk you through the process of creating two different kinds of pitches: the logline and the short synopsis. Both will be instrumental to you and your novel-writing career regardless of what path you choose to follow. But they will be especially important if you choose to pursue the path of traditional publishing (selling your novel to a major publisher). Because on this path you, the author, are the first link in a long chain of people who have to be able to effectively sell your novel to someone else.

I call this the **chain of awesome.**

Basically, the chain of awesome consists of multiple levels of people who have to convince other people that your book is awesome.

To get your book published by a major publisher, you first have to get a literary agent. And to get a literary agent, you have to convince an agent that your book is awesome so they'll represent you. The agent will then have to convince an editor at a publishing house that your book is awesome so they'll buy it. But to buy the book, the editor has to convince a whole bunch more people at the publishing house—sales team, marketing team, publicity team—that the book is awesome.

But the chain of awesome doesn't stop there. Once the book is sold to a publisher and getting ready to be released, the sales team has to sell the book to the bookstores. The booksellers in the bookstore have to sell the books to the readers.

Then on the promotional side, the publicity and marketing teams have to sell the book to people like reviewers, bloggers, and the media.

And let's not forget about your agent, who's still out there selling your book to foreign publishers and movie producers!

And remember: the chain of awesome starts with YOU.

So, let's dive in, shall we?

The Logline

The logline is another handy tool that we novelists are borrowing from our screenwriting cousins. It's usually used for internal purposes to sell your book to agents, publishers, and movie producers, but it can also be a great tool for quickly selling directly to readers.

By definition, a logline is a one-sentence description of your story. Yup, just one.

"Lunacy!" you might be saying right now. "It can't be done!"

Well, allow me to prove it to you.

Can you guess what novel this is?

On the verge of losing her home, an out-of-work alcoholic, who frequently blacks out, becomes entangled in a missing persons investigation; but when the man she's convinced is guilty is released, she must confront her inner demons once and for all before the key suspect turns his sights on her.

What's this novel?
Answer: *The Girl on the Train* by Paula Hawkins!

What about this one?

On the verge of melancholy due to crippling loneliness, a girl with a rare disease that prohibits her from ever going outside starts a relationship with the new boy next door;

but when she realizes she's falling in love with him, she must decide whether to risk everything before her disease tears them apart forever.

Recognize this recent young adult best seller?
It's *Everything, Everything* by Nicola Yoon.

Did you notice these two loglines were about very different stories but shared a very similar structure? Good for you! You're a pattern-seeking genius now!

They *did,* indeed, have the same structure because I wrote them with the same awesome Save the Cat! logline template. And here it is!

THE SAVE THE CAT! LOGLINE TEMPLATE

*On the verge of a **stasis = death** moment, a flawed hero **Breaks Into 2**; but when the **Midpoint** happens, they must learn the **Theme Stated** before the **All Is Lost.***

Ta-da! A logline that fits any story of any genre.

Why does this logline work? Because it creates urgency, delivers on a hook, and shows us why *this* protagonist is essential to *this* story and vice versa (the marriage of hero and plot!).

We use the phrase "on the verge of" (or an opening with similar urgency) and follow it up with a stasis = death moment to prove right off the bat that this story is *necessary.* This hero is doomed without it! We include the Break Into 2 (or at least a glimpse of what the Act 2 world will be) to prove that the plot moves. It doesn't just stay in the same old status quo Act 1 world forever. The mention of Act 2 also helps depict the hook (or premise) of the story. And we mention (or at least hint at) the Midpoint and the All Is Lost to show that this story has stakes—and they are going to be raised! And we reference the Theme Stated to show that the story has something to say.

Now, of course, you might have to fiddle around with the language a bit and replace some of the phrasing to make sure the actual syntax is clear and compelling. You don't want your logline to feel awkward just because you're trying to cram it into a template. But the beats should fit. If you're finding, however, that your logline falls flat, you might want to look at your Midpoint again and make sure it's *big* enough. Are the stakes being raised enough to send the story into yet a new direction? Or take a look at your All Is Lost again. Is *enough* on the line to make the story feel urgent?

Let's stick a couple more stories into the template and see what we get!

The Fault in Our Stars by John Green (Buddy Love)

On the verge of depression, a teen cancer patient meets a quirky, charismatic fellow patient who brings her back to life; but when one of them relapses, she must learn the true meaning of being alive before they're separated forever.

The Martian by Andy Weir (Dude with a Problem)

After getting left for dead on Mars by his crew, a cocky astronaut figures out the impossible: how to grow food on a barren planet; but when all of his crops are destroyed and his supplies are running out, he must solve the biggest problem of all: getting off the planet before time runs out.

Ready Player One by Ernest Cline (Golden Fleece)

On the verge of succumbing to a life of poverty, a lonely gamer is the first player to find a clue to the whereabouts of the most valuable video game "Easter egg" in history and kicks off a worldwide treasure hunt; but when an evil corporation tries to kill him, he must team up with his fellow competitors to stop the corporation from finding the treasure before it's "game over" for good.

Harry Potter and the Sorcerer's Stone by J. K. Rowling (Superhero)

On the verge of wasting away with a horrible foster family, an awkward orphaned boy discovers he's a wizard and sets off to attend a magic school; but when an attempt is made on his life, he must finally prove his worth before the most evil wizard of all time gets his hands on a powerful totem that could bring about the end of the magic world.

Are you worried that this template gives too much away? Don't be. Think about this: Did any of the loglines above make you *less* inclined to read the book? Probably not. They probably made you want to read the books *more* because they spoke to that innate story DNA that lives inside all of us. These loglines included everything that a great story needs. And your logline must too. You must prove to whoever is on the receiving end of this logline that this is a novel *worth* their time. This novel won't disappoint, because it's got *all* the crucial elements:

- A flawed hero (*who* the story is about and *why* they need this journey)
- A Break Into 2 (*where* your story is going)
- A Theme Stated (*how* this story is universal)
- An All Is Lost (*what* the major stakes are)

But if you're still worried about your logline giving too much away, feel free to make it a tad more vague. If your Midpoint or All Is Lost is a huge spoilery twist, then don't spell it out; just give us a hint. But be careful not to hide *too* much or your pitch can sound abstract and unfocused. This is called **hiding the ball**, and it can often leave the reader feeling blasé about your story because they can't quite grasp what it's about. You've hidden *too* much!

For example, take a look at this alternate logline for *Harry Potter and the Sorcerer's Stone* and tell me if it's as interesting as the one I just presented:

> *On the verge of wasting away with a horrible foster family, an awkward orphaned boy discovers a life-changing secret about himself and sets off on an exciting adventure; but when things take a dangerous turn, he must step up and stop the forces of evil from destroying everything.*

Not quite as compelling, is it? Why? Because it's *too* vague. I've hidden everything—including the hook! Which is the fact that Harry discovers he's a wizard and attends a magic school. *That's* the kind of stuff that gets readers to click "Buy."

So take heed. There's a delicate balance between avoiding spoilers and giving the potential reader enough information to get 'em hooked.

The Short Synopsis

Now that we've mastered the logline, let's take a look at the other very important pitch: the short synopsis! This is often called the jacket flap or back cover copy by publishers or sometimes just a book summary or book description. It's typically a two- to three-paragraph summary of your novel, designed to do one thing: entice readers to read it!

The best part about learning to write a stellar short synopsis is that there are *so* many to study. And they're all so accessible. Just flip to the back cover of your favorite paperback. Or look up your favorite novel on Amazon, Barnes and Noble, IndieBound.org., Goodreads .com, publishers' websites, and anywhere the book is being pitched to readers.

Unlike the logline, the short synopsis will be seen by *everyone* who comes across your book. It will be what nearly every potential reader uses to determine whether they want to buy/read your book—and that includes agents and publishers too!

So in other words . . . it better be good.

But don't worry! You know I'd never leave you high and dry.

Let's look at a few book summaries taken straight from the back covers of popular novels and see if we can identify some of the beats that publishers are using to pitch the book to readers.

Cinder by Marissa Meyer (Superhero)

> Humans and androids crowd the raucous streets of New Beijing. A deadly plague ravages the population. [Setup] From space, a ruthless lunar people watch, waiting to make their move [stasis = death]. No one knows that Earth's fate hinges on one girl. . . .
>
> Cinder, a gifted mechanic, is a cyborg. She's a second-class citizen with a mysterious past, reviled by her stepmother and blamed for her stepsister's illness [flawed hero]. But when her life becomes intertwined with the handsome Prince Kai's [Catalyst], she suddenly finds herself at the center of an intergalactic struggle [Fun and Games] and a forbidden attraction

[Midpoint]. Caught between duty and freedom, loyalty and betrayal, she must uncover secrets about her past [Theme Stated] in order to protect her world's future [All Is Lost hint].

Me Before You by Jojo Moyes (Buddy Love)

Louisa Clark is an ordinary girl living an exceedingly ordinary life—steady boyfriend, close family—who has barely been farther afield than their tiny village [Setup/first flawed hero]. She takes a badly needed job working for ex–Master of the Universe Will Traynor [Catalyst], who is wheelchair bound after an accident. Will has always lived a huge life— big deals, extreme sports, worldwide travel—and now he's pretty sure he cannot live the way he is [second flawed hero].

Will is acerbic, moody, bossy—but Lou refuses to treat him with kid gloves [Fun and Games], and soon his happiness means more to her than she expected [Midpoint]. When she learns that Will has shocking plans of his own [All Is Lost hint], she sets out to show him that life is still worth living [Theme Stated].

Sharp Objects by Gillian Flynn (Whydunit)

Fresh from a brief stay at a psych hospital, reporter Camille Preaker [Setup/flawed hero] faces a troubling assignment: she must return to her tiny hometown to cover the murders of two preteen girls [Catalyst]. For years, Camille has hardly spoken to her neurotic, hypochondriac mother or to the half-sister she barely knows: a beautiful thirteen-year-old with an eerie grip on the town. Now, installed in her old bedroom in her family's Victorian mansion [Fun and Games], Camille finds herself identifying with the young victims—a bit too strongly [Midpoint]. Dogged by her own demons, she must unravel the psychological puzzle of her own past [Theme Stated] if she wants to get the story—and survive this homecoming [All Is Lost hint].

As you can see, there are definitely specific beats that appear again and again in these summaries, meaning you can easily write your own synopsis using beats you already have. Do you sense another template coming your way?

Voilà!

THE SAVE THE CAT! SHORT SYNOPSIS TEMPLATE

PARAGRAPH 1: Setup, flawed hero, and Catalyst (2–4 sentences)

PARAGRAPH 2: Break Into 2 and/or Fun and Games (2–4 sentences)

PARAGRAPH 3: Theme Stated, Midpoint hint and/or All Is Lost hint, ending in a cliffhanger (1 to 3 sentences)

Compared to loglines, there's a little more wiggle room in the synopsis format. There's space for more pizzazz, more style, and more tone. So feel free to mix things up and be creative. But these three paragraphs should be included. This is how you effectively pitch a book in one page. And yes, this short synopsis should *not* exceed the length of one page . . . double spaced! (You hoped I might forget about the spacing, didn't you?)

If you can't effectively pitch your novel in one page, then you haven't quite figured out what you're trying to say about it yet. All great novels can be effectively pitched in one page.

You'll notice in the template provided above that I mention a Midpoint *hint* and an All Is Lost *hint*. When pitching directly to readers, you want to provide enough information to give a sense of the stakes and the looming danger, but never so much that you spoil the whole book. And every short synopsis should definitely end in a cliffhanger.

Why?

To leave the reader wanting more, of course! The short synopsis is *not* a play-by-play summary of your book. It's another pitch. Another tease.

In Paragraph 1, we introduce a flawed hero and their world (Setup) to give the reader the sense of who the hero is and why they are best suited for this story. We also evoke the Catalyst that will soon change that world.

In Paragraph 2, we dive into the upside-down world of Act 2 to show the general direction of the plot and to give the reader our hook (the promise of the premise).

And in Paragraph 3, we hint at the stakes (the urgency) and the internal journey, which, combined, make up the *why* of the whole novel. While at the same time we leave the reader wanting more.

Your short synopsis is a vital, indispensable component of your novel package. Once you master it, you can use it over and over again. Basically, any time you need to pitch your novel to another human being in written form, out it comes! Like guns drawn! It's your ultimate novel-selling weapon.

Those of you on the self-publishing path can cut and paste this short synopsis right onto retailer sites, your website, and the back of your book.

Those of you on the traditional publishing path can cut and paste this short synopsis right into your query letter to agents. And if it's *really* good, chances are your agent will cut and paste it right into *their* query letter to editors. And your editor might even cut and paste it (or at least parts of it) right onto the book's jacket flap. I mean, why reinvent the wheel? Especially when you've crafted such a flawless, nonsqueaky wheel.

And for those of you currently just dabbling in the novel-writing process, unsure of what will become of it, this summary can be used anywhere you want to post information about your book or sent to anyone to whom you want to submit your book for feedback.

The short synopsis is a test to make sure you've nailed your beats and that your story resonates. If, after following this template, your short synopsis isn't quite working, it's time to go back and look at your beats again and those handy beat checklists in chapter 2. Perhaps your Catalyst isn't big enough to rip your hero from their Act 1 world. Perhaps your Act 2 world isn't quite different enough from your Act 1 world. Perhaps your Midpoint or All Is Lost stakes aren't weighty enough.

If you fix up those beats, I promise you, your short synopsis will shine.

Now it's time for you to do a little research of your own. Go to your favorite bookstore or online retailer and read one synopsis after another, looking for these patterns. My guess is you'll find they're almost always there. Which means the publishers—who are usually the ones writing these book descriptions—are using this same template . . . whether they realize it or not.

Save the Author!
You Got Problems, I Got Solutions

Well, folks, we've reached the end of the Save the Cat! novel-development process. We know what it takes to create story-worthy heroes; we know how to craft fifteen compelling story beats that will leave our reader breathless; we've studied the ten Save the Cat! story genres and know what specific elements need to be included in each one; *and* we're well versed on how to write a compelling logline and short synopsis.

Sooooo . . .

How are you feeling?

If your answer is *A little freaked out, to be honest*, don't worry. I've jam-packed a whole novel-writing career's worth of wisdom into these pages. It's certainly understandable for you to feel a little over-whelmed. Which is why I've included this chapter, dedicated entirely to the most frequently asked questions and concerns that I hear from authors implementing the Save the Cat! methodology.

So let's get you sorted out.

Help! Where Do I Start?
The Foundation Beats

In my Save the Cat! workshops, often we'd go through the fifteen beats extensively, with explanations and examples and thorough analysis, and at least one student would be staring at me, totally bewildered. When I asked, "What's wrong? Are you still not understanding the A and B Story connection? Should we go back and tackle the Theme Stated again?" the student would continue to stare and blink, and I'd continue to guess at what might be puzzling them, until finally they would be able to put their bafflement into words and say, "Um . . . where do I start?"

Aha! Excellent question!

Reason would dictate that you start at the beginning. You tackle your Opening Image, then you move on to your Theme Stated, then your Setup, and so on. After all, that's the order in which they appear on the beat sheet and the order in which the reader will read them in the finished novel. Sounds logical, right?

But actually, you might be surprised to learn, it's not how *I* tackle the beats.

I'll admit, the prospect of coming up with fifteen beats *is* a little bit daunting. Which is why I usually start with what I like to call the Five **Foundation Beats**. These beats make up the pillars upon which all the other beats stand. They are also all single-scene beats, so they're easier to tackle up front. These are the directional beats of the story, meaning each of these beats sets a new direction for the plot. Once you establish these beats, the rest of the beats tend to fall into place a bit more naturally, based on the simple mechanics of the beat sheet.

The Five Foundation Beats are

- Catalyst
- Break Into 2
- Midpoint
- Break Into 3
- All Is Lost

However, before you tackle *any* of the beats, figure out the three components of your story-worthy hero—a problem (or what makes your hero a flawed hero), a want or goal, and a need. Only when you've got a good idea of *who* your hero is will you be able to figure out what kind of transformative journey they require.

Although everyone is different and the creative process is unique for each writer, here's how I tackle the beat sheet using these Five Foundation Beats:

First, I nail down the three components of my story-worthy hero (problem, want, and need). This starts to create a picture of what the hero's Act 1 world will look like.

Then I work through the following questions:

- What does the hero's Act 2 world look like? How is it different from Act 1? Is it different *enough*? This starts to shape my Break Into 2 beat.

- How would my flawed hero change the wrong way, based on what they *want*, not what they *need*? This continues to shape my Break Into 2 beat.

- What kind of major event would be enough to kick this hero out of their status quo and into this strange new world? This forms the Catalyst beat.

- Does my hero generally flounder or excel in this new world? This determines the Midpoint and whether it's a false victory (the hero excels in the new world) or a false defeat (the hero flounders in the new world).

- How does my hero, then, change the right way, based on what they need? This helps me start to discern my Break Into 3.

- Finally, what kind of rock-bottom life-changing event would be enough to eventually convince my hero to change the right way? This informs my All Is Lost beat—which you may recall is usually another Catalyst.

Help! I Need More Structure! Using the Save the Cat! "Board"

Ah, so you're a structure hound like me, are ya? The beat sheet itself just isn't enough? Like a mouse who's been given a cookie, you gotta have *more*, do ya? Well, fear not. I got more. I got lots more where that beat sheet came from.

I got . . .

The board.

The Save the Cat! board is exactly what it sounds like . . . a board. A corkboard, to be more exact. The biggest you can find at the store. Or, if you're more digitally inclined, check out the Save the Cat! software at

SavetheCat.com for a virtual board that you can put on your laptop and take with you wherever you may roam.

The corkboard is then filled with index cards (I recommend the 3 by 5-inch size), arranged in a particular order to illustrate the Save the Cat! Beat Sheet. It's also a great tool for more visual learners who need to *see* the beats laid out in front of them.

I've found that the board can be super beneficial when you're stuck (while plotting, writing, or revising), to *see* your story in a new way. Literally. By laying out the beats on the board, you get a better view of the BIG picture of your story. And as I said in the last chapter, authors tend to struggle with seeing the big picture. Especially when they're standing in the middle of the picture. (Like on page 120, trying to find a synonym for the word "face." Trust me, there aren't any good ones. Just use "face.")

Once you have your physical corkboard (or your Save the Cat! software), divide the board into four rows. (See the illustration below.) I like to use masking tape. These rows represent Act 1, Act 2A (the first half of Act 2), Act 2B (the second half of Act 2), and Act 3. (Note: The Save the Cat! software is already set up this way.)

ACT 1

ACT 2A

ACT 2B

ACT 3

Now we start laying out our cards, each representing a scene or chapter in our novel. Each card should reflect *one* piece of information. So if you write longer chapters that encompass multiple scenes or pieces of information, then you'll have multiple cards per chapter. But don't worry too much about that right now. Just focus on getting your ideas down on cards.

For example, if you know your Catalyst is going to be that Aunt Clementine gets murdered, that would be one scene or piece of information. And you would create a card that says:

> **Penny finds Aunt
> Clementine's body**

Or if you know that somewhere in your Fun and Games you're going to have a scene where Penny interviews Aunt Clementine's butler and discovers he doesn't have an alibi for the night she was killed, you would create a card that says something like:

> **Penny interviews butler.
> No alibi!**

Or perhaps you know that a few weeks have to pass between two plot points in the Bad Guys Close In and you don't yet know what's going to happen during those weeks; you could create a card that says:

> **Two weeks pass . . .
> ???**

Remember back in chapter 2, when I told you that some of the beats were single-scene beats (like the Theme Stated, Catalyst, and All Is Lost), and some were multi-scene beats (like the Setup, Fun and Games, and Dark Night of the Soul)?

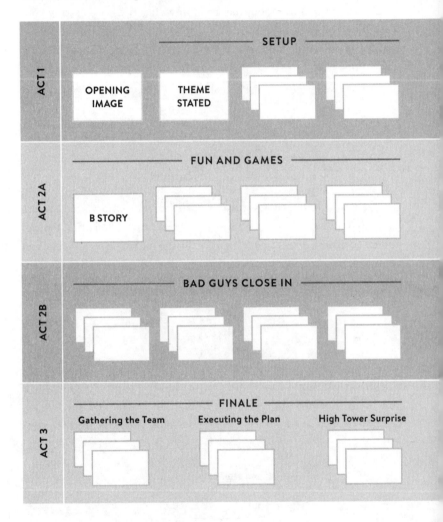

SAVE THE CAT! WRITES A NOVEL

Well, when we start to lay out our cards on the board, we see much more of how that comes into play.

Here is what the board should look like when it's set up:

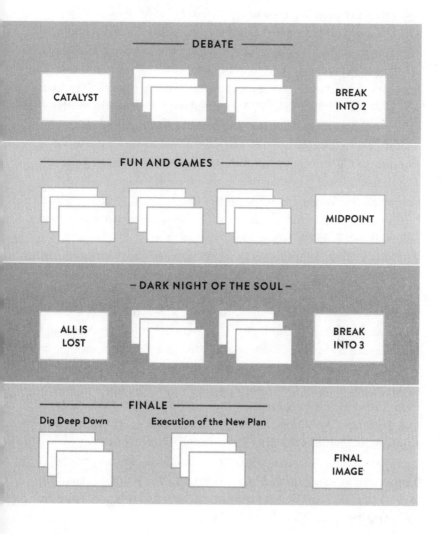

WOWZA! It sure does help to see it all laid out like that, doesn't it?

But by now you might be thinking, *Dang, that Fun and Games section is LONG!*

And you're right. There are a *lot* of scenes to cover before we reach that exciting, stakes-raising, life-changing Midpoint. Which is why the story gods invented B stories and C stories and sometimes even D stories! To fill in those long stretches of pages with something *other* than the A Story. The A Story should still be front and center. For instance, if you're writing a murder mystery, then the ups and downs of solving that mystery better make up the majority of those cards. But you can (and should!) give your reader a break from the A Story every once in a while and talk about something else for a scene or two. What's going on with the love interest? The best friend? The hero's family? That annoying guy at work? What happened to that email from the ex that the hero found back on page 70? Make sure to give your reader some breathing room between major plot points. It will keep the A Story fresh and exciting.

Now, it's important to note that the number of cards depicted in the preceding graphic is by no means the number you're limited to *or* required to have. This is just an illustration to show you that while the Catalyst usually consists of one card or one scene, the Setup, Debate, Fun and Games, Bad Guys Close In, Dark Night of the Soul, and Finale contain multiple cards/scenes. Your specific number of cards will change depending on the number of pages/words in your novel and how you structure your scenes and chapters. But a general rule of thumb is to have approximately 30 cards for every 25,000 words or 100 pages of story. So for a 75,000-word novel, you might end up with somewhere around 90 cards.

However, if you're building the board in the brainstorming phase, I say create as many cards as your awesome little brain can come up with. You can always delete cards later as you start to write. I'm a big fan of the "no limits" method of brainstorming.

If, on the other hand, you're building or updating your board in the writing or revision phase of the novel, chances are you have a target word count or page count goal dictating where your beats go (see the guidelines at the beginning of chapter 2), and you might have to be a little more strict with your card numbers.

But what makes the cork (or virtual) board so functional is that it's highly adaptable! If you get an aha! moment and suddenly figure out that your brilliant bike crash scene belongs not in the Fun and Games but rather in the Bad Guys Close In, then presto change-o! Just move it! This flexibility is why I recommend cork or virtual boards over writing out scenes on a whiteboard. You can add as much detail or information about the scene as you want on that little index card, and when it's time to move it, all the information goes with it.

The board allows you to build and rebuild your story with the touch of a button or relocation of a pin. You can shuffle up your novel whenever you please and see what comes out of the new configuration. Because sometimes all you need is that one simple turn of the kaleidoscope, and suddenly the whole picture comes into focus.

Help! I Might Have More Than One Main Character! A Look at Novel Narratives

After reading chapter 1 of this book, you know that you're supposed to pick *one* character to be your primary hero of the story. And you might remember I gave the example of Aibileen from *The Help* by Kathryn Stockett. Although there are two other characters whose point of view we *do* see, I still consider her the primary hero of that novel, the one who changes the *most*. But that doesn't mean Minny and Skeeter didn't have their own transformative arcs. They most certainly did, so they *also* have beat sheets. (Check out the breakdown of *The Help* on page 124 to see how their three beat sheets weave together.)

So, yes, if you're writing a novel with multiple main characters, chances are you're going to need multiple beat sheets, one for each character, in order to track each character's transformative arc throughout the story. I still recommend nailing down your *primary* hero first, but the best way to juggle multiple arcs is to create multiple beat sheets and then weave them together to form a compelling narrative.

Some beats might overlap. For instance, in *The Help*, Aibileen and Skeeter experience the same Break Into 2 beat when Aibileen agrees to share her stories with Skeeter. But the two have different Catalysts. And Minny's beats are very separate from Aibileen's and Skeeter's until the Midpoint, when the story lines converge.

On the other hand, you may write a novel with multiple main characters in which *none* of the beats overlap. This happened to me when I was writing my young adult novel *Boys of Summer*. The story is told from the viewpoints of three boys—Grayson, Mike, and Ian. They are best friends who share a very transformative summer on a vacationers' island, but their experiences are quite different. For the most part, they have very different beat sheets. Their only overlapping beat is the All Is Lost, which is fitting because it's when they all realize how each of their actions are affecting the others, and this ends up strengthening their friendship. But yes, it means I created three distinct beat sheets—one for each character—before I started writing. And I was constantly juggling those beat sheets as the novel developed and changed.

The best way to get good at juggling multiple beat sheets is to study authors who have done it. I recommend finding at least three novels starring multiple protagonists (preferably in the same story genre as the book you're writing) and writing a beat sheet for each one. Study where the beats overlap and where they differ. Take note of how the author interwove the stories together to create their tapestry. Then set out to do the same.

So how do you know if you *need* multiple beat sheets?

Well, the best places to look at are your narration and point of view.

How many narrators does your novel have? (Or, if you haven't started writing yet, how many narrators do you *plan* to have?) If you're undecided on this point, the following breakdown might help you decide. Let's look at the various types of novel narratives and see how many beat sheets each one most likely requires.

SINGLE FIRST-PERSON NARRATIVE

- **DEFINITION:** The novel is told from the direct point of view of one main character, using pronouns like *I*, *me*, and *my*.

- **EXAMPLES:** *The Hunger Games, Prey, The Hate U Give, Ready Player One, The Outsiders, The Adventures of Huckleberry Finn, The Handmaid's Tale.*

- **BEAT SHEET COUNT:** One. One narrator = one hero = one beat sheet.

MULTIPLE FIRST-PERSON NARRATIVE

- **DEFINITION:** The novel is told from the direct point of view of multiple main characters (usually told through alternating chapters), using pronouns like *I*, *me*, and *my*.

- **EXAMPLES:** *The Help, The Girl on the Train, The Sun Is Also a Star* by Nicola Yoon, *An Ember in the Ashes* by Sabaa Tahir, *The Time Traveler's Wife* by Audrey Niffenegger, *Wonder, All American Boys* by Brendan Kiely and Jason Reynolds, *Children of Blood and Bone* by Tomi Adeyemi.

- **BEAT SHEET COUNT:** Multiple, usually one for each narrator.

SINGLE THIRD-PERSON NARRATIVE (LIMITED)

- **DEFINITION:** The novel is told from the point of view of an outside narrator (someone not *in* the story), who has access to only one character's thoughts, using pronouns like *he, she, they, hers, his,* and so on.

- **EXAMPLES:** *Harry Potter and the Sorcerer's Stone, Misery, 1984, The Statistical Probability of Love at First Sight, The Deep, Heart-Shaped Box.*

- **BEAT SHEET COUNT:** One. Whoever's thoughts the narrator has access to.

MULTIPLE THIRD-PERSON NARRATIVE (LIMITED)

- **DEFINITION:** The novel is told from the point of view of an outside narrator (someone not *in* the story), who has access to multiple characters' thoughts, but only one character at a time (usually told through alternating chapters), using pronouns like *he, she, they, hers, his,* and so on.

- **EXAMPLES:** *Big Little Lies, Six of Crows, Eleanor and Park, The Da Vinci Code, A Game of Thrones, Far from the Tree.*

- **BEAT SHEET COUNT:** Multiple, usually one for each major character whose thoughts the narrator has access to.

THIRD-PERSON NARRATIVE (OMNISCIENT)

- **DEFINITION:** Usually found in older books (less common today), the novel is told from an outside narrator's point of view (someone not in the story) who has access to everyone's thoughts at once, using pronouns like *he, she, they, hers, his,* and so on.

- **EXAMPLES:** *Emma, And Then There Were None, Les Misérables, A Christmas Carol, Matilda.*

- **BEAT SHEET COUNT:** One or multiple, depending on how many of the characters have significant transformative arcs.

Help! I'm Writing a Series! The Series Beat Sheet

You probably guessed by now that if you're writing a series with multiple novels in it, you're going to need multiple beat sheets—one for each novel. But you'll also need an overarching beat sheet that covers the entire series.

This Series Beat Sheet doesn't necessarily need to have *all* of the fifteen beats, but it should track a larger arc for your hero or heroes. One that stretches over the entire series. And it should follow a three-act structure similar to a single-book beat sheet.

Think about trilogies, for example. Each book will have three acts and fifteen beats, but the first book, as a whole, is often the setup book, depicting an Act 1 world for the series. It brings us and the hero into the story, introduces all of the players, and lets us know what's what. Then it usually ends with a Catalyst, a Debate (or a choice for the hero), and a Break Into 2, effectively setting up the second book in the trilogy, or the Act 2 book. Then the second book in the trilogy usually ends with an All Is Lost moment, followed by a wallowing Dark Night of the Soul and finally another decision: a Break Into 3 that leads us to the final installment. And don't third books in trilogies always feel like one giant Finale? It's where we find the most epic battles, the most characters lost, the highest stakes, and the greatest victories!

So, a Series Beat Sheet for a trilogy might look something like this:

> Book 1 – Series Act 1
> Book 2 – Series Act 2
> Book 3 – Series Act 3

This is the way I set up my sci-fi Unremembered trilogy. In book 1, *Unremembered*, I introduce my hero, Seraphina, who has literally crash-landed in an unfamiliar world (our world). By the end of the first book, I've revealed exactly where Seraphina is from and how she happened to arrive in our world. Then, in her *series* Break Into 2 (the decision that leads to the second book), she escapes our world. By the end of book 2, *Unforgotten*, Seraphina has had a *series* All Is Lost and a *series* Dark Night of the Soul and makes a very fateful and sacrificial decision to return to her world. This is the *series* Break Into 3, which leads us straight into *Unchanged,* the third book, and the *series* Finale, where Seraphina finally faces up to people who made her who she is and who have been trying to control her for the entire trilogy.

A four-book series or "quartet" can also be broken down in a similar way. Here's a possible Series Beat Sheet for a four-book series:

> Book 1 – Series Act 1
> Book 2 – Series Act 2 (up until a Midpoint twist)
> Book 3 – Series Act 2 (up until the Break Into 3)
> Book 4 – Series Act 3

And yes, while you're doing *all* of this, you're also juggling character arcs for your hero—one for each novel *and* one for the series as a whole.

Yikes!

No one said writing a successful series was easy! All of that strife and torment you deal with when beating out *one* novel? Well, multiply that times three, and that's what it's like to plot a successful trilogy. But with a little thoughtful planning and some storytelling ingenuity, it *can* be done well. And it has been.

Let's look at one of the most famous novel series of our time: the Harry Potter series by J. K. Rowling. Each of the seven novels in the series has an excellent beat sheet in which Harry grows and changes, learning little pieces about himself and his destiny along the way. But the series, as a whole, also has a transformative journey, as Harry goes from a shy, insecure orphan boy to the mature, confident, magical warrior who fulfills his destiny and defeats Voldemort. Each of the mini arcs he experiences in the seven books adds up to the larger arc of the entire series. Which is why he can't just defeat Voldemort in book 1; rather, he has to *temporarily* maim him, learning a little something about his own abilities in the process.

When you plot a series, every book has to count. You can't have a series with one or two important novels and a bunch of filler novels. Every book has to have a purpose. A *why*. A Theme Stated and a lesson learned for our hero. And they can't all be the same. Related and interlinked, yes, but not the same.

Which is why, as I've mentioned, often not every book in a series will fall into the same genre. As the *purpose* of each installment will vary, so might the *type* of story. *The Hunger Games* (book 1 in the trilogy) is a Dude with a Problem. It's the story that brings Katniss Everdeen *into* the system. The choice of how she's going to deal with that system isn't broached until book 2, *Catching Fire*, which makes it an Institutionalized story. Only when she's decided to "burn it down" can she start coming to terms with being the savior and rebel leader that she's become, making the third book, *Mockingjay*, a Superhero story.

Three books. Three beat sheets. Three genres. One phenomenal story. And you can do it too. I believe in you!

Help! My Hero is Unlikable! How to Save a Cat

Back in 2011, when I was writing *52 Reasons to Hate My Father*, my young adult novel about a spoiled teen heiress who has to take on fifty-two low-wage jobs in order to earn her twenty-five-million-dollar trust fund, I immediately confronted the likability issue, which many authors have asked me about since. My hero was a filthy rich girl who's never worked a day in her life, grew up traveling the world on yachts, lives in a mansion in Bel-Air, drives a five-hundred-thousand-dollar Mercedes, and oh yeah . . . she's an insufferable spoiled brat. Now that's a character you can root for!

Here's the problem. I told you way back in chapter 1 that you need to create a hero who has somewhere to go. Someone with flaws. Someone imperfect. Someone for whom change is a necessity. You gotta back *way* up on the runway so you have some takeoff room to fly that hero where they need to go. And sometimes, in order to do this, you gotta start with a hero who is less than a peach.

But you *still* have to make sure the reader will stick around to see that transformation take place.

So what do you do?

YOU SAVE A CAT!

As I mentioned in the introduction, "save the cat!" actually started as a fancy writer trick designed to take an unlikable hero and make them a little more likable. It originates from the imaginary scenario that you've got a douchebag of a hero, desperately in need of some de-douchebagging, walking around doing douchebaggy stuff when suddenly he sees a cat stuck up in a tree. He stops, he climbs up in the tree, and he saves the cat, at which point you, the reader, stop and go, *Wait a minute; this guy can't be* all *bad. He's got a good heart.* And voilà! Now you've got a *redeemable* unlikable hero—instead of just an unlikable one.

Okay, so you don't literally have to save a cat! It's just an expression that means you need to employ some writerly sleight of hand to convince your reader there's something worth rooting for in your hero.

Although I'll admit that in *52 Reasons to Hate My Father*, I actually did make the hero's dog an insecure, emotionally damaged rescue. So yes, she quite *literally* saved a dog! But you don't have to rescue animals to solve your likability problem; you have other options.

GIVE YOUR HERO ONE REDEEMING QUALITY, ACTION, OR HOBBY

Is your hero meek? Bossy? Vengeful? Whiny? Depressed? Ungrateful? Nothing can spoil a great Setup like an annoying hero you just want to shake and say, "Snap out of it! Life is not that bad!"

And that's exactly what you need to do in this situation. You need to make life *not that bad.* You need to give your hero *one* little thing that the reader can cling to. Do they have a cute niece, nephew, or neighbor kid who looks up to them? Do they have a secret notebook filled with really bad, yet endearing, poetry? Do they volunteer once a week at the dog shelter? Give 'em *something* that we can latch onto and think, *Well, at least they've got that.*

In my young adult novel *The Chaos of Standing Still*, the hero, Ryn, was struggling to get over the death of her best friend. And let's just say she wasn't exactly a bundle of laughs. When my friend and critique partner, Joanne Rendell, read the first draft, she said, "Well, the story's good, but Ryn is kind of a downer. She has no passions. No interests. No hobbies. It's sort of depressing to read. Can't you give her *something*?"

And of course, Joanne was right. Critique partners usually are! So we brainstormed for days trying to figure out what Ryn's *thing* was. We finally came up with drawing. It was a passion she'd given up after her best friend died because her grief was clouding her ability to draw things the way she saw them. I was able to talk about her lost passion for drawing and flash back to times when she did draw and it made her happy. I truly believe this small tweak not only fixed my likability issue but also gave me a cool metaphor to use to show how Ryn gets over grief: by learning to draw again.

Or think about *The Hunger Games*. Gruff, severe Katniss Everdeen is not exactly warm and inviting when you first meet her. What makes her likable? The fact that she'll do *anything* for her sister, Prim—something we witness on page 22 when she volunteers for the reaping in Prim's place. But even before that, the author gives us so much to love about this tough young girl. Like the fact that she'll break the rules of the Capitol to feed her sister. Or, don't forget page 1, where Katniss tells us she spared the cat's life because Prim cried when she tried to drown him in a bucket.

Save the Cat!

GIVE YOUR HERO A (REALLY BAD) ENEMY OR SITUATION

Recent studies have shown that reading fiction can make you more empathetic. It gives you X-ray vision into other people's thoughts, feelings, and struggles. It allows you to peek in the windows of other people's lives and see why they are the way they are. A gift we're rarely given in real life. And learning about someone else's struggle can go a long way toward helping us not only understand that person, but *sympathize* with them as well.

Which is why another great way to bring a reader around to an unlikable character is to pit them against an even *less* likable character. A villain, a nemesis, a complicated best friend, even a horrible parent can do the trick. Once we see how horrible *that* person is, we no longer can bear to hate the hero! Instead, we *understand* the hero. We think, *Well, no wonder they're so horrible; look what they have to put up with!*

Understanding why a person is the way they are helps us sympathize with that person. It's a lesson in empathy that I think we can all stand to learn these days. What makes someone act the way they do? What horrors is this person living with? Although in real life we can't always go behind closed doors and find out, we can certainly do it in fiction. And we should!

In *The Kite Runner* by Khaled Hosseini, we're introduced to the hero, Amir. Let's face it: Amir isn't very nice to his best friend, Hassan. In fact, he's just plain awful to him most of the time. Why do we root for this character? Why do we keep turning the pages to find out what will happen to him?

Because of his father.

We get a peek at what Amir's life is like: his struggle to win the affections of his seemingly cold-hearted father, his desperation to prove to his father that's he not the worthless son his father thinks he is. And *that* is enough. We don't forgive Amir for the things he does to Hassan, at least not until the end. But we can start to *sympathize* and understand his actions a little bit better.

I used this same parental trick in *52 Reasons to Hate My Father*. Actually, the trick is in the *title*. Lexington Larrabee is pretty horrible, but wait until you meet her dad. He's seemingly unloving, uncaring, and never around. No wonder she acts like such an irresponsible brat! She's trying to get her father's attention.

A similar way to accomplish this same task is to put your hero in a bad situation. Or at the very least, *explain* their situation.

Emma Woodhouse in *Emma* by Jane Austen lost her mother at a very young age. No wonder she's so wary of attachment! Rachel in *The Girl on the Train* was cheated on by her husband with a woman he went on to marry and have a child with. No wonder she drinks! Jean Valjean went to prison for nineteen years for stealing a loaf of bread. No wonder he's been hardened and turned against society! Even the infamous Ebenezer Scrooge has a reason for how he turned out: he was kicked out of his house by his father when he was a boy. No wonder he has such trouble empathizing with others!

Characters are never unlikable for no reason. They don't emerge that way from the womb. We all start as a blank slate. So what was drawn on that slate to turn the hero into the person we meet on page one of the book? Giving us a glimpse of their past, their parentage, and/or their present situation can really help us wrap our head around who this person is and why they are the way they are. And once we get a firm grasp on the *why*, we can start sympathizing with the hero's plight to fix it.

Help! I'm Stuck!
Some Parting Words of Wisdom and Inspiration

There's no such thing as writer's block.

There! I said it!

If you're awake, you can write. If you can sit down in a chair, you can write. If you have fingers, you can write.

I didn't say the writing was going to be any *good*. But you're never actually *blocked* from writing. You can always write something.

Regardless of what stage you're at, you *will* get stuck in this process. I guarantee it. You will have good days and bad days. You will write scenes you love and scenes you throw away. You will change your Catalyst beat a million times until you come up with the right one. You will get to the end of the novel and realize your Fun and Games is all wrong.

It's called a creative *process* for a reason.

But that doesn't mean I'm going to end the book without giving you some helpful tips for dealing with that process!

So, here's what I got for you.

GIVE YOURSELF PERMISSION TO WRITE/PLOT BADLY

There's no such thing as writer's block or plotter's block. There's only perfectionist's block. (Thank you to author Emily Hainsworth for this brilliant, brilliant phrase!) We're terrified that what we write or plot will be *horrible*. Well, then, just give in to that fear and *let* it be horrible. Write something horrible. Plot out a dreadful, disgusting, cringe-worthy beat sheet. Let yourself SUCK!

Here's a little secret for you: If you write something horrible, no one but you *ever* has to read it. And *you* can always go back and fix it later.

Nora Roberts says, "You can't fix a blank page." And how true is that? Write something bad so Future You has something to fix! Otherwise Future You will be very bored and disappointed that Past You didn't live up to your end of the bargain and put something down on that page. Don't disappoint Future You. Don't put Future You out of a job. Write something awful and let Future You deal with it. That's what Future You does best.

So don't be afraid to write badly. Embrace the bad! Or as I like to say, "Don't be afraid to write crap. Crap makes great fertilizer."

BE FLEXIBLE! BEATS WILL CHANGE

Whether you're a plotter or a pantser—whether you spend days, weeks, months, or even *years* drafting your beat sheet and making sure every single detail is figured out before you start writing, or you simply jot down a few ideas and hit the page—either way, your beats *will* change. It's inevitable. You may get to the final page of your novel and realize that your Setup is all wrong. You may be halfway through your first draft (or even your *final* draft) and realize your All Is Lost needs to come *way* earlier, or be *way* more devastating.

Your beats are not carved in stone. Nor should they be.

Author Terry Pratchett says, "The first draft is just you telling yourself the story." In fact, some people even call the first draft "the discovery draft." Because that's what you're doing. You're discovering the story. You're exploring the world. You're getting to know the hero. Plotting a novel and thinking you can stick to everything you planned is about as delusional as plotting your life and thinking nothing will ever go astray.

Yes, hammering out your fifteen beats in advance can certainly help you figure out where you *want* to go with the story and will probably even set you in the right direction, but it won't ever help you figure out *exactly* how to get there.

Writing a novel is a Golden Fleece. The daunting white page (or screen) you face every day is your road. "The End" is your prize. I, and your critique partners and fellow writers, are your team. And there *will* be detours along the way. There will be road apples that stop your journey cold and force you to reroute. Rebeat.

Be flexible and let your beats change as your story and your hero come more and more into focus.

And when you get lost, remember to come back to your wants and needs. They are your signposts on this journey. As you drive toward the Midpoint, keep your sights on what your hero wants. And then, as you drive toward the Final Image, keep your sights on what the hero needs. These two things will help guide you through the dark spots on the road.

DON'T COMPARE YOUR WORK IN PROGRESS TO SOMEONE ELSE'S FINISHED MASTERPIECE

As you read the beat sheets in this book, and as you set out to analyze other novels and find the patterns in them, keep in mind that these are *finished* products. Not works in progress. They represent months, sometimes even *years*, of struggle. Not to mention countless revisions, editorial letters, copyedits, and professional proofreads. It's hard *not* to compare ourselves to the great works we find on our shelves, because what else do we *have* to compare ourselves to? It's not like any of our favorite authors are posting their messy, hideous rough drafts on their website for all to see. But I guarantee you, they exist. Those authors have them. We *all* have them. Novels don't spill onto the page in finished form. Usually (at least for me!), they spill onto the page as grotesque, misshapen Rorschach test images that I have to squint and tilt my head at for hours on end to attempt to make any sense of.

And along the same lines, try not to compare your beat sheet in progress to any of the beat sheets featured in this book. Remember, those are analyses of stories that are already finished and perfected. I can guarantee you they don't resemble anything like the outline the author started with when they first sat down to write (if they even started with an outline!).

This is what I call the difference between a **Before Beat Sheet** and an **After Beat Sheet**. A Before Beat Sheet is what we plotters create before we start writing—a road map for our story to help us stay on target to our destination. An After Beat Sheet is an analysis of a finished, completed, revised, edited, copyedited, proofread novel to study the patterns in the story.

To illustrate how different these two beat sheets can be, and how much a beat sheet can change as you write the novel, I've included Before and After Beat Sheets for my novel *The Geography of Lost*

Things. Read it, and you'll see how sparse the Before Beat Sheet is, how many holes there still are, how little I had figured out before I started writing, and how much the beats changed as I spent more time with the story and the characters. In the After Beat Sheet, you'll notice many of the beats have moved, while others are just more fleshed out, and some beats were rewritten altogether.

So, be kind to yourself. You won't have it all figured out at the very start. Or even if you do, as I said before, it most likely *will* change.

THE GEOGRAPHY OF LOST THINGS

BY: Jessica Brody
STC GENRE: Golden Fleece
BOOK GENRE: Young adult contemporary
PAGE COUNT: 464 (Simon Pulse Hardcover, 2018)

1. Opening Image

BEFORE: An envelope arrives with the title and keys to the classic car belonging to Ali's dead father, Jackson. She hates her father and the car (because he was always driving away from her in it). Jackson left Ali and her mother with a lot of debt.

AFTER: A messenger arrives with an envelope from Jackson, Ali's recently deceased father, who walked out on her and her mother years ago. What's inside won't be revealed until later.

2. Setup

BEFORE: Ali sets off to sell the car to a buyer in Fort Bragg. She needs the money to save her foreclosed house and help get her mother out of debt (A Story/wants). She can't drive a stick shift. so her ex-boyfriend, Nico, has to come with her to drive the car. Somewhere, we see Ali throwing things away. She's constantly decluttering her life.

Her biggest flaw: She's too quick to discard things before giving them a chance to prove their worth.

AFTER: Ali's mom leaves for a week-long catering job while Ali is left to pack up her house, which is being foreclosed by the bank. Ali wants to try to save the house, but her mother has given up on saving it. As she packs, Ali throws most things away (she is an obsessive declutterer) and thinks about what got them into this mess of debt. It was all Jackson's fault.

Jackson was constantly in and out of Ali's life. He was never reliable and was constantly opening credit cards in her mother's name (and not paying them off). We learn that Jackson's two favorite things in life were his 1968 Firebird 400 convertible and a 1990s post-grunge band called Fear Epidemic. Ali is harboring a lot of anger and resentment toward her father.

We also learn that Ali loves doing personality quizzes. She likes that they distill people down into easy-to-define boxes. This ties into her flaw of labeling people too quickly so she can "throw them away" just as quickly.

3. Theme Stated

BEFORE: While visiting Glass Beach in Fort Bragg, someone says to Ali (re: a piece of sea glass): "The ocean forgives." Meaning the ocean can take something old and seemingly invaluable like trash and turn it into something shiny and worth keeping.

This is a reference to Ali's inability to forgive her father and how quick she is to throw things away (including Nico), deeming them worthless. One man's trash is another man's treasure.

Ali's Life Lesson: Forgiveness (giving people the opportunity to show you who they really are before you label them and discard them).

AFTER: On their last day of high school, Ali's best friend, June, gives her a scrapbook she made, documenting their friendship. "You're not going to throw it away, right?" June asks, to which Ali vehemently replies, "I'm not going to throw it away. *Ever.* I love it." June then says, "That's right. And you don't throw away things that you love."

Ali knows June is referring to her ex-boyfriend Nico, but really this is the life lesson that Ali will learn about her father as well. Don't discard people too quickly. There might be things about them that you don't know or understand.

Later, the theme is restated by a man on the beach in Fort Bragg who says (re: a piece a sea glass that Ali found), "The ocean forgives." Meaning the ocean can take something old and seemingly invaluable like trash and turn it into something shiny and worth keeping.

Ali's Life Lesson: Forgiveness (giving people the opportunity to show you how valuable they can be).

4. Catalyst

BEFORE: The buyer tells Ali the car isn't worth as much as she thought it would be. Her dad didn't take care of it as well as she thought (maybe because he was getting sick in recent years?).

AFTER: A knock on the door. Ali opens it to find the messenger we saw in the Opening Image. He claims to have lived with Jackson before he died. He gives Ali an envelope and inside Ali finds the key to Jackson's most prized possession: his 1968 Firebird 400 convertible.

5. Debate

BEFORE: How will Ali get the money to save her house now?

Nico tells Ali about "trading up" on Craigslist. They can start with something small and through a series of bigger and better trades, end up with something worth the amount of money she needs to save the house.

At first, Ali thinks he's nuts. It'll never work. But what does she have to lose?

AFTER: What will Ali do with the car?

Almost immediately she puts the car up for sale on Craigslist, figuring the money she makes from it can go to save her house.

The next day she goes to the computer lab at school to check if she got any responses, and Nico is there. The two share an awkward encounter, fraught with animosity, and we learn that Nico is Ali's ex-boyfriend. They broke up one month ago (for reasons we don't yet know).

Ali finds a ton of responses to her Craigslist post. The man who offers her the most money lives in Crescent City, CA (five hours north of there). She tells him that she'll drive the car up tonight. The amount he's offering is enough to save the house from foreclosure (wants).

When Ali gets back to her own car in the parking lot, she finds Nico waiting for her. He read the email over her shoulder and knows about the sale of the car. He snarkily reminds her that she can't drive a stick shift, so how will she ever get the car up to Crescent City? Ali realizes the only person she knows who *can* drive a stick shift is Nico.

6. Break Into 2

BEFORE: Ali agrees to go along with Nico's crazy scheme. They put their first item up for trade on Craigslist.

AFTER: Ali really doesn't want to ask Nico for help, but she has no other choice. She offers to give him one thousand dollars from the sale of the car in exchange for driving it up to Crescent City with her. He agrees.

7. B Story

BEFORE: Rediscovering Nico and learning about his secrets (the things she never stayed around long enough to learn about before breaking up with him; i.e., "throwing him away").

Also, the B Story will be flashbacks of Ali and Nico's relationship, leading up to their breakup. The real reason they broke up will be a mystery to the reader, until it's revealed through the flashback.

AFTER: Nico is the B Story character. Through flashbacks of what their relationship was like when it was good compared to how bad it is now, Ali will learn more about herself and her flaws.

But ultimately it will be this journey with Nico that opens her eyes to what really happened the night they broke up and, more important, teaches her the theme of forgiveness.

8. Fun and Games

BEFORE: Upward path: Trading up on Craigslist, Nico and Ali fighting, meeting new people through the trades.

We also learn more about Jackson's obsession with a 1990s postgrunge band called Fear Epidemic and how he left Ali and her mom to tour with them when they got back together in the late 2000s.

AFTER: **Downward path**: Ali and Nico do *not* get along. It's clear they're both still angry at each other about the breakup, and the car ride is tense.

As they reach their first pit stop, Fort Bragg, Nico tries to convince Ali that she shouldn't sell the car. She should keep it because it's a classic. Instead, she can earn enough money to save her house by "trading up" on Craigslist. He explains that you start with something small and, through a series of bigger and better trades, end up with something worth a lot of money. Ali thinks he's nuts and won't agree to it. Nico says he's going to do it anyway and prove to her that it works. He starts the trades on his own.

As they travel farther up the coast, they hit a literal roadblock, which forces them to turn around and take an alternate road (setting back Ali's goal of reaching Crescent City by the end of the day).

They have to spend the night together in a hotel room and it's beyond awkward.

Also, through scattered flashbacks we learn more about Ali's relationship with Nico and her childhood with Jackson.

9. Midpoint

BEFORE: **False victory**: trades have been going well but stakes are raised at a Midpoint party when Ali and Nico almost kiss.

AFTER: **False defeat**: They reach Crescent City and the buyer examines the car, quickly coming to the conclusion that it's a "clone." It's not a 400 like her father claimed. It's a regular Firebird that Jackson stuck a fake 400 emblem on.

Ali considers this just another way that Jackson has let her down. The car is worth only a fraction of what she thought and not nearly enough to save her house.

By this point, Nico has already traded up to something worth $200. He convinces her to keep the car (for now) and join him on his "trade up" journey. She reluctantly agrees, figuring she has nothing left to lose.

10. Bad Guys Close In

BEFORE: Downward path: Trades slow down? Or they run into trouble with the trades? Ali and Nico's relationship is heating back up, which summons Ali's internal bad guys to screw it up.

Ali starts to put together pieces about Nico and the night of the breakup.

AFTER: Upward path: The quest is going well. Ali and Nico continue up the coast, going where the trades take them, and eventually trading up to something valued at $5,000.

Miraculously, Nico and Ali are also starting to get along better, maybe even having fun. Nico teaches Ali how to drive a stick shift. Then, when they go to watch a movie at a drive-in theater, they kiss, causing Ali to reexamine her feelings for Nico.

Meanwhile, more flashbacks about Jackson are triggered by the various people Ali meets from Craigslist and the things they're trading. These flashbacks start to reveal another side of Jackson, beyond just his disappointments.

In the trunk of the car, Ali finds a picture of Jackson with the lead singer of Fear Epidemic (from when Jackson was a roadie for them on their reunion tour).

11. All Is Lost

BEFORE: The car breaks down and it'll cost way too much money to fix it. Their journey is stalled.

AFTER: Someone from Craigslist scams them and they lose the last item they traded, bringing them back down to $0 (**road apple**). Ali blames Nico for not seeing the scam coming, and the two fight. But it quickly becomes clear that this fight is not about Craigslist. This is a continuation of the fight from the night they broke up, except this time Nico is saying things to Ali that he didn't say before, namely, the truth. And it stings.

Ali storms off, takes the car, and leaves Nico alone in the parking lot.

12. Dark Night of the Soul

BEFORE: Ali wants to quit and go home. Nico comes clean about the night of the breakup and what really happened.

Ali realizes she was too quick to judge him and cast him aside. She was working under false assumptions (because she didn't stick around long enough to learn the truth).

Ali finds a rare vinyl Fear Epidemic record in the trunk of the car. It once belonged to her father, and it's worth a lot of money.

AFTER: As Ali wallows in the car, she has one final flashback about Nico: the night they broke up. Finally, the details of that night are revealed.

Ali is pulled out of the flashback by the sound of Nico's phone beeping with a series of text messages. What Ali reads on the phone reveals the final missing piece of what happened the night of the breakup (**Dark Night epiphany**). And it's a piece that absolves Nico of everything Ali had accused him of. Ali realizes she misjudged him and threw him away too quickly. That's why Nico has been so angry at her during this trip.

Realizing her mistake, she goes back to find him. Nico and Ali have a heart-to-heart on the beach and all is forgiven. But she has yet to forgive the first person who ever let her down. The one person she never thought she could forgive . . .

Ali goes to a classic car repair shop to sell Jackson's Firebird. It's not worth as much as she thought, but it's enough to get them both home. And, after everything they lost from the Craigslist trades, they need all the money they can get. But before she hands over the car, she finds a cassette tape in the player that belonged to Jackson. She listens to it, hearing a recording made when Jackson was on tour with Fear Epidemic. Apparently, Jackson wrote a song during that tour that was supposed to be on the band's new album, but they broke up before they could record it. Ali has a feeling the song is about her, and she wants to know what the lyrics say. She realizes she wants to understand her father.

13. Break Into 3

BEFORE: Ali decides to continue the journey and get the rest of the money she needs through Craigslist trades. She and Nico (now reconciled) put the vinyl album up for barter on Craigslist.

AFTER: Ali makes a decision not to sell the car (yet) and instead to drive it north to Tacoma, Washington, where the lead singer of Fear Epidemic now lives. He's the only one who she thinks might know who her father really was.

14. Finale

BEFORE: The lead singer of Fear Epidemic responds to their Craigslist post and summons Ali to his house. He remembers her father (who was a roadie for the band on their reunion tour). He gives Ali the missing piece she needs to forgive her father (something about her father she didn't know?). He tells her how much her dad really loved her.

Then, after hearing about their quest, the singer offers to trade her something for the vinyl record. But the item he offers is way more valuable than the record because he wants to help. Ali gets the money she needs to save the house, but instead decides to save the car? Or spend it on something else? She learns that some things are worth keeping and some things you have to let go of (and at first you may not know which is which).

AFTER: Ali meets with Nolan Cook, the man from the photograph Ali found in the trunk of the Firebird. Nolan Cook tells Ali something about her father that she never knew—a detail about one of her flashbacks that changes the meaning of the entire flashback and starts to explain why Jackson *really* left. It wasn't for the reasons Ali always thought.

Then Nolan digs up the lyrics that Jackson wrote. They *are* about Ali, and when Ali reads them, her father starts to take shape before her eyes. She understands him on a deeper level. A level that finally allows her to forgive him.

15. Final Image

BEFORE: Ali and Nico drive the car back home, reunited.

AFTER: Ali and Nico get back in the Firebird to drive home (Ali is now behind the wheel). She's not heading home with the money to save her house. But she's heading home with something better—closure.

Final Image

I have no idea what in this book will resonate with you and what won't. What will help you through your own writing Dark Night of the Soul and what you simply skimmed over. That's why I put *everything* I have into these pages—over a decade of story wisdom—hoping that something you read will not only stick but also serve to *transform*.

Yes, it is my sincerest hope that you close this book as not only a better writer, but a changed person. What flaws did you uncover in yourself? What imperfections did you perfect? What *wants* did you abandon in service to your more worthy *needs*?

You, my friend, are the true hero of this story. You are the reason I wrote this book. Right now, yours is the only transformation that matters to me. So, go out there and be the storytelling superhero that I know you're destined to be.

ACKNOWLEDGMENTS

This book would not exist if it weren't for some pretty stellar people. Thank you first and foremost to Blake Snyder, for introducing this magical method to the world and for guiding me and inspiring me through your written words. I hope I have done you proud with this installment. And to B. J. Markel for carrying on Blake's legacy and trusting me to write this book. You have been my champion from the very start, and I truly couldn't have done this without you. Also thanks to Rich Kaplan for your tireless efforts in spreading the magic of Save the Cat! to so many writers around the world and for believing in me and my quest to adapt this methodology for novelists. Thank you to Scott Brandon Hoffman for introducing me to Save the Cat! (waaaaaay back when). You are the Catalyst for everything! And of course, thank you to my agent, Jim McCarthy, for always saying, "Cool!" when I pitch you a new idea (well, *almost* always), but especially for saying, "Cool!" when I came to you with the idea for this book.

I am forever indebted to Lisa Westmoreland at Ten Speed Press for taking a chance on this project and for guiding me through the writing of my very first nonfiction book (which often felt like an All Is Lost). Your patience, wisdom, and gentle nudges in the right direction were always exactly what I needed. Thank you! Also thank you to my exquisite copyeditor, Kristi Hein, who whipped this book into shape and delighted me with our amusing sideline exchanges about jacket flap spoilers, vampires, and corkscrews. And to the wonderful people at Ten Speed Press who have worked so hard to get this book out into the world. That includes, but is by no means limited to, Daniel Wikey, Eleanor Thatcher, and Chloe Rawlins.

Giant, overflowing buckets of gratitude go to Joanne Rendell, Jessica Khoury, José Silerio, and Jennifer Wolfe for not only listening to me whine incessantly about the genres, but also offering sage advice just when I needed it most and for guiding me down the path to finding "the perfect ten." But when it comes to the writing process, my husband, Charlie, always deserves the *most* thanks of anyone. After all, he has to live with me during the Fun and Games *and* the Bad Guys Close In *and* the All Is Lost. Thank you for being my constant Break Into 3, my B Story, and my heart. And as always, thank you to my parents, for being my first and still most fanatic cheerleaders, and especially to my dad, Michael Brody, for passing on the "writing gene."

But most of all, thank you to all my students. All of you. Whether you came to my writing workshops, or took one of my online classes, or we're just meeting now, for the first time, through this book. Just know that this book was inspired by you, is made possible because of you, and is wholeheartedly dedicated to you. Your creativity, energy, and determination to fill the world with stories are what keeps me going through the darkest nights of the soul. I wrote this book for you. Go forth and tell beautiful tales.

ABOUT THE AUTHOR

Since leaving her job as a studio executive for MGM Studios in 2005, Jessica Brody has sold more than fifteen novels to major publishers. She writes books for teens, tweens, and adults, including *The Geography of Lost Things* (Golden Fleece), *The Chaos of Standing Still* (Rites of Passage), *Better You Than Me* (Out of the Bottle), *52 Reasons to Hate My Father* (Fool Triumphant), the Unremembered trilogy (Superhero), and the forthcoming *Sky Without Stars* (Institutionalized), the first installment in a new sci-fi series pitched as "*Les Misérables* in space." She also writes books for Disney Press, including the Descendants: School of Secrets series, based on the hit Disney Channel original movies, and the LEGO Disney Princess chapter books. Jessica's novels have been translated and published in over twenty-three countries, and *Unremembered* and *52 Reasons to Hate My Father* are currently in development as major motion pictures. When not working on her own novels, Jessica teaches online writing workshops at Udemy.com. She lives with her husband and three dogs near Portland, Oregon.

Visit her online at JessicaBrody.com. Follow her on Twitter or Instagram @JessicaBrody.

INDEX

Published in the United States by Ten Speed Press, an imprint of the
Crown Publishing Group, a division of Penguin Random House LLC,
New York.
www.crownpublishing.com
www.tenspeed.com

Ten Speed Press and the Ten Speed Press colophon are registered trademarks
of Penguin Random House LLC.

Save the Cat! is a registered trademark of Blake Snyder Enterprises, LLC.

Library of Congress Cataloging-in-Publication Data
    Names: Brody, Jessica, author.
Title: Save the cat! writes a novel : the last book on novel writing you'll
    ever need / Jessica Brody.
Description: First edition. | Berkeley, California : Ten Speed Press, 2018. |
    "Based on the best-selling screenwriting books by Blake Snyder." | Includes
    bibliographical references and index. |
Identifiers: LCCN 2018017675 (print) | LCCN 2018022433 (ebook) |
Subjects: LCSH: Fiction—Authorship. | Fiction—Plots, themes, etc. | Creative
    writing. | BISAC: LANGUAGE ARTS & DISCIPLINES / Composition &
    Creative Writing. | LANGUAGE ARTS & DISCIPLINES / Publishing. |
    LANGUAGE ARTS & DISCIPLINES / Study & Teaching.
Classification: LCC PN3355 (ebook) | LCC PN3355 .B734 2018 (print) |
    DDC 808.3—dc23
LC record available at https://lccn.loc.gov/2018017675

Trade Paperback ISBN: 978-0-399-57974-5
eBook ISBN: 978-0-399-57975-2

Printed in the United States of America

Design by Chloe Rawlins

Cover art © GK Hart/Vikki Hart and malerapaso

18th Printing

First Edition